Somebody Else's Problem

Consumerism, Sustainability and Design

SOMEBODY ELSE'S PROBLEM

Consumerism, Sustainability & Design

Robert Crocker

Greenleaf
PUBLISHING

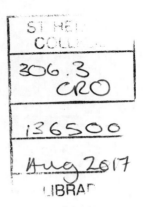
© 2016 Robert Crocker

Published by Greenleaf Publishing Limited
Aizlewood's Mill
Nursery Street
Sheffield S3 8GG
UK
www.greenleaf-publishing.com

The right of Robert Crocker to be identified as Author of this Work has been asserted by him in accordance with sections 77 and 78 of the Copyright, Designs and Patents Act 1988.

Cover by Christopher Thornton.

Printed and bound by Printondemand-worldwide.com, UK.

MIX
Paper from
responsible sources
FSC® C004959

British Library Cataloguing in Publication Data:
    A catalogue record for this book is available from the British Library.

    ISBN-13: 978-1-78353-491-3 [paperback]
    ISBN-13: 978-1-78353-503-3 [hardback]
    ISBN-13: 978-1-78353-493-7 [PDF ebook]
    ISBN-13: 978-1-78353-492-0 [ePub ebook]

For Rose,
and to the memory of my parents,
Walter and Claire

Contents

Part I: From consumption to consumerism

Part II: The escalation of consumption

Part III: Towards sustainable consumption

List of illustrations

Foreword

Stuart Walker

I was sitting on a beach in a sheltered cove in Greece. I was on one of the lesser visited islands and this place was quite secluded – a lengthy walk from the nearest road. The water was calm, the sky was blue – it was a perfect scene. One could imagine Odysseus dropping anchor in such a cove, and wood nymphs playing among the shadows of the tamarisk trees that came down to the sand.

The beach here was not the usual golden colour but a dark grey. I dragged my fingers through the sand, and picked up a handful. The granules were blue-black schists, volcanic in origin, but among them were larger fragments – whites, turquoises, reds and greens. I separated these out, put them to one side, and repeated the process. Within a few minutes, without moving from my position, I had accumulated a pile of plastic fragments – bits of bottles, toys, wrappers, nylon ropes and other assorted junk that had been discarded in the sea and forgotten, and had ended up here, polluting and sullying this small piece of paradise.

In Britain, because of a long austerity programme, funding to local councils has been severely reduced. This means there is less money to deal with the clean-up of our consumptive lifestyles. Perhaps one of the few benefits of economic recession is that one becomes aware of the things we so easily take for granted in more affluent times. It brings our reality into sharper focus and makes visible the real costs of our profligacy. This can be depressing but it is also a more honest picture of who we are and what we have become.

I live close to some of the most beautiful areas of England – the Yorkshire Dales and the Lake District of Cumbria. When my wife Helen and I go hiking in these places at weekends, I am uplifted and restored by the sheer beauty of the moorlands and valleys, the mountain streams and the lakes, the misty mornings, the rain-soaked mosses and the vibrancy of colour in the sunny interludes. But I am also appalled and disheartened by the amount of refuse on the roadsides; verges and hedgerows are often thick with bottles, cans, plastic, and packaging thrown from passing cars. Plastic wrap from hay bales – caught in branches and fluttering in the breeze like tattered flags – is also a common sight. Even in remote places – places renowned for their special significance and beauty – one cannot escape the blight of litter and waste. This is as true here as it is in a secluded cove thousands of miles away. This is the dark side of consumerism, and the curse of 'convenience', and it is devastating the planet. We are quite literally laying waste to the oceans, the lands, and the very air we breathe.

The critical and increasing pressures of contemporary consumption-based living are manifold – environmental breakdown, species extinction, mega-cities, population growth, resource depletion, climate change, mass migration from poorer to richer regions, and continuous war. These pressures are symptomatic of ways of living that are out of balance – ways that prioritize particular concerns to the detriment of others. Essentially, this is a question of values: what we choose to focus on and give precedence to, and what we choose to ignore. And so it is a moral concern – the morality of waste and the morality of the illusory, often misleading, messages of marketing and corporations whose vested interests are neither benevolent nor benign.

In modern times, and especially since the mid-nineteenth century, industrial growth, scientific and technological innovation, urbanization, mass-production and mass-consumption have been key priorities of human development. Within a capitalist economic system that seeks continual growth, these priorities have exacted an enormous toll on people and planet. They have been accompanied by unprecedented and ever-increasing resource consumption and inordinate levels of waste. A rapacious commitment to the constant production of short-lived consumer 'goods' within a globalized corporate system that seeks rising profits with little or no consideration of the costs is, as is entirely to be expected, trashing the planet. And the corporate hegemony that seeks to expand Western-style consumerism into every corner of the world is creating socio-cultural tensions that cannot be divorced from the rise of so-called asymmetric warfare. What the

West refers to as violent fundamentalism is a child of the late-modern condition and a world characterized by 'consumer' choice, advertising, relativism, social atomization and, increasingly, a sense of meaninglessness and hopelessness. But it is a world stripped of depth and significance. And it is difficult to have confidence in a better tomorrow when evidence of climate change, melting icecaps and species extinction is constantly met with ambivalence, procrastination and prevarication. In our enthusiasm for short-term gains and the new, we have assiduously avoided, and continue to avoid, the question 'To what end?' We are now becoming all too aware of where our technological means are taking us. But a future without hope is formula for despair.

A primary factor in this contemporary condition is consumption. Our economies are perilously dependent on it, and corporate agendas constantly encourage it. Billions of dollars each year are channelled into persuading us to be dissatisfied, and the solution is always the same: buy something, buy anything, and buy more. Politicians endorse this agenda and news channels affirm its significance by continuously reporting rises in share prices and consumer spending in highly positive terms. We have all been enculturated to believe that ever-increasing consumption is a constructive and progressive achievement; we have accepted it as normality.

An economic system that is premised on activities tied to the exploitation and destruction of the planet on which we all depend for our survival is self-evidently foolish. Although rooted in the Enlightenment and the Industrial Revolution, this system gained new momentum with the post-Second-World-War boom in mass-consumption, which means that, in its contemporary form, it has been in full swing for less than a century. Yet, in this short time, its consequences have been devastating.

In this important, fascinating and insightful new study, Robert Crocker traces the history of consumption, and examines the basis of the modern phenomenon of consumerism. He looks at consumerism's relationship to social behaviours, morality and deception; to waste production, its causes and effects; to sustainability; and to design. Today, this kind of critique is vital because consumerism is so pervasive and so commonplace; it is how we live. The very familiarity of its seductive veneer has the effect of masking its ruinous core. His systematic approach to this topic in *Somebody Else's Problem* provides a clear, timely and thorough dissection of something we all take for granted. It is a wide-ranging examination that enables us to see properly, perhaps for the first time, something that has been in plain sight all along. Robert Crocker enables us to realize that this is quite definitely *not* somebody else's problem.

Stuart Walker
Professor of Design for Sustainability, Lancaster University
Lancaster, England
April 2016

Preface

About 20 years ago, in Adelaide, South Australia, I helped start and manage a small pedestrian advocacy group called 'WalkSafe SA'. As Secretary of this little group of volunteers, I spent five years listening to disturbing and sometimes heart-breaking stories of injury and death among pedestrians, and representing their interests to local and state authorities, journalists and politicians. In my daytime job I was lecturing in design history and theory at the University of South Australia, and, influenced by these stories, began looking with increasing scepticism at the heroic story of modern design, the rise of the motor car and its conquest of the city.

This experience led me to question many of the assumptions behind our car-centred transport system, including its largely hidden costs, and our continued willingness to sacrifice so much – in money, resources and lives – to maintain and improve it. Over time, I also began to consider the advantages of more sustainable forms of transport and urban design, and I found myself taking a greater interest in other environmental problems, and their relationship to our way of life.

Following this rather unusual route into environmentalism, about ten years later, in 2006, I became involved in helping develop a cross-disciplinary Masters in Sustainable Design. My colleagues and I found that although our students could readily engage with the environmental and aesthetic application of design for sustainability, they had difficulty in understanding the larger social contexts of our environmental crisis. Many subscribed to the then popular idea that individuals could somehow change the world by influencing others, and by demonstrating, in their own work and life, how this change might occur. This was a view, given my experience, I could not accept.

However, part of our problem in starting this Masters programme was that, with a few exceptions, most books on sustainable design at that time, like the more popular scientific texts, encouraged this myth of 'individualization'. They did not really address the problem of consumerism, preferring to leave this problem to others. Indeed, none of these texts seemed to reference the many books on consumer culture, its history, sociology or psychology, perhaps because these at this time did not deal at all with the environmental implications of their own subject. I found similar gaps in the business and economic literature. These treated 'consumption' as a necessary part of the business equation; the few dissenting voices were pushed aside, their work largely dismissed by the mainstream.

The more confrontational environmentalism I had witnessed in the sixties and seventies seemed now to be a distant memory, and instead had been replaced with an extraordinary accommodation. Even environmental NGOs, I soon found, were using the same appeals, trying to individualize the problem, putting it back onto the consumer, as though she could somehow disengage herself from the world around her. Their advertisements suggested that if you joined the club you could help them save the world. Like an elephant in the room, consumerism was almost everywhere, it seemed, treated with kid gloves. It was as though all we needed to do was change a few routines around the house, and things would start to get better.[1]

This situation led me to develop a course on 'Consumer Culture, Technology and Sustainable Design' for our Masters programme. This book loosely follows the structure and intent of this course, even though I have considerably changed and refined its original arguments. I have tried here to confront the individualization of the problem of consumerism from a series of linked historical, social and psychological perspectives. In doing this, my intention is to speak more directly to those engaged in design and its many related disciplines, hopefully including also those from other related disciplines like planning and engineering, and also of course the intelligent general reader.

To suit this rather wider audience I have tried to walk a narrow bridge over the crocodiles of theory on the one side and of data overload on the other.

---

1 See Maniates, M. (2002) 'Individualization: Plant a tree, buy a bike, save the world?' in Princen, T., Maniates, M. & Conca, K. (Eds.), *Confronting Consumption*. Cambridge, MA: MIT: 43-65.

For this is indeed a very large topic, and in a book this size I cannot hope to more than skim the surfaces of many, often very divergent, academic fields. So I have avoided here peppering my text with references, limiting myself to a few useful footnotes on each page and appending a list of 'further reading' that might be helpful to the reader at the end of each chapter.

My main argument is that consumerism is now the most serious problem we are faced with, far greater than many of the issues that appear at the top of the first page of the newspapers. It lies behind the diplomatic shadow-play of international agreements on emissions and the frequent weighty scientific reports on climate change. In its expanding global context consumerism *is*, directly or indirectly, the main engine driving this climate change, and all its many and manifold results. It should be of concern to everyone. It especially concerns designers, those charged with its continuous priming and realization, in the images, products, systems and environments with which we now must live.

Acknowledgements

Through conversation and friendship, many have contributed to this book. Firstly, I would like to acknowledge seven years of wonderful conversations with my students in the Masters programme; they have often challenged me and forced me to change my own cherished opinions, or to question again the arguments of others.

I should also thank here those colleagues and friends who took time to read parts or all of this book in various earlier drafts, often making useful comments and suggestions, notably Julie Collins, Martin Freney, Gini Lee, Vaughan Levitzke, Gjoko Muratovski, Paul Keath, Esther Ratner, Jonathan Sobels, Chris Thornton, Kate Thornton and Sam Wells. Their comments have helped make this book a much better one.

The research and conversation of my current and former PhD students have also influenced my own thinking in writing this book. These include Aaron Davis, John Devlin, Gabriele Fitzgerald, Chris Thornton (again), Belinda Paulovich, Martin van der Weyer and Atiq Zaman. Added to this list I must also thank Janette Gay, Gini Lee, John Devlin, Stephen Schmitz, Chris Thornton and Belinda Paulovich, who have kindly contributed photographs, for which I am very grateful. I must also thank Chris Thornton, again, for the cover design, and Brett Cole for the photo on the cover.

Vaughan Levitzke, in his capacity as Director of Green Industries SA (formerly Zero Waste SA), has also been a good friend to this book, in his support for the various research initiatives in which I have been involved over the last five years. And I would also like to thank here my friend, Stuart Walker, Professor of Design for Sustainability at Lancaster University, for the Foreword that graces this book. My patient and helpful editors at Greenleaf,

Victoria Halliday, Anna Comerford and Rebecca Macklin, should also be mentioned, along with the editing skills of Kate Thornton and Janette Parr.

Last but not least, I thank my family for their love and support, and especially my wife, Merrie, and daughter, Rose, to whom this book is dedicated. Both also have read slabs of this book at various times, and I owe them much for their patience and comments. Rose in particular I owe much to, for our many conversations on the background scientific issues and their implications for the topics covered here. I should also thank them both for their patience, putting up with the writing of this book for so long.

Introduction:
The problem with consumerism

From access to excess

In *Life, the Universe and Everything*, one of his *Hitchhiker's Guide to the Galaxy* books, Douglas Adams describes a cricket match, at Lords in London, in an imagined future, where both players and spectators become so absorbed in the game that they fail to notice a giant spaceship slowly moving into position overhead. It turns out that this deadly ship is hidden from their sight by a special type of shielding device. This exploits a recently discovered 'field', which Adams, tongue-in-cheek, calls the 'Somebody Else's Problem Field'. This natural field is difficult for observers to focus on, since it always appears to be just outside their range of attention or interest.[1]

I would like to suggest here that the mental game of consumerism – of thinking about what we like or dislike, comparing what we have with what others have, and imagining what we might just need – has a similarly distracting and blinding effect. It has become so absorbing and apparently urgent that it is difficult to see outside its magic circle, and the 'invisible' opponents gathering in the background, even if these have become increasingly apparent to science.

Bombarded by the media with deceptive information encouraging us to buy more, or at least to have as much as the next person, most of us cannot make much sense of how our way of life might influence climate change. It seems too 'far away', too big in scale and slow-moving, and too long-term in

---

1 Adams, D. (1982) *Life, the Universe and Everything*. London: Pan Books: 28-9; and see also Gardiner, S.M. (2011) *A Perfect Moral Storm: The Ethical Tragedy of Climate Change*. Oxford: Oxford University Press.

its effects. And most scientists are not so good at telling us what we should be doing about it.

In fact, few now really understand the connection between their everyday lives and climate change. After years of publicity campaigns that feature scary science and target the damaging effects of individual behaviour, too many people now imagine that they are somehow at fault. Feeling unfairly blamed for what they cannot control, some react by denying the problem in the first place: the scientists must be wrong; climate change is all 'natural'; it is all about sunspots, long-term trends, or something else 'out there'.[2]

Talking about consumerism and sustainability in the same sentence might be easier than talking about consumerism and climate change, but it is still not easy, since most people immediately resort to a moral stance, and a blame game. The very term 'consumerism' reflects the likes, dislikes, interests and beliefs of those who use it. Most of us, when we use this term, instinctively refer to 'other' people, those 'over there' – perhaps the very rich who waste money on 'rubbish', unlike us – or perhaps to some obnoxious individual whose behaviour we personally dislike. Consumerism is thus a moral, judgemental, ideological term, with significant political and social implications.[3]

A glance at the history of this term shows that it has never attained the status of an objective concept like the economists' 'consumer' or 'consumption'. Instead, 'consumerism' is one of those key terms that suggest conflict and tension – in this case conflict over resources, over what we receive for what we do, and over why others seem to have more or less, sometimes undeservedly. In modern societies there has always been a tension between the promise of industrialism to provide *access* to essential goods and services for everyone, according to our needs, and the reality, which often comes down to a life of hard work and sacrifice, as we attempt to earn enough to pay for what we think we need.

This ideological, moral inference in the word 'consumerism' is evident in the way it has been used in in three quite distinct ways: first, as a collaborative, political movement to protect consumers and their interests

2   Maniates, M. (2002) 'Individualization: Plant a tree, buy a bike, save the world?' in Princen, T., Maniates, M. & Conca, K. (Eds.), *Confronting Consumption*. Cambridge, MA: MIT: 43-65.

3   See Brulle, R.J. (2013) 'Institutionalizing delay: Foundation funding and the creation of US climate change counter-movement organizations', *Climactic Change*, 122.4: 1-14; and Norgaard, K.M. (2011) *Living in Denial: Climate Change, Emotions and Everyday Life*. Cambridge, MA: MIT.

from predatory retailers and pay-day lenders; second, as an approach to economic policy that emphasized the benefits of manufacturing more consumer goods as a means of generating prosperity; and, more recently, as a wasteful excess in consumption, a cycle of endless shopping, accumulation and discard, stimulated by a remorseless, ubiquitous media.

Since the late 1970s sociologists have added a fourth, only slightly more objective, definition of this term. Typically, this depicts consumerism as something of a material-cultural accompaniment of industrial mass-consumption – 'a way of life' and 'state of mind' involving the many thoughts and activities associated with consumption. This definition reflects the fact that more and more people now feel obliged to think about, compare, evaluate, purchase, use, and then discard what they think they need, in ever larger volumes, and in an increasingly rapid cycle of 'buy, use, and trash'.[4]

Our increasing engagement in this last type of consumerism reflects large scale, long-term changes, including a steady rise in the amount of money available for 'discretionary spending'. Average spending on food, for example, has fallen in the developed world from about half of most people's incomes to less than 10% today. The price of many goods and services has also fallen relative to the cost of production, advertising has become more pervasive, and the idea that we can improve ourselves through consumption itself has taken hold in more and more people.

Encouraged by rapid technological change, economic globalization, unprecedented population growth, massive urbanization, and a global 24-hour mass media, since the early 1980s consumerism has become the most visible universal cultural expression of economic life. For individuals everywhere, even for the poor, it has become a vehicle for self-expression and social aspiration. Labourers in South America and Thailand now aspire to own a pair of Nike shoes or Rayban sunglasses, even if they must make considerable sacrifices to do so.

Because consumerism today requires such a rapid cycle of purchase, use and discard, it also results in premature wastage, since what we have will seem 'older' much sooner. For example, of the approximately 1.5 million

---

4   See Swagler, R. (1994) 'Evolution and applications of the term consumerism: Theme and variations', *Journal of Consumer Affairs*, 28.2: 347; Smart, B. (2010) *Consumer Society: Critical Issues and Environmental Consequences*. London: Sage, especially 8ff.

new Apple iPhones sold across the world on the first day of sale in 2010, over three-quarters were bought by people who already possessed an iPhone.[5]

This increasingly rapid cycle of purchase, use and discard is made possible not only by greater technological efficiencies, but also by a steady reduction in the many obstacles that once limited our capacity to purchase new products. Lower prices, easy credit, new ways of purchasing online, instant transactions, and more intensive, invasive forms of advertising and branding, all make buying so much easier. A hundred years ago only the wealthy could be so blasé about shopping as so many are now.

The rise in the volume of consumption per person over the last 30 years not only creates more waste and takes up more time, but also consumes more energy and resources. When mobile phones first became popular in the 1990s we might have predicted that the average user would need up to 20 or so handsets over the course of a lifetime; at current rates of consumption, we can now assume this figure is over 30. We can add to the environmental load of this figure the much longer tail of extraction and manufacture, including water, energy and mineral resources, and the eventual costs of each product's disposal: yet another environmental cost that is never paid.

Consumerism as deception

As many have argued, current resource consumption rates are entirely unsustainable, even if we factor in increasing technological efficiencies. In a field of continuous technological innovation and expanding consumption rates, efficiency gains are soon overwhelmed by increases in demand and use. For example, India's new Tata car has a tiny motor with relatively low emissions; it retails for the equivalent of US$2,500.[6] However, its sales to India's burgeoning middle class are expected to amount rapidly to millions. This necessarily outweighs the greater efficiencies of its motor – a phenom-

---

5   Kim, S. & Paulos, E. (2011) 'Practices in the creative reuse of e-waste.' *Human Factors in Computing Systems: Proceedings of SIGCHI*, Vancouver, Canada: 2,395-6; and see Wilhelm, W., Yankov, A. & Magee, P. (2011) 'Mobile phone consumption behaviour and the need for sustainability innovations', *Journal of Strategic Innovation and Sustainability*, 7.2: 20-40.

6   See Vail, J. (2008) 'The Tata Nano strikes back: Does Jevons' Paradox apply to productivity, too?' *The Oil Drum*. http://www.theoildrum.com/node/3561, accessed 1 May 2013.

enon evident in the sale of many other supposedly greener cars, appliances and devices.

At first sight, we can see the benefits of this consumerism; through individual choice and the availability of such low priced goods someone who could not afford a car can now do so, opening up possibilities they could never have entertained before. However, as with so many other technological consumer products, once the car is adopted, it soon edges out its slower, less convenient, but more sustainable rivals, and 'locks' its users into a dependence that cannot easily be escaped. Where there is a poorly organized public transport service, or none, it is unlikely the consumer can choose *not to drive*, or do anything except what her neighbours do.[7]

In many cities around the world driving is now 'compulsory', since it is extremely difficult, even heroic, to live without a car when there are few available alternatives. Our currently expanding rates and volumes of consumption are enabled and encouraged through means like these. What the individual does cannot count for much when everyone else is obliged to drive.

Developed over many years, systems like these necessarily involve massive 'sunk costs', or irrecoverable investments in money, time, energy, materials and skilled labour. Over time, such systems also produce cultural and social effects, sometimes termed 'sunk-cost effects'. These 'legacy effects' normalize how we experience the system concerned, its rules or norms, and the behaviour it enables.[8]

We display an apparently unshakeable commitment to the forms of modernization we have inherited, along with their more obvious disadvantages. This is what lies behind many of the political and economic compromises over the environment we have witnessed over the last three decades – from the famous Brundtland report of 1987, which outlines the need for 'sustainable development' (and consumption), to this year's Paris agreement.

7   See Sanne, C. (2002) 'Willing consumers – or locked-in? Policies for a sustainable consumption', *Ecological Economics*, 42: 273-287; and Soron, D. (2009) 'Driven to drive: Cars and the problem of "compulsory consumption"', in Conley, J. & McLaren, A.T. (Eds.), *Car Troubles: Critical Studies of Automobility and Auto-Mobility*. Farnham, UK: Ashgate: 181-197.
8   See Kelly, T. (2004) 'Sunk costs, rationality and acting for the sake of the past', Nous, 38.1: 60-85; and also Arkes, H.R. & Blumer, C. (1985) 'The psychology of sunk cost', *Organizational Behavior and Human Decision Processes*, 35.1: 124-40.

The effects, or more properly, 'fallacies', of our larger provisioning systems necessarily blind us, as users, to their disadvantages, and to the advantages of established alternatives. Such sunk-cost fallacies also underwrite our *deception* as consumers. This 'deception' is not the simple fact of being misled, as in the case of bogus advertising, but a long-term, mutually beneficial agreement to remain in ignorance; we literally don't want to know the negative effects of our everyday, seemingly necessary but convenient actions. This deception is shared between consumers and producers, who also gain their own advantages from maintaining the status quo.

This deception starts with the consumer's commitment to a product that promises to satisfy an identified 'need', perhaps one that the media has defined or reminded her of. Perhaps it is a 'wrinkle-reducing' face cream. Its value to her is then increased through the transaction itself, which encourages her to believe that what is now hers is good, and does what it claims to do. Such everyday commitments give consumerism its cumulative power and moral weight; as we buy and use, we become committed to the product for which we have sacrificed our money, and the time and effort this represents to us.

Consumerism as waste making

Consumerism is also characterized by waste-making. It requires the removal of the seemingly 'old' to make way for the new, the latest and the 'best'. To persuade us to throw away something like a mobile phone that might only be one or two years old, or to encourage us to use items that can only be used once, depends on self-deception, and a willingness to 'discount' or devalue what we might hold in our hands.

A familiar example of this relationship between consumption, deception and waste can be seen in our present coffee culture. To 'save time', we now drink coffee from throwaway plastic-lined paper cups, even though they are most often unrecyclable and generate substantial emissions in their manufacture and disposal. Starbucks alone is said to need eight million of these cups every day. In many parts of the world, such plastic/paper cups, along with plastic bags, soft drink cartons, and plastic snack packets, end up, more or less immediately, in the waste stream.

We want to believe they are recyclable, and that 'someone' will fix this problem. Those who recognize that there is, in fact, no one behind the curtain managing this problem, and that there is just a large and growing pile of these rapidly discarded things 'out there', will attempt to change their behaviour. They might adopt the 'Keep-cup' approach, or bring their own mug or glass. But this will probably not change the behaviour of others, who will regard the 'Keep-cup' as strange, unless the café concerned really tries to encourage more pro-environmental behaviours.[9]

In the argument that follows in this book, I emphasize that consumerism *necessarily* involves this kind of deception, and also a waste making which remains largely concealed from us. This is in part stimulated by stylistic or technical obsolescence, and in part by a mental 'discounting' of the value of what we have. This is a process that starts in comparison. When we see something newer and seemingly better than what we already have, this renders what we have less valuable, until it becomes 'old', in our eyes, and ready to be given or thrown away.

The problem of this increasingly rapid and extensive creation of waste has three related dimensions. Firstly, present global rates of production for consumption generate waste in unmanageable quantities. These volumes cannot be dealt with effectively, except in a few clean, post-industrial cities like mine, which have advanced engineering services and good collection systems. In the rest of the world, we are looking at an unmanageable regime that tries to 'catch up' with the waste created. After all, only about half of the world's population presently experiences a 'formal' collection of waste, just as only 50% of our global population has access to modern sanitation. This means for more than three billion people waste is a form of pollution.

Secondly, most wastes now contain large proportions of environmentally persistent or toxic substances — chemicals, plastics, metals and cements — often fused together, which are then broken down into smaller, less visible, pollutants. These soon 'escape' from their short-lived homes, and most cannot be easily recaptured and reused in any useful form. Marine scientists can now photograph plankton that glow with micro-plastics from cosmetics and other products inside them, and regularly find young dead seabirds

9   See Wright, S., Gregory, S. & Kalaian, S. (2011) 'Environmental purchasing practices and environmental beliefs of stand-alone coffee shop owners and managers', *Journal of Foodservice Business Research*, 14.2: 180-8; and McCollough, J. (2012) 'Determinants of a throwaway society: A sustainable consumption issue', *Journal of Socio-Economics*, 41.1: 110.

with their stomachs full of brightly coloured plastics, fed to them in innocence by their parents.[10]

Thirdly, consumerism's reliance on the rapid removal of the 'old' to make space for the new, the 'discounting' noted above, has turned waste making and the deception it involves into an almost universal commercial strategy. Reuse, second-hand markets and recycling, for all their obvious value, cannot keep up with the massive volumes of stuff being created. Recycling might convert around 20% of our managed waste globally to resources that can be used once again, and this percentage might rise to 60% in well-managed cities like mine, but globally this means that a large proportion of our waste becomes pollution more or less immediately, or shortly after discard, even if it is technically 'recyclable'.

FIGURE 0.1: RUBBISH IN THE CILIWUNG RIVER, JAKARTA, INDONESIA

Photo: J. Devlin (2015)

10   See Liboiron, M. (2015/6) 'Redefining pollution and action: The matter of plastics', *Journal of Material Culture*, 21.1: 1-24; and IWSA (2014) *Waste Atlas: 2014*. ISWA. http://www.atlas.d-waste.com/Documents/Waste-Atlas-report-2014-webEdition.pdf, accessed 1 May 2015.

A brief history of modern consumerism

Historians have traced the development of our consumer society in Europe and America, over the last 500 years, back to the first European attempts to gain safer access, by sea, to the fabled spices, silks, jewels and other luxuries of the East. This first stage in the development of a modern consumer society is often associated with the adoption of new and exotic novelties and luxury goods, including tea, coffee, spices, silks, cottons, ceramics, exotic woods, plants and drugs.

At this time questions of access to consumption were couched in terms of 'luxury'. Indeed, debates about these new luxuries became a way of talking about many related things, including trade itself, manufacturing, money, and the morality of spending. This early first phase of our developing consumer society was mainly restricted to an urban elite, who could afford these goods, even if some of these goods, such as cotton cloth, coffee and tea, were soon within the reach of many more ordinary people.[11]

The second phase of this development, beginning in late eighteenth- and nineteenth-century Europe and America, has been associated with industrialization and the rise of a larger urban middle class, who by the beginning of the nineteenth century made up to about 10% of the population of Britain. In this larger society of consumers, the economic terms 'consumption' and 'consumer' were used more widely to talk about the spread and use of new manufactured goods.

As cities grew and the numbers of consumers increased, the 'consumer' and her needs attained a greater economic and political importance. Closely tied to the cooperative movement and the early history of the labour movement, concern for the well-being of the consumer generated associations to protect consumers and ensure they had access to the necessities of life. This political defence of the consumer's interests was later retrospectively termed 'consumerism'.[12]

11 See Berg, M. (1999) 'New commodities, luxuries, and their consumers in eighteenth-century England', in Berg, M. & Clifford, H. (Eds.), Consumers and Luxury: *Consumer Culture in Europe, 1650–1850*. Manchester: Manchester University Press: 63-85.

12 See Gurney, P. (2005) 'The battle of the consumer in postwar Britain', *Journal of Modern History*, 77.4: 956-987; Hilton, M. (2007) 'Consumers and the state since the Second World War', *The Annals of the American Academy of Political and Social Sciences*, 611: 66-81.

From the 1880s to about 1920 we can insert a third phase into this brief history of our consumer society, when the politics of consumption, of access to the necessities of life, and the receipt of a 'living wage', became a dominant concern in all industrial societies. This was marked by the rise of modern economics, modern socialism, trade unionism and political parties associated with the defence of the 'working class'.

One of the more significant early economists (after Karl Marx) to explore the tension between consumption's promise to provide access for the majority, and the 'conspicuous consumption' of the wealthy, was Thorstein Veblen (1857–1929), whose key ideas I will be occasionally referencing here. His *Theory of the Leisure Class* (1899) remains a perceptive study of the role of emulation in turning consumption itself, along with 'conspicuous leisure' and 'conspicuous waste', into a means for asserting social distinction, and a model for others to follow.[13]

A little later, in the 1920s and 1930s, 'consumerism' came to be understood as an economic strategy that stimulated or favoured an increase in the production of consumer goods. It was believed that an increase in the circulation of goods would help raise the nation's living standards – an idea that became especially attractive in the Depression. By working and then consuming, ordinary people would benefit others, whose consumption would in turn benefit them, in an unceasing virtuous circle that would provide employment and rising incomes for all.[14]

The myth of the 'consumer as citizen' established in the late nineteenth century was early associated with this second definition of so-called 'economic' consumerism. Revived and slightly reconfigured during the Cold War, and again after 9/11 in the 'war on terror', the 'consumer citizen' involves another form of consumer deception, since it enables a rhetorical link to be made, not only between the self-interest of the individual consumer and that of the corporation, but also between these and the nation's own interests.

13   Dwyer, R. (2009) 'Making a habit of it: Positional consumption, conventional action and the standard of living', *Journal of Consumer Culture*, 9.3: 328-347; and Veblen, T. (2007) *Theory of the Leisure Class*. Oxford: Oxford University Press.
14   Dickinson, G. (2005) 'Selling democracy: Consumer culture and citizenship in wake of September 11', *Southern Communication Journal*, 70.4: 271-284; Marchand, R. (1998) *Creating the Corporate Soul*. Berkeley, CA: University of California Press; and Cohen, L. (2004) *A Consumers' Republic*. New York: Vintage Books.

The allied victory in the Second World War and the rise of America as a global power ensured that, after the war, this model of democratic 'economic consumerism' became the dominant strategy of Western governments and a means of distinguishing the West from the Communist East. The spread of this economic ideal resulted in what might be seen here as a fourth phase in the development of today's 'consumer society' – a 'democratization' of a type of consumerism that in the nineteenth century had been largely restricted to the middle classes.

The first part of this book overviews the main themes to be found in the development of this consumer society, at least up to the 1970s. These include the role of luxury in stimulating consumption (Chapter 1), the role of imitation in production, consumption and design (Chapter 2), the role of idealization and ideology in design, production and consumption (Chapter 3), and the development of large-scale technological systems enabling mass-consumption in an increasingly urbanized world (Chapter 4).

Consumerism in the post-war economy

The fourth phase of our little history of consumer society was marked by the widespread acceptance in the West of the idea that a modern democratic society required not only wider access to education and employment based on ability and skill, but also an economy based largely on the production and distribution of consumer goods. This, it was believed, would raise living standards, avoid the social conflicts that had marred the inter-war period, and increase prosperity for all.

As the economist and business consultant Victor Lebow explained in a remarkably candid and often-quoted article for the *Journal of Retailing* in 1955:

> Our enormously productive economy demands that we make consumption our way of life, that we convert the buying and use of goods into rituals, that we seek our spiritual satisfactions, our ego satisfactions, in consumption. The measure of social status, of social acceptance, of prestige, is now to be found in our consumptive patterns. The very meaning and significance of our lives today are expressed

in consumptive terms ... We need things consumed, burned up, worn
out, replaced, and discarded at an ever-increasing pace.[15]

Lebow went on to summarize the purpose of this more intensive expression of 'economic consumerism', which was to benefit production as well as
consumption, and to lift the standard of living, in this way keeping workers
in the West safe from the siren song of communism. As he claimed, 'the total
effect of all the advertising and promotion and selling is to create and maintain the multiplicity and intensity of wants that are the spur to the standard
of living in the United States.'

While individual campaigns for certain products might or might not be
successful, he declared, the overall effect was to shift consumers' commitments to new wants and expectations. This candid admission explains precisely how advertising works in the economic system: not necessarily in
the individual terms of one product over another, but in shaping the wants
of large numbers into needs, which then, through emulation, over time,
becoming 'essentials' for everyone at a certain income level.[16]

The post-war economic 'long boom' of the 1950s and 1960s was accompanied by a massive increase in oil production and a decline in its price
relative to that of other goods and services. Termed the '1950s Syndrome'
by the environmental historian Christian Pfister, this 'growth economy' was
enabled by the expansion of new post-war industries, particularly large-
scale car-manufacturing, chemicals, plastics and electronics – all heavy
emitters in their own right.

The car itself was a key vector in this transformation, extending cities and
creating a range of dependent practices in its wake. In this book, much of
my discussion about systems refers to this period, and the dynamic nexus
between cheap energy, industrial expansion, and rising levels of consumption – most typically based on the car and its transformation of the city. This
entered a dramatically accelerated phase from the early 1980s as this growth
model was gradually exported to the rest of the world.[17]

15   Lebow, V. (1955) 'Price competition in 1955', *Journal of Retailing*, 31.1: 5-11;
      and see Trentmann, F. (2011) 'Consumers as citizens: Tensions and synergies',
      in Ekstrom, K.M. & Glans, K. (Eds.), *Beyond the Consumption Bubble*. London:
      Routledge: 99-111; and Cohen, L. (2004) *A Consumers' Republic*. New York: Vin-
      tage Books.
16   See Alexander, J., Crompton, T. & Shrubsole, G. (2010) *Think of Me as Evil? Open-
      ing the Ethical Debates in Advertising*. Godalming, Surrey: PIRC, WWF-UK.
17   Pfister, C. (2010) 'The "1950s Syndrome" and the transition from a slow growing
      to a rapid loss of global sustainability', in Uekoetter, F. (Ed.), *Turning Points of*

What seemed most urgent in the 1950s was an economic transformation that would raise living standards and increase a broadly democratic commitment to a modern, progressive consumer society. At the time, this growth economy was explained using the rhetoric of the Cold War: a national, democratic, consumption-driven modernization would guarantee access to essential goods and services for all.

This was envisioned and shaped by the application of science, technology and design. It is no accident that the 1950s are widely regarded by design historians as a 'golden age' for modern design. Certainly, the design and production of consumer goods, along with marketing and advertising, became key economic and political strategies among the Western allies. Likened to an economic perpetual motion machine, it was thought that growth based on consumption, and enabled by cheap energy and the application of technology, would benefit all. It could save the world from the terrors of the past and, along with pre-emptive nuclear armaments, from the dangers of the Cold War.[18]

However, at the very moment when this dream of access for all was closest to being realized, the word 'consumerism' was adopted again – this time with its more typical contemporary meaning of *excess*, or *excessive devotion to consumption activities*. This more negative use of the term was also, and for the first time, directly related to the growing threat of environmental damage, and to the implicit contradiction between the claims made of this consumer democracy and the realities of the economic, social, gender and racial inequalities that were to be found within it. The Vietnam War made this contradiction more sharply felt as concerns with industry's capacity to wreak environmental damage became more widespread, and anxieties about the threat of a possibly imminent nuclear war grew.

The now widely adopted interpretation of consumerism as 'excess' was also shaped by the rhetoric of the 1960s counterculture. Individual choices in consumption became opportunities for revealing and remaking identity,

Environmental History. Pittsburgh, PA: University of Pittsburgh Press: 90-118; and see McNeill, J.R. & Engelke, P. (2014) *The Great Acceleration: An Environmental History of the Anthropocene since 1945*. Cambridge, MA: Harvard University Press.

18 Crowley, D. (2008) 'Europe reconstructed, Europe divided'. in Crowley, D. & Pavitt, J. (Eds.), *Cold War Modern: Design, 1945–1970*. London: Victoria and Albert Museum: 43-65; and Oldenziel, R. & Zachmann, K. (Eds.) (2009) *Cold War Kitchen: Americanization, Technology and European Users*. Cambridge, MA: MIT Press.

a way of showing off a dedication to peace and social equality, and a commitment to saving the environment. Young radicals interpreted everyday consumerism, as promoted by the TV, the newspapers and magazines, as a means of social control by the 'establishment'. The counterculture contested this 'control' of consumption and argued instead that consumption was an opportunity for self-expression and personal transformation – a theme I return to in the second part of this book.

In the late 1960s, then, what a person chose to consume came to be seen in moral terms, and as a form of commitment, which could make all the difference to the individual and the world. Music, clothes, new 'personal' technologies and, later, personal computers, all became 'tools for living', in opposition to the addictive, damaging products of the corporate 'establishment' and 'TV culture'.[19]

The fifth and final stage in the journey towards today's consumer society, most evident from the late 1970s onwards, was accompanied by an exponential increase in consumption associated with globalization and computerization. This was accompanied by an equally exponential rise in greenhouse gas emissions – 'a great acceleration' that has at last brought consumerism to the attention of governments, economists, policy makers and business leaders.

As I try to show in the second part of this book, this historical trajectory has developed a momentum of its own that has become embedded in the 'sunk-cost effects' of our technological systems, and in the norms and expectations of consumerism. In this more recent period the individual consumer's goals and values have been progressively reset to the terms, rhythms and needs of the market, which is itself driven by the engine of demand created by a now global consumerism.[20]

Starting from the meritocratic, democratic idealism of the Cold War, we have entered a world where economic and political survival now seems to depend on an expansive consumerism, whose direct results are the environmental crisis that we can see around us. In the second part of this book I look at what I take to be the main accelerators of this final, and most seriously dangerous phase in the development of our consumer society, from

---

19 Rome, A. (2003) '"Give Earth a Chance": The environmental movement and the sixties', *Journal of American History*, 90.2: 525-554; and Turner, F. (2006) *From Counterculture to Cyberculture: Stewart Brand, the Whole Earth Network, and the Rise of Digital Utopianism*. Chicago: University of Chicago Press.

20 Steffen, W., Crutzen, P.J. & McNeil, J.R. (2007) 'The Anthropocene: Are humans now overwhelming the great forces of nature?', *Ambio*, 36.8: 614-621.

the mid-seventies to the present. This includes an intensification of social comparison and competition (Chapter 5), the acceleration of communication unleashed by computerization (Chapter 6), and the transformation of our understanding and experience of nature and environment (Chapter 7).

Returning to sustainability

Since the 1980s, and influenced by a growing environmental movement, three distinct approaches to solving the problem of consumerism and its impact on our environment have risen to prominence.

The first is sometimes termed 'green growth' or 'eco-modernization'. Its history stretches back to the sixties' 'back to the land' environmentalists' fascination with alternative technologies, including solar panels, the use of wind-turbines to drive generators, and composting toilets. Despite its 'alternative' tag, it has become a dominant technocratic response to our environmental crisis, and is now driven largely by various forms of engineering and environmental science.

This approach emphasizes the importance of changing our technological systems, methods of generating energy, of designing and manufacturing products, to more sustainable ones, and measuring these against the lower environmental standards of the past. 'Low-carbon' products and systems, so this argument goes, will reduce our emissions, largely through evidence-based interventions that prioritize technological innovation and efficiency gains. America's LEED rating systems for new buildings, along with the use of PVC solar panels for electricity generation, are representative of this more widely supported approach.[21]

The second approach, in part a reaction to the first's evident neglect of the problem of consumerism and its escalatory dynamic, advances the idea of 'de-growth' and a more radical reduction in the volumes of consumption itself. Its methods range from voluntary lifestyle changes, to the imposition of controls on industry and limiting economic policies. The aim is to reduce overall volumes of production and consumption, in readiness for

21   See Jakob, M. & Edenhofer, O. (2014) 'Green growth, degrowth, and the commons', *Oxford Review of Economic Policy*, 30.3: 447-468; and Schneider, F., Kallis, G., & Martinez-Alier, J. (2010) 'Crisis or Opportunity? Economic degrowth for social equity and ecological sustainability', *Journal of Cleaner Production*, 18: 511-518, and the other articles in this special issue.

a 'post-carbon world'. The main targets of de-growth advocates are not the technical advances suggested by proponents of 'green growth', but the prevailing neoliberal economic system and its prioritization of consumerism, typically at the expense of the environment.

The third approach is more closely related, in many respects, to the first than to the second. It emphasizes the value of a 'circular economy' – one where each supplier extracts more value from a product or service, by reusing resources and employing more people to do so, and by exchanging unwanted resources with others. Closely associated with the work of Walter Stahel and his associates working for the original Club of Rome in the 1970s, this approach emphasizes the importance of a more systematic pathway to a reduction in energy and resource use. In some respects it refers back to the more 'circular' world of our grandparents, when most useful things were kept for much longer and reused.[22]

Now of particular interest in China and the EU, the circular economy aims to transform production and consumption, but also to reinterpret that much abused idea of 'efficiency'. For proponents of the circular economy desire us to move from a situation where we might rush a product to market, sell it for the highest price to the greatest number, and then do the same again, to one where we can create added value by reusing every part of a product, either before or after use. So in this approach, for example, there is much interest in strategies like product service systems, which try to extend our relationship with the product by turning it into a complete service system, as manufacturers of some photocopiers do already.

It does not take much to realize that, while each of these approaches has value, their main weaknesses seem to be centred on how they approach consumerism. For example, the first appears to accept consumerism as a necessary evil that will be more or less automatically reduced through technological innovation and increasing eco-efficiencies. The evidence for such assumptions is clearly insufficient. The second makes no such assumptions and at least takes consumerism seriously. However, there seems to be considerable difficulties explaining how consumption levels might be practically reduced without considerable social disruption. The third is still grappling with the implications of the problem that consumerism presents.

22   Strasser, S. (2003) 'The alien past: Consumer culture in historical perspective', *Journal of Consumer Policy*, 26.4: 375-393; and Webster, K. (2013) *The Circular Economy: A Wealth of Flows* (online) at http://www.ellenmacarthurfoundation. org/publications/the-circular-economy-a-wealth-of-flows, accessed 1 July 2015.

For while the circular economy may reduce the consumption of resources, it is not always clear how this reduction will translate into changed consumer behaviour.

To these approaches a fourth might be added, which also has its share of supporters, myself included. This derives from development economics, and argues that a sustainable economy must not only recognize the value of the environment, but also the value of social welfare and well-being. This means, for example, typical non-monetary exchanges, such as those involving volunteers, should be included in our understanding of what the economy is, and how we can judge its health. Well-being, certainly, can't be mapped or enumerated by GDP, but it is reflected in a myriad of daily activities, many of which cannot be recorded as transactions.

As the economist Amartya Sen notes, in his work on famine, the mere presence of a market cannot define an economy and its purpose. It cannot even guarantee that food will be available for the hungry, or be equitably distributed, as he discovered. The 'standard of living', he argued, is never guaranteed by the presence of a free market. It is only ensured through stable institutions and strong community relationships, which, like many societies' 'volunteer economy', pre-exists and upholds the regular market economy. The work of most women as carers, for example, cannot be rewarded in financial terms; yet without this work, all known economies would cease to exist.[23]

I treat this fourth strand here with considerable interest, since Sen's argument tries to make clear that the purpose of the economy, and of consumption itself, is to ensure the development of the individual's capabilities, and not just to encourage 'growth' through consumerism. In this approach what is and should be prioritized is the removal of those basic obstacles that prevent the development of our capabilities, such as hunger, thirst, lack of shelter, education and meaningful employment. To this, we might add the need to reduce and eliminate the deception, waste-making and social competition consumerism engenders, since this undermines the stable institutions and strong community relationships on which the market itself depends.

From this brief overview, I would like to suggest that all four general approaches to generating more sustainable systems of production and

23   See Jackson, T. (2006) 'Consuming paradise? Towards a social and cultural psychology of sustainable consumption', in Jackson, T. (Ed.), *The Earthscan Reader in Sustainable Consumption*. London: Earthscan: 367-395; and Robeyns, I. (2005) 'The Capability Approach: A theoretical survey', *Journal of Human Development*, 6.1: 93-117.

consumption are important, and can inform an approach to imagining and progressively implementing more sustainable forms of consumption and production. In their own ways each aims to increase human well-being, to eradicate poverty, and to reduce the damage we are inflicting on the environment.

In the last part of this book I return to look at the problem of sustainable consumption from this perspective (Chapter 8). Drawing on the history, psychology and social organization of consumption, I suggest how some very simple changes in approach, led by design, can help us reconfigure the values, attitudes, relationships and practices presently generating over-consumption in so many areas (Chapters 9 and 10). While I provide few 'solutions', I try to suggest those means to solve our problems that seem most promising, and less destructive of the environment.

Further reading

Dauvergne, P. (2008) *The Shadows of Consumption: Consequences for the Global Environment*. Cambridge, MA: MIT Press.

Dittmar, H. (2008) *Consumer Culture, Identity and Well-being*. Hove, UK: Psychology Press.

Fry, T. (2009) *Design Futuring: Sustainability, Ethics and New Practice*. Oxford: Berg.

Goodwin, N.R., Ackerman, F. & Kiron, D. (Eds.) (1997) *The Consumer Society*. Washington, DC: Island Press.

Lee, M.J. (Ed.) (2000) *The Consumer Society Reader*. Oxford: Blackwell.

McNeill, J.R. & Engelke, P. (2014) *The Great Acceleration: An Environmental History of the Anthropocene since 1945*. Cambridge, MA: Harvard University Press.

Miller, D. (2010) *Stuff*. Cambridge: Polity Press.

Sassatelli, R. (2007) *Consumer Culture: History, Theory and Politics*. London: Sage.

Smart, B. (2010) *Consumer Society: Critical Issues and Environmental Consequences*. London: Sage.

Strasser, S. (1999) *Waste and Want: A Social History of Trash*. New York: Henry Holt.

Tatzel, M. (Ed.) (2014) *Consumption and Well-Being in the Material World*. London: Springer.

Urry, J. (2011) *Climate Change and Society*. Cambridge: Polity.

Veblen, T. (2007) *Theory of the Leisure Class*. Oxford: Oxford University Press.

Walker, S. (2011) *The Spirit of Design: Objects, Environment and Meaning*. London: Earthscan.

Part I
From consumption to consumerism

1
Pleasure and luxury in consumption

Pleasure in consumption

Small children are great pleasure seekers. Toys, games, little outings with their parents in the park, eating and drinking, and perhaps, more meditatively, exploring Mummy's cupboards or Daddy's shoes, all these activities are pursued with an innocent hedonism that is, by turn, both delightful and frustrating to their parents. And what brings pleasure can change very rapidly: one moment it might be an ice cream and its sweet, creamy, coldness in the mouth, and next the delight of riding a tricycle in the house, or bouncing on the bed.

Young children also experience great joy and pride in using and possessing things they label as 'mine', particularly clothing and toys, from a pair of shiny red shoes, or a warm woollen coat with fascinating buttons, to a little red truck pulled clattering around the living room floor. Some of these things, particularly small toys, dolls and pets, are magically transformed into 'friends', to be talked or sung to and played with. Many children's stories offer an insight into this process of 'vitalization', where favoured objects are turned into creatures of the imagination.[1]

Children have the capacity to make things come alive, to live in the moment, and to engage deeply in the sensual. They are always anticipatory, with short attention spans: little Jill or Johnny will not wait, they want it now! These qualities make them ideal consumers. Indeed, going shopping

[1] See LaMothe, R. (2001) 'Vitalizing objects and psychoanalytic psychotherapy', *Psychoanalytic Psychology*, 18.2: 320-339.

with young children can be especially challenging. 'Daddy!... I want that!...' Desperate to hush their shouting, many parents give in to their children, and buy them some small treat to restore peace.

A child will display the same 'hedonic adaptation' we notice as adults but in an accelerated mode. This is the tendency for the newly purchased object to decline in value over time as we become used to it. But in children this week's treat (or upset) is soon forgotten as other more interesting or exciting things come into view. And so begins the child's passage into consumerism – an unfair contest that is really between the parent and the store or the media, but is often turned into one between parent and child.[2]

Over the last 50 years or so marketers have entered the world of childhood and made it their own. Children, like most adults, are now subject to an average of 3,000 or so advertisements each day, and most online games they play or TV programmes they watch have pop-up or full-length ads. As Juliet Schor points out, 'the typical first grader can evoke 200 brands. And he or she has already accumulated an unprecedented number of possessions, beginning with an average of 70 new toys a year.' Although these might be American statistics, more and more children around the world are starting life in a similar, heavily commercialized childhood.[3]

In some respects, this targeting of children is not new; shops have been seducing children since the eighteenth century. However, today's media is another matter. Ubiquitous and immersive, it now captures a lot of 'spare time' in many lives, especially those of children. With a TV in most bedrooms, children are now exposed to almost continuous media manipulation. As one friend, a schoolteacher, told me recently, at least two to three children in each class of seven- or eight-year-olds will now answer the age-old question of 'What do you want to do when you grow up?' with something like 'I want to be rich', or 'I want to be famous'.

As they grow up, children look to the models of behaviour and possession they see around them – especially those in the media – to work out what adult life is about. For example, even though I was born in the 1950s and, as a child, had limited access to most media, I remember, as a boy of about 12, suddenly becoming fascinated with expensive Italian sports cars. I leafed through old

2   Tatzel, M. (2014) 'Introduction', in M. Tatzel (Ed.), *Consumption and Well-Being in the Material World*. London: Springer: 1-10.

3   Schor, J.S. (2004) *Born to Buy: The Commercialized Child and the New Consumer Culture*. New York: Scribner: 20, cited in Hill, J.A. (2011) 'Endangered childhoods: How consumerism is impacting child and youth identity', *Media, Culture and Society*, 33: 347-362.

magazines and gazed lovingly at their designs, colours, powerful engines and lavish interiors. I couldn't drive, my father was not really interested in cars, and I had seen only one or two such cars on the streets. But looking at the pictures, and perhaps influenced by the comics and adventure books I was reading, I would imagine myself 'one day' owning one, and tearing around at high speed, doing all those exciting things I imagined real adults did.

Emerging from the chrysalis of childhood, teenagers now are more vulnerable to the siren song of consumerism, since their paths to adulthood have been more intensely and deliberately shaped by the media than children of my generation ever were. This emphasizes the importance of having the 'right' stuff to become who they want to be. In a famous recent case, a group was arrested for breaking into the houses of celebrities in Hollywood and stealing their clothes and other possessions, a catalogue of 'cool', especially elevated for them by its intimate links with their most admired celebrities. These young people were all from middle-class backgrounds, and had no history of crime.[4]

In their confessions to the LA police, and to *Vanity Fair*, which immediately published a remarkable story about their adventures, it became clear that these 18- to 20-year-olds thought of themselves as apprentices to their victim-heroes. Bizarrely, one of the perpetrators showed up at court with her own small film crew, to create what was to become part of an episode in her self-penned fashion and celebrity blog. The thrill for these kids was not so much gaining money from their thefts, for they had access to this at home, but from possessing and using the luxury branded clothes and accessories they aspired to own. The things they took from their heroes' homes had a special, almost magical aura through their intimate associations. In true Hollywood style, this curious story was turned into a film, Sophie Coppola's remarkable *The Bling Ring*.

Deception and choice in consumerism

Like young children in the supermarket, or teenagers hanging out in the mall, as adults we too face an abundance of advertisements for competing

---

4   Sales, N.J. (2010) 'The suspects wore Louboutins', *Vanity Fair*, 28 February 2010, http://www.vanityfair.com/culture/2010/03/billionaire-girls-201003, accessed 12 November 2015; Coppola, S. (2013) *The Bling Ring:* I am grateful to Katharine Thornton for this example.

goods and services. Often with insufficient or deceptive information, we are obliged to work out whether we really need them, or if we can afford them. While most choices in consumption are relatively straightforward, with few negative consequences, others are more challenging. For example, buying a house or car, perhaps involving large debts, can undermine our peace of mind and, in some circumstances, lead to conflicts with families or friends.

Choice with regard to consumption can be tension-filled; so much seems to hang upon the choices we have to make, and dealing with them takes up a lot of mental space. So we might find ourselves buying a new suit for a job interview, upgrading our phone to make sure no one at a meeting will think worse of us, or even paying too much for a car, simply because we do not want to look bad in the eyes of others. Many of these decisions are now driven by time pressure, by a desire to do the right thing, or perhaps to avoid others' negative judgements.[5]

Deception is built into consumerism, not just because advertisers want to trick us or seduce our children, but because deception, and self-deception, are essential aspects of consumption itself, and are part of the everyday experience of both buyer and seller. As buyers we have to believe in the 'good life', or at least a better life, that the new product or service promises, and that the particular house or car we are interested in will indeed satisfy our hopes and needs. When we are given the keys, or take the new car home, we are also committed financially, so we now believe in the virtues of that house or car, and it becomes an essential part of our lives, and of who we think we are.

Sellers, too, have to believe that the product or service they are offering is worth its price, and that advertising, and selling it, is worth the effort required. Owning a Ford franchise, for example, will influence a business-man to 'appreciate' the virtues of what he is selling, and also commit him to the brand, and to a belief in its superiority to other similar cars. Having paid money for one of his cars, we have also committed ourselves to a belief in the value of our purchase. We now have to believe, or at least half-believe, in the myth of the brand, and in the car's unique features.[6]

5   Binkley, S. (2009) 'The civilizing brand: Shifting shame thresholds and the dis-
     semination of consumer lifestyles', *European Journal of Cultural Studies*, 12:
     21-39; Scheff, T.J. (2003) 'Shame in self and society', *Symbolic Interaction*, 26.2:
     239-262.
6   See Boush, D.M., Friestad, M. & Wright, P. (2009) *Deception in the Marketplace:
     The Psychology of Deceptive Persuasion and Consumer Self Protection.* London:
     Routledge.

While all marketing and advertising must 'create the need' for consumer products, the process also involves confronting and influencing this deeper psychological bonding between person and product or experience. It means the advertiser must somehow create or excite in the consumer a sense that something is lacking. Like the child in the sandpit who notices another child has the bigger, newer and better truck to play with, we are constantly made aware that what we have is perhaps not quite as good as it might be, compared with what someone else has. This gives all consumers an 'itch' for more, a more that can bring them only temporary satisfaction, until the 'next best thing' comes along. From the other side, the seller must entice the buyer, and present the object for sale as 'the best' in its category, as full of promise, and personally transformative – a veritable pot of gold at the end of the consumer's particular rainbow.

The idea of luxury

Consumerism presented in this way is necessarily delusive – a process of imagining, comparing, and possessing that is frequently entangled in our hopes and dreams. Its delusive qualities are binding, influencing our commitments and beliefs, and our sense of who we are. These qualities are particularly clear when we consider luxury goods; their intense desirability, and the very idea of the elusive and exclusive nature of 'luxury', are used to present and sell many products today. Luxury, by definition, is what we imagine to be the 'best', the most valuable, or the ultimate in a particular class of goods. What is designated as a 'luxury' is usually something that we can physically possess, use or enjoy – such as clothing, cars, houses, personal accessories, food or drink.

In the 'Bling Ring' case, the police had to believe that the kids involved were stealing luxury goods for their market value – 'for money' – and this was the prosecutor's case. One detective, however, admitted to *Vanity Fair* that there was something 'weird' going on, and that there was something 'stalkerish' in their desire to wear what their celebrity heroes had worn. These luxury goods had, by association, become unique, the very best of the best, the ultimate prize in a fashion-loving teenage world saturated with images of elusive and otherwise impossible to earn luxuries.[7]

---

7   Sales, N.J. (2010) 'The suspects wore Louboutins', *Vanity Fair*, 28 February 2010, http://www.vanityfair.com/culture/2010/03/billionaire-girls-201003, accessed 12 November 2015.

The 'spookiness' the detective noticed is an essential component of the delusion of consumerism: it is the belief that a particular desired product, and especially a luxury one, will somehow transform us, and our experience, into something better, or even the best we can imagine, and also of course something socially superior. For luxury has always been held up as the ultimate social standard or measure of value, and a signal that the owner is 'higher' up the social tree, and somehow beyond the ordinary.

Indeed, in the distant past luxury was restricted to kings and princes, and only later 'allowed' to descend to merchants and those socially 'below' the very wealthy. So luxury has always had a powerful and dynamic role in shaping consumption practices 'below it', provoking both the cupidity of the buyer who desires it more than anything else, and that of the seller, who wants to exploit this unquenchable 'need' or desire for her own profit. Since luxury is so desirable, it is the pot of gold at the end of the rainbow, not only for the buyer, but also for the seller.[8]

The word 'luxury' seems to behave more like an adjective than a noun. In the minds of the elite who can afford such 'heavenly goods', it is attached to something, and then, when the luxury item in question has been copied cheaply, and loses its original rarity and exclusivity, something else that is also rare and expensive will take its place. In a memorable passage, the historian Fernand Braudel lists dozens of now everyday items that in the past moved, much more slowly than most luxuries do today, from the category of 'luxury' to that of 'ordinary'; he includes sugar, pepper, ceramic plates, metal forks, glass windowpanes and chairs in this list.

Availability and price are critical in this 'descent', or 'democratization', of luxury. As Braudel explains: luxury 'has many facets, according to the period, country or civilization in question. In contrast, the social drama, without beginning or end, with luxury as its prize and its theme, scarcely changes at all...' Luxury, he concludes, not only represents 'rarity and vanity, but also social success, fascination, the dream that one day becomes reality for the poor, and in so doing immediately loses its glamour'.[9]

The word's curious history helps illuminate this strangely mobile and elusive term. It derives from the Latin word *luxuria*, which meant 'sensual excess' or 'indulgent pleasure' (and not *lux* or 'light' as is sometimes

8   Berry, C.J. (1994) *The Idea of Luxury: A Historical and Conceptual Investigation.* Cambridge: Cambridge University Press: chapter 1.
9   Braudel, F. (1984) *Capitalism and Material Life, 1400–1800.* New York: Harper: 122, cited in Berry, C.J. (1994) *The Idea of Luxury: A Historical and Conceptual Investigation.* Cambridge: Cambridge University Press: 35.

assumed). Indeed, in the ancient world it was regarded with evident sus-
picion as a potential misuse of wealth for private indulgence. For this reason the term soon became a negative one, associated by the first Christians
with 'pagan' indulgence and sexual licence, often of a rather legendary kind.
Medieval preachers denounced luxury and sexual excess in the same breath,
sometimes describing this category of sin in lurid detail for their fascinated
audiences. The Italian word *lusso* retains something of the sensual guilty
pleasure the word once suggested. But since luxury was associated with a
certain elevated social rank, this attack on luxury was invariably controver-
sial, and potentially divisive.

In the Renaissance period, because of increased expenditure on luxury in
princely courts, the term began to lose its more negative associations. Many
of the Italian rulers, for example, felt obliged to establish their legitimacy in
the eyes of their subjects, and so commissioned artworks, collected ancient
objects and manuscripts, and redesigned their fortresses into neoclassical
palaces, replete with formal gardens, theatres, galleries and lavish public
spaces.

Their appetite for luxuries such as silks, fine ceramics and furniture, silver and glassware, and of course specially commissioned artworks, quickly
spread by example to the wealthy merchant elite. For the Medici princes
of Florence, the commitment involved in the consumption of such luxury
entailed a self-justifying belief system or ideology, Christian Neo-Platonism.
Its heavily symbolic spiritualization of nature and experience was elaborated in poetry, literature, philosophy and art, and remains one of the great
magnets for visitors to Florence to this day.[10]

The rising demand for exotic luxuries that accompanied the growth of
European courtly culture was also linked to the 'discovery' and colonization
of the New World. For luxury is not only precious to its possessors but also to
its sellers, who stand to make a fortune from this transaction. Originally the
result of seaborne attempts to find safer routes into distant Asia, and avoid
the conflicts then occurring in the Middle East, the opening-up of seaborne
trade routes not only changed Europe in economic terms, but also transformed its elite's understanding of the world and their place in it.

Printed textiles and rare spices, sugar, ceramics, silks and tea from the
East, American silver, exotic hardwoods, coffee and chocolate, were all
imported in increasing quantities. Many of the evils we now associate with

---

10   See Cole, A. (1995) *Virtue and Magnificence: Art of the Renaissance Courts.*
     New York: Abrams.

this period – from the slave trade to the violent colonization of the Americas, South Africa, Indonesia and India – can be traced back to the intense, rising demand for luxuries, and the extraordinary profits to be made by selling them in Europe. The quest for luxury in this way became a quest for power, wealth, conquest, empire, colonization and more capital.[11]

In response to this growing expansion of overseas trade, there was a huge growth in the number of professional lawyers and bankers, agents of various kinds, merchants, shopkeepers, manufacturers, public servants or 'placemen', and naval and army officers. These 'middling' people became the new luxury's essential facilitators and chief beneficiaries. European artisans and manufacturers imitated the most coveted imported luxuries, creating in time their own fine porcelain, silk clothing, silverware, ceramic tableware and glassware for drinking and eating. While they were not able to match Indian textiles or Chinese porcelain in quality or refinement for many years, they made up for this in other ways, especially in clever technical innovations, which made the luxuries the market craved more accessible, and more affordable.

The democratization of luxury

It is no exaggeration to say that this hunger for luxury transformed Europe and the world. It brought in its train new forms of capitalism, credit and indebtedness, and eventually of an imitative 'mass' manufacturing that the world had never seen before. As Saint-Simon, the disgruntled but perceptive chronicler of Louis XIV's glittering court, complained, this increasing desire for luxury had transformed both the court and the kingdom itself. The king, he said, had

> made luxury meritorious in all men, and in some a necessity, so that
> gradually the entire Court became dependent on his favours for their
> very subsistence ... Once it had begun this rottenness grew into that
> cancer which gnaws at the lives of all Frenchmen. It started, indeed, at
> the Court but soon spread to Paris, the provinces, and the army, where

11 Trentman, F. (2009) 'Crossing divides: Consumption and globalization in history', *Journal of Consumer Culture* 9.2: 187-220; and Guy, J. (2014) '"One thing leads to another": Indian textiles and the early globalization of style', in Peck, A. (Ed.), *Interwoven Globe: The Worldwide Textile Trade, 1500–1800*. New York: Metropolitan Museum of Art: 12-27.

generals are now assessed according to the tables that they keep and
the splendour of their establishments.[12]

The pursuit of 'abundance', excess or luxury in the courts created a strong
incentive to overspend and to become indebted, as Saint-Simon suggests.
This became most pronounced in the later seventeenth century, when there
seemed to be more and more on which to spend increasingly large sums, to
maintain appearances at court or in the city. But soon, cheaper versions of
the more desirable objects were invented and produced; this reduced the
price while increasing demand further.

For example, very expensive large, flat mirrors that were once the monopoly of Venetian craftsmen were, through Louis's enticements soon produced
in France, in a factory largely built to service the court and the homes of
the aristocracy. French craftsmen trained in the Venetians' secrets were
then paid by the Duke of Buckingham to start manufacturing these items
in London, so that by the end of the seventeenth century, large, flat mirrors
had become a staple of polite luxury in many English homes.

In the late seventeenth and eighteenth centuries, in Britain as in France,
in a world of increasing mobility in wealth and status, the pursuit and open
display of luxury soon became the norm, and this was closely related to the
enhancement of social reputation. It is not surprising that the first literary
and philosophical works about consumption were discussions about luxury,
its alleged dangers, and its significance in political and economic terms. This
large and diverse literature, sometimes rather misleadingly presented as
a 'debate', ranged from hostile denunciations, like those of Saint-Simon, to
attempts to relate the increasing consumption of luxury to the wealth of the
nation, through the benefits it had brought to trade and manufacturing.[13]

In many discussions of luxury in the period, a distinction was made
between the 'decent' and 'polite' use of luxury in the better regulated homes
of the upper and middle classes, and the excessive use of luxury by a previous generation of aristocrats, particularly the drunken adventures of the
English cavaliers of the Civil War era, and famed 'rakes' like Rochester,
whose exploits were closely associated in popular memory with the court of

12   Saint-Simon, L.d.R. (1958) *Saint-Simon at Versailles*. Translated and edited by
     L. Norton. London: Hamish Hamilton: 261.
13   Hilton, M. (2004) 'The legacy of luxury: Moralities of luxury since the 18th cen-
     tury', *Journal of Consumer Culture*, 4.1: 101-123; Berg, M. (1999) 'New commod-
     ities, luxuries, and their consumers in eighteenth-century England', in Berg,
     M. & Clifford, H. (Eds.), *Consumers and Luxury: Consumer Culture in Europe,
     1650–1850*. Manchester: Manchester University Press: 63-85.

Charles II. Indeed, it seems the term 'rake' migrated downwards, from those brilliant, gifted and rather flawed characters, to anyone who seemed to be following the trail these men had blazed.[14]

The so-called rakes were often the sons of aristocrats, young men of means, the heirs of fortunes but with limited social or political responsibility. They gained an outsized reputation because they could enjoy their pleasures – seemingly with few moral or financial restraints – outside the limits of 'decency' prescribed by religion, tradition, or the increasingly evident 'polite' use of luxury by their more settled, usually older, peers. Their role in the late seventeenth century was akin to that of today's young Hollywood celebrities, whose late night exploits might fill the pages of gossip magazines, websites and social media. And in retelling their tales in a witty way, the rakes gained a notoriety that was strangely attractive, or repulsive, to others.

Here is Jonathan Swift, tongue in cheek, referring to this double role, simultaneously the subject of religious and political denunciation, and a role-model for aspiring young men, who could recount these exploits in humorous tales, and don their caps, with sly admiration, to these 'superior' wealthy young men of 'reputation':

> They Writ, and Raillyed, and Rhymed, and Sung, and Said, and Said Nothing; They Drank, and Fought, and Whor'd, and Slept, and Swore, and took Snuff: They went to new Plays on the first Night, haunted the Chocolate-Houses, beat the Watch, lay on Bulks, and got Claps: They bilkt Hackney-Coachmen, ran into Debt with Shopkeepers, and lay with their Wives: They killed Bayliffs, kick'd Fidlers down Stairs, ate at Locket's, loyterd at Will's.[15]

Each act of drunkenness, outrageous nocturnal exploit, or sexual adventure, soon had to be excelled, or replaced by some even more risky indulgence that might also live on and make its perpetrators famous in the retelling. The English rake at the end of the seventeenth century in this way seemed to walk a moral tightrope between the rising standards of polite refinement that commerce had brought to Britain, and the temptations created by large cities like London and Paris, where everything, it seemed, was now for sale.

---

14   See Bryson, A. (1998) *From Courtesy to Civility: Changing Codes of Conduct in Early Modern England.* Oxford: Oxford University Press.

15   Swift, cited in Mackie, E.S. (2009) *Rakes, Highwaymen and Pirates.* Baltimore, MD: Johns Hopkins University Press: 38.

By turning the standard of polite luxury consumption on its head, and revelling openly in its sensual and sexual possibilities, the rake was both the ultimate hedonist and someone who revealed in his own life the dangers of unrestrained consumerism. He was the 'heroic' individualist, the 'pure' consumer – the young man who could indulge in sins only dreamed of by the young apprentice, who worked hard at the lathe in his shop. He embodied the secret, guilty dream of every consumer, to 'have it all', without the worry of how 'it all' would be paid for. Like today's young celebrities, the rake was, by definition, a man of wealth, but usually of limited responsibility.

Hogarth's A Rake's Progress

One of the first literary and artistic studies of this individualized excess of consumption, or perhaps, more accurately, of 'consumerism' is *A Rake's Progress*, William Hogarth's famous series of prints with their own commentary in verse, published in 1735. Like today's many imitators and admirers of celebrity culture, not so unlike the 'Bling Ring', Hogarth's rake is a 'wannabe', as much a victim of his own circumstances as a perpetrator of outrage.

Certainly neither a wealthy aristocrat, nor a hard-working writer or playwright trying to impress the court, Hogarth's 'Tom Rakewell' is a middle-class boy on the make, but without a clear idea of how he could achieve his goal of 'becoming somebody'. With considerable insight, Hogarth makes him the sadly neglected son of a mean-spirited London merchant. Indeed, Hogarth makes it clear that Tom's father's absence is the main source of the rootlessness that makes him aspire to be a rake, an argument also pursued by the author of the article in *Vanity Fair* on the leaders of the 'bling ring'.[16]

Tom Rakewell, like many younger consumers today, is not sure who he really is, or what he really wants, but fantasizes and imagines whom he might become, if given the opportunity. And it is clear in Hogarth's story that this is to be accomplished through the means afforded by consumption. His father's death provides Tom the opportunity to seek out the good life, since he had bequeathed him a fortune, which Tom sets about

16   Reproduced in Fort, B. & Rosenthal, A. (Eds.) (2001) *The Other Hogarth: Aesthetics of Difference*. Princeton, NJ: Princeton University Press: 22-29.

spending on 'remaking' himself, his appearance, and his way of life, and modelling himself on his much wealthier aristocratic fellow students he had met at Oxford.

In real life Hogarth's own father had been a schoolteacher and scholar, who, like Tom Rakewell, had ambitions to be a writer. Also like Tom, he was imprisoned for debt while Hogarth was still a child, and his suffering and early death obviously made a powerful impression on his young son. Brought up by his sisters and mother, in straitened circumstances, Hogarth was aware of the dangers of debt, and of the pursuit of luxury and hedonism; this is reflected in some detail in many of his prints and paintings, beyond this particular series. For Hogarth the pursuit of pleasure was a new form of madness, an attempt to climb the social ladder by mimicking the behaviour and extravagant spending of those who had the position and money to live such a life.

So in the first plate of *A Rake's Progress*, we find Tom in his father's room after the latter's sudden death, being fitted out in smart new clothes by a tailor. The central action of this plate is Tom's attempt to buy off a young woman, Sarah Young, whom he had evidently seduced and made pregnant while a student at Oxford. The deceptive letters he had written to her, promising marriage, spill from the apron of her angry mother who stands beside her. Sarah's tears, it is clear from Hogarth's portrait, move Tom not at all, so intent is he on the fantasy of becoming a 'man about town', a 'somebody' like the wealthy young men he had so admired at Oxford.[17]

In the second plate, reproduced here, we see how Tom will use his new-found wealth; he is being 'remade' with the assistance of various 'masters', who all offer their services to the aspiring young man about town. Tom stands against a fashionably Palladian architectural background, holding a play that he hopes to complete and produce, perhaps for the court. Several of Charles II's favourite rakes, including the notorious Rochester, were also famed playwrights and poets.

Arranged around the young man are all the predatory 'assistants' of the time: the music master, the architect and designer, the dancing master, and even the cudgel-bearing stand-over man, whom Tom might need should he be involved in some late-night argument or fight. These all promise to help 'make' him into the man of fashion he aspires to be. Like many modern consumers, Tom believes all that he needs to become the

17   See Hallett, M. (2001) 'Manly satire: William Hogarth's A Rake's Progress', in Fort & Rosenthal (Eds.), *The Other Hogarth*: 142-161.

person of his dreams are the 'right' props, as he learns to perform the role to which he aspires.[18]

FIGURE 1.1: WILLIAM HOGARTH, TOM RAKEWELL 'SURROUNDED BY ARTISTS AND MASTERS', PLATE 2, *A RAKE'S PROGRESS* (1735)

Courtesy Savannah College Art & Design, Georgia, USA

Hogarth here makes it clear that Tom has learned nothing, neither from his education and religious heritage, nor from his neglectful father. In the third plate, the famous Rose Crown tavern scene, we find Tom drunk and undone, one prostitute helping him to drink more and another stealing his watch, while the 'posture lady' (whose explicit performance was the main attraction of many brothels at this time) undresses in the foreground. In the

18   See Campbell, C. (2004) 'I shop therefore I know I am: The metaphysical basis of modern consumerism', in Ekstrom, B. & Brembeck, H. (Eds.), *Elusive Consumption*. Oxford: Berg: 27-44.

scene, this perceptive author underlines the reduction of human beings to commodities in the new commercial city.

FIGURE 1.2: WILLIAM HOGARTH, 'THE TAVERN SCENE', PLATE 3, *A RAKE'S PROGRESS* (1735)
Courtesy Savannah College Art & Design, Georgia, USA

In this, and in subsequent plates, Hogarth aims to show how Tom's self-indulgence has moral, as well as spiritual roots, and serious personal consequences. We see Tom dishevelled and drunk after his encounter with the prostitute. His 'manly' sword is symbolically unsheathed at his side and his lantern, representing the light of reason, and the soul, lies broken on the floor. On the wall behind him are the cruel visages of Roman emperors who stare blankly down at him, perhaps there to remind him of the ultimate emptiness of his indulgence, and a classical reference that would have been well understood by Hogarth's audience.

The following plate depicts a nasty confrontation with a bailiff over debts, from which Tom is rescued by his ever-faithful Sarah, the mother of his child, now dressed as a respectable milliner. In this scene Tom is on his way to being 'received' at the Court. It is as though Hogarth wants to underline the contrast between the virtues of honest hard work that Sarah embodies, and the dangers of the dream that motivates Tom, that of becoming 'some-one' at last, at least in the eyes of his social betters.

As Hogarth puts it in an accompanying verse, 'Poverty [is] ... Ready to seize the poor Remains That Vice hath left of all his Gains.' Tom's pursuit of pleasure fails to get him the position he wants, and requires more and more of the dice, the bottle, and the brothel, while his real fortune ever more quickly melts away. The role of debt and speculation, as Hogarth well understood, is vital in creating and maintaining the excess enabled by con-sumerism: by borrowing or 'winning' at the table (or share market) we can extend our capacity to consume, even beyond our means.[19]

Compassionate and tragic, Hogarth's moral vision illuminates his detailed study of the new consumerist economy of pleasure and luxury. The city was now built on trade, and everything, including people, was for sale. In the last three plates of A Rake's Progress, Hogarth forces us to confront the con-sequences of this life, in excruciating, visceral detail. After shamefully mar-rying an old widow in order to steal her fortune, an evil act again confronted by a weeping Sarah and child, in the last two plates we witness Tom's rapid descent into ill health, madness and death. His debts can never be repaid, and his way of life has led to an incurable venereal disease that soon sends him mad.

The final plate, pictured here, shows the ultimate conclusion of Tom's 'pro-gress'. He is in the madhouse, where, attended by the ever-faithful Sarah and his child, he struggles towards death. Around him is an assortment of other madmen, possessed by more traditional delusions – religious, 'scientific', and political. But Tom's madness, Hogarth is suggesting here, is an impor-tant new kind of delusion, a speciality of his own more 'commercial times'. Summarizing this, Hogarth declares in the accompanying verse, that these are the 'ghostly ... Shapes of Pleasure' that now torment Tom, and which he has pursued to his own financial, mental and bodily ruin, and finally to his own early death.[20]

19   Hogarth, plate 4, in Fort & Rosenthal (Eds.), The Other Hogarth: 25; and see Crown, P. (2001) 'Hogarth's working women: Commerce and consumption', idem.: 224-239.
20   Hogarth, plate 8, in Fort & Rosenthal (Eds.), The Other Hogarth: 29.

FIGURE 1.3: WILLIAM HOGARTH, 'IN THE MADHOUSE', PLATE 8, A RAKE'S PROGRESS (1735)

Courtesy Wellcome Museum, London

Somebody and nobody

This tragic story is very significant. It is one of the first literary and artistic productions to explore the essential double bind underlying modern consumerism. As the 'pure' consumer, with no productive work and no aim to live a fulfilling life, Tom has embarked on a journey he cannot afford, in order to remake himself into someone he can never become. Throughout the series Hogarth hints at Tom's neglect of his capabilities, his potential skills and his capacity to work, with an abandoned, half-written play left in plain sight in several of the plates.

Caught up in his dream of 'becoming somebody', Tom ignores what he could do with his own talents. Instead he pursues the empty symbols of success, on a path that leads, as Hogarth emphasizes, directly to self-destruction, madness and death. Hogarth implies that nothing can satisfy someone in such a delusive state – a conclusion not so different from that of modern psychologists, who emphasize the incommensurability of consumerism's materialism and perfectionism with our intrinsic well-being.[21]

For Hogarth the pursuit of pleasure and luxury was necessarily tied to mounting indebtedness and theft (if we assume the old lady Tom married was his victim), with Tom's gambling somehow promising to make up for his losses. Hogarth had witnessed the destruction of his own father through debt, and there are many signs in A Rake's Progress, and elsewhere, that he considered debt to be the main means through which reality catches up with the consumer's dream of self-transformation. Debt allows us to possess *immediately* what seems most desirable, rather than wait to accumu late the money necessary to buy what we need. Credit, like speculation and gambling, dangles before its victims the hope of a rapid 'solution' to the urgent problem created by consumerism, allowing us to enjoy it now and pay for it later. As Hogarth rightly divined, 'loss aversion' intensifies Tom's gambling, since in his mind he hopes that he might at last recover what he had 'before', when he first inherited his father's estate.

Tom's underlying problem is that he feels he 'needs' to possess the clothes, home, servants, attributes, money, and above all the fashionable style required to be recognized as 'a man about town'. He hires expert designers, trainers, music and even poetry masters to make him more visible to those he aspires to join. It is Tom's negative sense of personal value that supplies his inner motive, an inadequacy the clear-eyed artist recognizes, and to which he repeatedly draws attention. Tom is chasing a dream because he secretly believes he is 'not good enough'; by becoming a rake like his wealthy friends, he thinks he will become 'somebody' – recognized and valued at last.

For Hogarth the developing British class system was the context of this inner contest between the 'somebody' we want to be recognized as, and the 'nobody' we fear we might be. In a brilliant sketch from this period, in a frontispiece to a little book of 'peregrinations' by Ebenezer Forrest, Hogarth depicted a traditional folk figure called 'Somebody'. He is a well-dressed young man without a head – in fact, an empty suit of fine clothes.

21   See Dittmar, H. (2007) 'The costs of consumer culture and the "cage within": The impact of the material "good life" and "body perfect" ideals on individuals' identity and well-being', Psychological Inquiry, 18.1: 23-31.

For the tailpiece, Hogarth sketched his distinctly working-class companion, 'Nobody', who lacks a body, and is merely a grinning face with hands grasping forks, knives and spoons; perhaps for Hogarth this is the person who nevertheless understands his real needs.[22]

* * *

Tom's story seems a useful starting point for a discussion of consumerism in this book. Hogarth deftly weaves together the three dimensions of consumerism like coloured thread in a string: its moral and psychological basis, in the consumer's emotive commitment to possession and ownership; its social and comparative drivers, which suggest the consumer must 'be' or look like some admired others; and its financial and economic risks, typically large amounts of debt, and the consequences this can lead to. Tom's actions involve him in a series of increasingly troubling personal, social and economic obligations, and these necessarily have a moral dimension that cannot be evaded. For there are significant costs involved in what, where and how we consume.

Tom's delusive pursuit of luxury and pleasure that promised to enhance, transform and elevate him to some imagined 'better life' was, for Hogarth, necessarily self-destructive. It was a product of materialism, and the lack of love, moral instruction, and familial example that should have been a part of Tom's upbringing; it was also the result of Tom's own neglect of his capabilities, shown in the abandoned play that appears cast aside on a side-table in two of the plates. The diversionary power invested in the dream of consumerism is something I will return to later.[23]

Like every consumer since, Tom wants to be accepted, and to be seen as successful. The imitative, emulative quality that drives consumerism is laid bare in Tom's story, but is worth examining in more depth. Our capacity for imitation informs not only consumerism, but also the productive systems that generate the goods and services that are the objects of the consumer's quest. It also informs the work of the designer, who must imitate and adapt what is most desirable, to entice the consumer to use what the manufacturer provides.

22   For a discussion of these points see Uglow, J. (1997) *Hogarth: A Life and a World*. New York: Farrar, Strauss & Giroux: chapter 11.
23   On this contrast, see Kasser, T., & Ryan, R. (1996) 'Further examining the American Dream: Differential correlates of intrinsic and extrinsic goals', *Personality and Social Psychology Bulletin*, 22.3: 280-287.

Further reading

Appleby, J.O. (1978) *Economic Thought and Ideology in Seventeenth Century England*. Princeton, NJ: Princeton University Press.

Berg, M. (2005) *Luxury and Pleasure in Eighteenth Century England*. Oxford: Oxford University Press.

Berry, C.J. (1999) *The Idea of Luxury: A Historical and Conceptual Investigation*. Cambridge: Cambridge University Press.

Bryson, L. (1998) *From Courtesy to Civility: Changing Codes of Conduct in Early Modern England*. Oxford: Oxford University Press.

Campbell, C. (2005 [1987]) *The Romantic Ethic and the Spirit of Modern Consumerism*. 2nd edn, London: Alcuin.

Crowley, J.E. (2001) *The Invention of Comfort: Sensibilities and Design in Early Modern Britain and America*. Baltimore, MD: Johns Hopkins University Press.

De Vries, J. (2008) *The Industrious Revolution: Consumer Behaviour and the Household Economy, 1650 to the Present*. Cambridge: Cambridge University Press.

Hallett, M., & Riding, C. (Eds.) (2007) *Hogarth*. London: Tate Museum.

Mackie. E.S. (2009) *Rakes, Highwaymen and Pirates*. Baltimore, MD: Johns Hopkins University Press.

McCracken, G.D. (1988) *Culture and Consumption: New Approaches to the Symbolic Character of Consumer Goods and Activities*. Bloomington, IN: Indiana University Press.

Melchior-Bonnet, S. (2001) *The Mirror: A History*. (K.H. Jewett, Trans.). London: Routledge.

Peck, A. (Ed.) (2014). *Interwoven Globe: The Worldwide Textile Trade, 1500–1800*. New York: Metropolitan Museum of Art.

Schwartz, D.T. (2010) *Consuming Choices: Ethics in a Global Consumer Age*. New York: Rowman & Littlefield.

Schor, J.S. (2004) *Born to Buy: The Commercialized Child and the New Consumer Culture*. New York: Scribner.

Tatzel, M. (Ed.) (2014) *Consumption and Well-Being in the Material World*. London: Springer

Trentmann, F. (2016) *The Empire of Things: How we became a world of consumers from the fifteenth century to the twenty first*. London: Allen Lane.

Uglow, J. (1997) *Hogarth: A Life and a World*. New York: Farrar, Strauss & Giroux.

2
Imitation in design and consumption

Imitation and global trade

As an adaptive art, design builds upon an innate, universal human imitativeness, which is also fully on display in consumerism. As children, we learn and develop through imitation. Imitation is the most effective way to learn, to teach and to pass on environmentally and culturally specific knowledge and skills, including language and design. By imitating their parents, children are able to learn whole languages within a few years; they are prime examples of the many evolutionary benefits to be gained from imitating others.[1]

This facility for imitation is also one of the sources of design, and the everyday practices of consumption with which designers must engage. For design is both an imitative and an adaptive art. It builds upon imitation and then adapts what has been learned to suit changing contexts. In this way, designers might borrow and adapt a form that belongs to another object or context, a landscape or a whole environment. The architect, Jorn Utzon, for example, referenced the sailing boats on Sydney Harbour, incorporating them into the design of the Sydney Opera House. An extraordinarily innovative and expressive work for its time, it took many years for many Australians to come to terms with it.

---

[1] Oughourlian, J.-M. (2011) 'Imitation in child development and adult psychology: From universal mimesis to the self formed by desire', in Garrels, S. (Ed.), *Mimesis and Science: Empirical Research on Imitation and the Mimetic Theory of Culture and Religion*. East Lansing, MI: Michigan State University: chapter 2.

In developing technological devices, other designers might imitate a technology or process and adapt or apply it to another context. The Dyson vacuum cleaner, for instance, is based upon extraction systems found in many factories. It took Dyson years of experimentation and work to create a working prototype he could sell, and then, as with the architect of the Sydney Opera House, he struggled to persuade others that his design would 'work' or sell, since it looked so unfamiliar and unlike other vacuum cleaners.

Nevertheless, new knowledge and experience can inspire a fresh round of adaptive imitation, sparking changes in behaviour, fashion, design and architecture. As a result of overseas trade in early modern Europe, the discovery of novel foods, drinks, spices and textiles stimulated many examples of adaptive imitation, with further developments and refinements created through design. The drinking of tea and coffee drove European artisans to develop a range of pots, cups, saucers and other implements to cater for this new practice; they based their designs on Chinese and Persian models, progressively refining their attempts against the standards set by these originals. This helped start a mania for collecting, using and displaying crockery in England and America.[2]

From the early 1500s, not long after the Portuguese 'discovered' India and Japan, overseas trade continuously stimulated adaptive imitation in Europe. The superior craftsmanship of Japanese and Chinese silk and ceramic manufacturers, of Indian carpenters, weavers, cotton printers and jewellers, all impressed and influenced European artisans. The wealthy commissioned tea sets and tableware from China, decorative chests and portmanteaus of ivory and silver from India, and of course gemstones and jewellery. The commissions themselves required various adaptations: Chinese potters had to place handles on their cups and Indian cabinet makers had to adapt to European tastes in the detail and intended use of their intricately decorated chests. The Japanese, Chinese and Indian rulers were also fascinated by the exotic differences they noted in their European visitors, and soon adopted their guns and instruments, and their love of tobacco.

The widespread adoption of oriental patterns in Europe is particularly revealing of the growing dependence of European elites on Asia for textiles, especially silks and cottons. Oriental patterns became favourites among

---

2   Berg, M. (2002) 'From imitation to invention: Creating Commodities in the eighteenth century', *Economic History Review*, 55.1: 1-30; and Trentmann, F. (2016) *Empire of Things*. London: Allen Lane: chapter 2.

European artisans, and they appeared in textiles and carpets imported into Europe, and were also reproduced on fabrics created in Europe. These imitative influences travelled both ways. Imported textiles commissioned by European consumers soon began to reflect their own preferences. For example, printed fabric from India was purposely given a lighter and more open background, more in keeping with European tastes (and climate). Such adjustments were again rapidly copied and further developed across Europe by artisans adapting Indian and Chinese patterns in their own products.[3]

Exchanges involving adaptive imitation also had significant intellectual, social and cultural parallels. These included the spread of Christianity into many parts of Asia, the serious study in Europe of Asian history, religions, literatures, languages, fauna and flora, and also the more practical adoption of exotic plants for use in European gardens, orchards, agriculture and medicine. From the seventeenth century, many paintings in India, Japan and China depict the strange features, dress and equipment of early European traders and their cargoes. There are also many paintings and prints in Europe, showing off this entanglement of East and West through trade. For example, there are a number of well-known seventeenth-century European portraits of sea captains, ambassadors, scholars, and others, wearing or using objects of exotic origin, from bird of paradise feathers in their caps, to Turkish rugs on their tables, and many other reminders of global trade, such as silks and tea implements in ceramic.[4]

Just as scholars and missionary-priests became the intellectual and religious conduit into Asia for their European audiences, so traders, designers and artisans became the cultural translators through which Asian goods were first copied and re-presented, interpreted and popularized for widespread use in Europe. Textiles are particularly valuable in revealing this increasingly interdependent world. Surviving examples show seventeenth-century silks made in London to Turkish patterns and colours for the Turkish market; Indian cottons were created in different colours and patterns not only for European customers but also for markets in Indonesia and Thailand. There was an extensive take up of favoured patterns, such as the (Persian) tree of life, or the (Chinese) rose and trellis, in both European and Asian workshops.

3   Guy, J. (2014) '"One thing leads to another": Indian textiles and the early globalization of style' in A. Peck (Ed.), *Interwoven Globe: The Worldwide Textile Trade, 1500–1800.* New York: Metropolitan Museum of Art: 12-27.

4   See for example Abraham van den Hecken (artist), *A Scholar in his studio,* c. 1655, in Bennett, J., 'Marege', in Bennett, J. & Kelty, R. (Eds.) (2015) *Treasure Ships: Art in the Age of Spices* (Adelaide: Art Gallery of South Australia): 183.

The desire for these luxuries in Europe prompted the manufacture of cheaper, more accessible substitutes, which in turn encouraged technical advances in production as well as adaptive imitation through design. This soon encouraged an expansion of consumption, as the middle classes took up cheaper versions of more desirable, exotic luxury goods. The eighteenth century saw the emergence of a pattern that became more common in the nineteenth: an expensive exotic luxury was soon replicated in a more accessible form as a 'semi-luxury' or 'popoluxe' product, more or less mimicking its expensive original. Printed cotton could be substituted for imported silk, new alloys for silver or gold, while jewellers and watchmakers invented lookalike substitutes, such as so-called 'paste' jewellery, to avoid the expense, and dangers, of wearing real jewels in public.

Adaptive imitation in design

Increasing demand for fashionable novelties, such as cottons and silks, lacquered and gilded furniture and mirrors, decorative ceramics and glassware, drove the search for cheaper substitutes, and led to the appearance of designers in every domain. The designer's expression of the object's more desirable qualities, in the fashionable taste of the time, reassured consumers of the value and utility of relatively new and untried objects, or objects that appeared to be copies of more luxurious ones. It was the designer's work both to understand and to anticipate consumer desires, and the formal elements that contributed to a dominant fashion.[5]

By the nineteenth century the collaborative application of professional design, marketing and technological improvement had become widespread. This was especially apparent in the manufacture of fast-moving packaged goods, furniture, wallpapers and textiles. In growing competitive markets, goods had to be more carefully designed and more effectively promoted. In this way professional design and marketing became intertwined, especially where goods were produced in large numbers for a mass market. Designers, in effect, found themselves between engineers or manufacturers, on the one hand, and retailers on the other, facilitating, translating and realizing innovations in more fashionable and attractive forms.

---

5   Kriegel, L. (2004) 'The culture of the copy: Calico, capitalism, and design copyright in early Victorian Britain', *The Journal of British Studies*, 43.2: 233-265.

Global trade today is vastly larger in volume than ever before, and more extensive in the variety of financial instruments, ideas, goods and services being traded. It is universal in its geographical spread, and the speed of transactions and technical innovations has greatly accelerated. Nevertheless, it remains tied to the social engine of adaptive imitation that would be easily recognizable to someone living in eighteenth-century London or Paris.

It is easier now to overlook the central role imitation has always played in design, and to focus instead on creative adaptation and invention. In the early modern period it was difficult for artisans to create exact copies, and therefore these were especially valued. From the 1780s onwards, however, in many areas original design became more widely valued, and was duly analysed and discussed in newspapers and journals; this is reflected in the expanding record of registered designs or patents. Original design could make a common object stand out clearly in a crowded field of competing products. Since mass-production created multiples of the same object or pattern, the designer was required to intervene continuously, to create apparent difference and variety.[6]

This is a central paradox in the relationship between industrialism and design. While *substitution* in materials, processes or products has become an essential building block in all advanced economic, scientific and technological systems and the knowledge that underpins them, human beings instinctively favour *variation and difference* within a recognizable field, as this is what is experienced in the apparently endless variations and similarities of the natural world.

So while the conversion of energy, labour and materials into more efficient and profitable forms of industrial innovation still requires many, and often subtle, forms of substitution, designers must intervene and mask this substitution with visual and material cues of distinction or difference. This involves a creative visioning that makes design an art both shaped by and in turn shaping industrialism and, ultimately, consumerism. The inventiveness of design begins in its ability to cut through the repetitiveness and similarities that industrial substitution inevitably creates, a skill closely associated with the generation of novelty and delight, to attract and fascinate the potential user or consumer.

6   Benhamou, R. (1991) 'Imitation in the decorative arts of the eighteenth century', *Journal of Design History*, 4.1: 1-13; and Saumarez Smith, C. (2000) *The Rise of Design: Design and the Domestic Interior in Eighteenth Century England.* London: Pimlico.

Adapting an earlier, often handmade model of an object or image into a renovated or different form that could be mass-produced, early Modernist design typically used abstraction and simplification to achieve its most powerful effects. Gio Ponti designed his famous *Superleggera* ('Super Light') chair, for example, after reflection and experimentation with a simple chair he had found in a fishing village not far from Genoa. His approach was not dissimilar to that used by William Morris in the development and design of his famous 'rush-bottomed chair' some 70 years earlier.[7]

However, Ponti spent many months experimenting with the chair's joints and legs in order to simplify the form, reduce the chair's weight, and increase its strength in use. He later described this process as an attempt to discover the primitive 'original' of all chairs, by working through the model provided by his chosen vernacular original.[8]

FIGURE 2.1: GIO PONTI, SUPERLEGGERA ('SUPER LIGHT') CHAIR

Photo: Gini Lee (2016)

7   See the photograph of this chair by Frederick Evans in William Morris's Kelm-
      scott Manor (1896), in Hart, I. (2010) *Arts and Crafts Objects*. Manchester: Man-
      chester University Press: 83.
8   See Vitra Design Museum (2015) 'Superleggera, no. 699; Gio (Giovanni) Ponti',
      http://www.design-museum.de/en/collection/100-masterpieces/detail-
      seiten/superleggera-no-699-ponti.html, accessed 1 May 2015; and also
      Lamonaca, M. (1998) 'Tradition as transformation: Gio Ponti's programme for
      the modern Italian home, 1928–1933', *Studies in the Decorative Arts*, 5.1: 52–82.

There are two complementary and interrelated aspects to adaptive imita-tion in design: a technical, scientific one, and a cultural or aesthetic one. In this process, cultural concerns and technical insights, largely based on pro-cesses of substitution, can combine to influence the designer, and in some cases – as in this one – to strike the gold of innovation. While we might admire Ponti's pursuit of the elegant minimum, his intensive structural experiments, and increasing fascination with a new, stronger triangular jointing system, combined to produce an extremely successful design.

This type of creative, adaptive imitation can also be seen at work in the prehistory of modern design. In the seventeenth century, as we have seen, the best dinner and tea sets enjoyed by the wealthy had been specially com-missioned and imported at great expense. European artisans were commis-sioned by several royal patrons to find the secrets of Chinese manufacture and produce their own versions, and these 'royal manufactories' soon inspired other entrepreneurial artisans. Emulating the 'polite luxury' of the courts, the commercial middle classes sought out their own cheaper din-ner and tea sets, and many rival potters attempted to satisfy this rapidly expanding demand.

Josiah Wedgwood's role in this field has been recounted many times, but is worth a brief mention here. It was through his efforts that the once sharp distinction between 'fine' imported porcelain and everyday table-ware began to change, largely through his energetic experimental pursuit of adaptive imitation and material and product substitution.[9]

Wedgwood was deeply interested in the technology and science of his calling. A tireless experimenter, he painstakingly recorded the results of using a particular glaze upon a carefully chosen batch of clay. This practice of meticulous experimentation, trial and comparison, is what some design-ers today might term a preliminary 'mapping' exercise, where the possibili-ties of substitution and variation are carefully laid out, assessed and then related to the aims of the exercise – in this case the creation of an English substitute for Chinese porcelain. Wedgwood was also a business pioneer. He developed new practices in management, manufacture and marketing, dis-playing an equally meticulous attention to detail, and again drawing on his understanding of the technical requirements of managing substitutability.[10]

9   For an introduction, see Dolan, B. (2004) *Wedgwood: The First Tycoon*. New York: Viking; and Forty, A. (1992) *Objects of Desire: Design and Society: 1750–1980*. London: Thames & Hudson: chapter 2.
10   McKendrick, N. (1982) 'Josiah Wedgwood and the commercialization of the potteries', in McKendrick, N., Brewer, J. & Plumb, J.H. (Eds.), *The Birth of a*

Wedgwood used this proto-scientific approach to wrestle with many of the typical problems that had beset production in his industry, including glazes that ran and colours that were unstable, lack of consistency in the size, shape and appearance of what was produced, and decoration that was often individualistic, non-standardized, and sometimes poorly executed by still largely independent craftsmen. These problems might have been unremarkable 200 years earlier but, with the tastes of his times shaped by far superior exemplars from China, they became the concern of many, including his great rival, Josiah Spode.

Wedgwood aimed for consistency, standardization and uniformity, and the way he ran his factory is suggestive of how changes in demand drove changes in production, increasing the importance of substitutability towards developing new techniques and expanding knowledge. By dividing his workers and dedicating their energies to separate processes within the production cycle – turning his 'men into machines' as he rather innocently put it – he managed to establish a much greater control over the production process.

Men (and women) in the factory became largely substitutable, the difference in their skill and their style of work becoming less noticeable and less disruptive to the process of ordered or planned imitation Wedgwood aimed for. Differences in colour, pattern and shape could be now regulated, and given to a single model-maker or designer to manage, before the manufacturing process commenced. Able to produce more uniform pots and plates, to carefully designed and recorded clays, patterns and moulds, Wedgwood could then have skilled painters decorate them, using simple stencils.

Wedgwood achieved great fame in his own lifetime due to a cream or ivory dinner set he made for the Queen; this work enabled him to use the title, 'Potter to Her Majesty'. Keenly aware of the 'engine of emulation' at work in his market, in 1764 he recorded his own surprise at Queensware's extraordinary success, wondering at how so many people seemed willing to follow the royal example:

> The demand for this said *Creamcolour*, alias *Queens Ware*, alias *Ivory* still increases. It is really amazing how rapidly the use of it has spread almost over the whole Globe, and how universally it is liked. How much of this general use and estimation is owing to the mode of its introduction – and how much to its real utility and beauty?[11]

Consumer Society: The Commercialization of Eighteenth-Century England. Bloomington, IN: Indiana University Press: 99-144.

11   Quoted in Blaszczyk, R.L. (2000) *Imagining Consumers: Design and Innovation from Wedgwood to Corning.* Baltimore, MD: Johns Hopkins University Press: 6.

FIGURE 2.2: WEDGWOOD CREAM-WARE PLATE (C. 1774), MARSH FROG DESIGN FOR
CATHERINE II OF RUSSIA

Courtesy Brooklyn Museum, New York

Given this background, it is not surprising that Wedgwood regarded his reproduction of the Duke of Portland's famous Roman cameo vase in 1790 as the ultimate triumph of his career. Probably dating from the first century, this vase, a delicate blue glass cameo reliquary, was one of the great classical treasures of the time. It is a measure of Wedgwood's wealth and success by this late stage in his career that, despite being dogged by ill-health, he was still willing to spend time and money to produce an 'exact' copy of this unique antique object. Some estimates suggest that he spent the equivalent in today's money of several million pounds. Although the venture was a commercial failure – perhaps only 20 were sold – his exacting copy of the vase became a successful promotional tool for both his company and his own ingenuity.[12]

12   Keynes, M. (1998) 'The Portland Vase: Sir William Hamilton, Josiah Wedgwood and the Darwins', *Notes and Records of the Royal Society of London* 52.2: 237-259.

Consumption and imitation

Wedgwood's vase was intended as a cheaper but more lifelike imitation or substitute for a famous antique vase. The neoclassical style required the production of a unified interior landscape of decorative patterns and forms, objects, furniture and furnishing, all in a matching, simplified 'classical' style. In England this resulted in artisans developing their work to match this demand, often using cheaper substitute materials like wood or plaster for metals or enamels. This can still be seen in many older fireplaces that have faux marble patterns in wood, and figures and decorative elements in gilded and raised plaster. Wedgwood's vase, in another substitute material, was part of this world of imitation and substitution, but was linked more directly to its authenticating original. While not itself commercially successful, as an extraordinary achievement in imitation it brought fame and further custom to his business; it was a triumph of craftsmanship as much as marketing.

FIGURE 2.3: JOSIAH WEDGWOOD AND SONS, LTD, PORTLAND VASE (C. 1790)

Courtesy Cleveland Museum of Art, Ohio, USA

Imitation and substitution always suggest an authenticating original, and so require knowledge of the past or the 'story' of the original, just as imitation from nature requires an understanding of what is being represented, and how it might be adapted to suit its new setting. Therefore, young designers in the nineteenth century were expected to spend many hours learning to draw plants, animals and birds, in a variety of styles, because most of the decorative elements they were expected to create were taken from these sources. These two reference points in time and place – the past and nature – in this way become frames that link the early development of modern design with mass-consumption.[13]

Imitation in design is strangely mirrored in the social imitation or emulation found in consumption. The 'engine of emulation', as Wedgwood called it, increased the sales of his cream-ware through the products' direct association with the Queen. Admiration and what Veblen called 'invidious' comparison, has always played a powerful role in consumer preference. What is desired is the original, the non-substitutable, but along the way the substitute becomes acceptable because the original is either not available or not affordable. But the substitute brings us closer to the original, or at least close enough to allow others to think we have in our possession something 'as good as' the best.

In this imitative landscape, even an innovation must build upon what has preceded it, and is often carefully designed in a form that will be familiar to the potential user. The link to the original must be self-explanatory and sufficiently visible in the object's design, and related to a familiar context to be accepted in the market. Even a revolutionary product like the iPhone was initially understood and accepted mainly because it was built upon the widespread and well-established experience of the mobile phone and the computer: it simply brought elements of these together in an elegant and evidently well designed new package.

Most design innovations are also geared to stimulate not only more consumption but also the more rapid discard of what is to be superseded or replaced. By making imitation and substitution seem innovative, a sense of value, of identification, can be transferred from what we already possess, which might now be made to look old-fashioned, to the 'next best thing'.

Substitution is thus intimately related not only to the generation of new, attractive objects for consumption, but also to the discard of what the new object is intended to replace. Novelty and discard in this way go together, for the promise of consumerism is embedded in the new, the latest and the

13   Keyser, B.M. (1998) 'Ornament as idea: Indirect imitation of nature in the design reform movement', *Journal of Design History*, 11.2: 127-144; and Brett, D. (1986) 'Drawing and ideology of industrialization', Design Issues, 3.2: 59-72.

best, and so we must make room for this 'better' object by devaluing and discarding the 'old', even if it still functions well. This is particularly obvious in interior design, where rooms are periodically remodelled or 'upgraded'.[14]

The consumer's commitment to a new product, perhaps something that resembles a more expensive and rare item, will coincide with a usually unspoken agreement that the substitute is both necessary to possess, and 'better' than its original. This widely accepted viewpoint is often expressed in the language of design promotion, sometimes termed 'lifestyle' or design advice. While many of Wedgwood's products sold very well following this type of substitution, his Portland Vase might have failed in the market partly because of its high price, and the fact that it was supposed to be an exact replica of an ancient and priceless antique, and not something simply 'suitable' for a neoclassical interior, easily matched with other more typical faux-marble wood panels and repeated decorative details.

The so-called 'Diderot effect' – named after the eighteenth-century Enlightenment thinker, Denis Diderot – is an important point of consideration here. It refers to a situation where we place our prized new object side by side with an old one, and notice how the old now stands out and suffers by comparison with the new. The new item makes the old appear imperfect and highlights the apparent age and stylistic incompatibilities between them. While the Diderot effect can lead simply to buying a new set of clothes, it can also lead to more expensive purchases. We start to perceive that what we have is 'not good enough' in comparison with the brand new, and then, for example, we might replace bathrooms, kitchens, and living room settings, and extend or change whole buildings.[15]

The Diderot effect has been understood for a long time and, in the nineteenth century led to the selling of furniture in matching sets, in fashionable historical style. This matching of form and colour, especially with goods that come with a provenance linking them to some valued or authentic original, is central to both the history of design and the story of consumerism. This is also echoed today in the world of the brand, where the brand summarizes a whole company and product history, and so embodies the qualities that the company is supposed to represent for the consumer.

14   Ryan, M. (2014) 'Apartment therapy: Everyday modernism, and aspirational disposability', *Television and New Media* 15.1: 68-80.
15   McCracken, G.D. (1988) *Culture and Consumption: New Approaches to the Symbolic Character of Consumer Goods and Activities*. Bloomington, IN: Indiana University Press: chapter 8; and see Hartman, T. (2007) 'On the Ikeaization of France', *Public Culture*, 19.3: 483-498.

We feel elevated when we buy a new car, not only because of the convenience, and the fact we might need one, but because such an important branded good becomes closely linked to our own sense of identity and social worth through the now public story of its origins and meaning, and its social worth. The 'story' associated with the car's brand becomes a myth that is attached to the object and helps elevate its value in our eyes, rather like a mental 'cookie' planted in the software of our minds: the new BMW, for example, might seem unique to us through this brand association, and seems to 'say' something about us – or at least so we like to imagine.[16]

The brand's story or myth, rather like Wedgwood's references to classical originals and to his royal customer, is deeply assumptive in its authority over us, because we all are led to assume a pre-existing perfection uniqueness or 'non-substitutability' in its mythical origins. Today, the luxury brand seems 'perfect' with its story carefully built up over time in many generations of advertising, mythmaking, logos and staged events. We bask in its reflected light, and feel elevated by our association with its carefully crafted 'authenticity'. This is often traced back to some workshop and dedicated individual craftsman, or family of craftsmen, as in the case of many famous 'luxury brands' today.

Through consumption, imitation allows us to try out the new, under cover of gaining access at last to a valuable 'authentic' object – in the form of an acceptable imitation or substitute. It also lets us assemble a series of these objects for ourselves in some relatively unique combination or collection, that seems to be ours and ours alone. In this way, identity and difference are developed and marked off against a shifting landscape of successive patterns of imitation and substitution. In time, the things we buy are then discarded in turn to make way for the new.[17]

A commercial opportunity is created by the time horizon of each manufactured good: the shorter the life, the more opportunity there is to produce a 'better' or more affordable substitute. Substitution based on adaptive imitation is thus attractive because it promises something 'as good as' the original object which may be a luxury, or just something beyond what we can normally afford. It promises more for less, and more more often.

16   Schembri, S., Merrilees, W. & Kristiansen, S. (2010) 'Brand consumption and narrative of the self', *Psychology and Marketing*, 27.6: 623-638.
17   See especially Miller, D. (2008) *The Comfort of Things*. Cambridge: Polity Press; and also Csikszentmihalyi, M. (1993) 'Why we need things', in Lubar, S. & Kingery, W.D. (Eds.), *History from Things: Essays on Material Culture*. Washington, DC: Smithsonian Institute: 20-29.

However, in an ever-widening market this creates a lengthy environmental tail, requiring more materials and energy, and creating more waste.

From imitation to hyper-consumption

Some years ago I visited Guzzini, a large Italian manufacturer of plastic kitchenware, tableware, sinks, baths and architectural lighting, and a very successful one in these highly competitive market sectors. Since the early 1960s Guzzini has used modern design as a strategic means of differentiating its products within a crowded and competitive market, its catalogues displaying every product like art in a museum, with each piece associated with its well-known designer.

During my visit the marketing manager confided to me that without this ongoing strategic use of design, without 'our designers', the company would be forced to compete directly with low cost producers in Asia. In a world of copies, he was suggesting, original design gave his company up to two years' advantage – he was explicit on this point – by producing an 'original' object for the consumer to value and enjoy.[18]

Indeed, within days of a successful design being released, it is now fairly common to find spies from other manufacturers photographing and copying, and then adapting what they have found; this can be seen in many domains, from fashion and shoes to toasters, cars and even planes. For example, during the same trip to Italy I stood before a shop window, admiring a beautiful pair of children's boots in red leather, only to see the same boots being photographed by a 'scout', presumably from a large international manufacturer. While such imitations are never 'exact' (for this has legal repercussions), they are usually, and sometimes very obviously close adaptations of the original.

This was brought home to me on returning to Australia. During my visit to Guzzini I had been given one of their fine plastic vacuum-jugs, and I was surprised to discover that a cheap knock-off was already being sold in my local Target store, at about a third of the price. The main difference was that the copyists had added a strange wavy skirt to the elegant Italian design, and changed the colour from an attractive, cool pastel green to a bright purple.

18   See Gentili, M. (2013) *Guzzini: Infinite Italian Design.* Milan: Skira; and Morello, A. (Ed.) (2002) *Culture of an Italian Region: The Marche, Guzzini and Design.* Milan: Mondadori Electa.

It was an ugly and offensive copy, but technically legal, as they had changed, arguably, more than 5% of the original design.

In a self-perpetuating spiral, competition based on price, substitution and imitation can drive down the quality of goods like this, lowering their value in the consumer's eyes. This might free the consumer to buy more, and so widen and democratize the market, but in turn it intensifies and accelerates the cycle of manufacture, purchase, use and discard, and compounds its environmental effects. Why retain something that is so cheap, when a new one can be had, perhaps in the latest style, for the same, or even a lower, price?[19]

Once consumers become accustomed to paying less and buying more products more often, they start to reveal a weaker commitment to the purchase; the product is effectively 'discounted' in their eyes. In turn, it will be replaced by another, perhaps more exciting, substitute. However, as the availability of cheaper goods within a product range increases, this excitement will possess the consumer less intensely, and pass from their minds more quickly. The rate of what the psychologists call 'hedonic adaptation' – our tendency to 'get used' to and tire of something we purchase – is tied to the ambient rate of the consumption and discard cycle itself, and the rising standard this comes to embody. This is an effect of the close ties between self-esteem and social esteem: we must have it when it is new, but we also must keep up with others, and so must seek out the new, and 'better', as soon as it appears.

When the background rate of purchase and discard speeds up, consumers will upgrade more frequently. Typically, the manufacturer will respond by further reducing the durability of what is being produced. In many fields, what were once durable goods have become more like 'consumables', even if their brand originally signified quality, durability and reliability. We have all seen the $100 ink-jet printers: they are 'loss-leaders' for the maker's more profitable ink cartridges.[20]

The advantage of this style of marketing, where the product becomes a cheap or even free 'gift' to attract the consumer, is that the consumer's

19   Cohen, M.J. (2011) '(Un)sustainable consumption and the new political economy of growth', in K.M. Ekstrom and K. Glans (Eds.), *Beyond the Consumption Bubble* (London: Routledge): 174-190.

20   Park, M. (2010) 'Defying obsolescence', in Cooper, T. (Ed.), *Longer Lasting Products: Alternatives to the Throwaway Society*. Farnham, UK: Gower: 77-106; and Slade, G. (2006) *Made to Break: Technology and Obsolescence in America*. Cambridge, MA: Harvard University Press.

custom for the attached service is assured. This is partly because of the arrangement's convenience, but partly also because we instinctively feel tied to the giver of a gift, especially one we think we need. Lock-ins like free 'gifted' mobile phones can generate regular sales of new service contracts, and tie consumers to the provider's brand family. This is now common across many product lines, particularly in electronic goods.

Marketing schemes like these require that the product be replaced within a limited time, for the benefit of the producer or seller. Buying something new in this way – as part of a contract we also often cannot understand – quickly dislodges the 'old' from our minds, and the 'new' becomes a lever to retain our loyalty. Since most mobile providers won't insure consumers' phones after their contracts expire, fear of phone failure becomes another incentive to upgrade.

Such rapid upgrading is now common in more and more domains. The period of retention of many everyday products, from toothbrushes and razors to cars and appliances, has become increasingly brief, through similarly strategic forms of waste making, generated through marketing and design. Meanwhile, an increasing proportion of these products end up in rivers, waterways and the ocean, our ultimate 'sink'. Off the coasts of much of South Asia, China, India and the United States, the same problem exists. Better waste management might be a temporary fix, but will not stop the creation of these wastes, nor the deception of the consumer this system requires.[21]

Our desire to emulate others and to improve upon what we have, through rapid substitution, plays a fundamental role in expanding and perpetuating consumerism. It has become increasingly, and devastatingly, self-destructive, for most of the traditional barriers to consumption, including even price, have been lowered as far as they can be. Instant transactions, cheap, distanced labour, heavily polluting manufacture, cheap, often plundered resources, cheap but polluting transportation, and easy ways of upgrading and then trashing what is no longer needed, all add their weight to the environmental load captured in climbing emissions since the 1950s.

Deception and waste-making are essential parts of the substitution cycle: the more easily deceived we are, the more readily we will make more waste, in buying what we do not necessarily need, and 'upgrading' even if what we

21   See below and Moore, C.J. (2008) 'Synthetic polymers in the marine environment: A rapidly increasing, long-term threat', *Environmental Research*, 108: 131-9.

have still works fine. Rather like the dilemma of the sorcerer's apprentice, played by Mickey Mouse in Disney's now classic version of the old children's story, the magic spell created by the growth economy cannot be stopped. Since the sorcerer has left the house, if you remember the story, Mickey has to keep trying to stop his buckets and mops producing more water, as everything in the house starts to sink under the rising magic tide which he cannot now reverse. Similarly, the constant increase in the volume of cheap, waste-ready goods, nearly all imitations of other, earlier, perhaps more robust ones, must be increased, to ensure the creation of surplus value, for reinvestment, to create even more of the same.

This continuous expansion, a treadmill of growth, makes it increasingly difficult for consumers to locate anything of more lasting value and personal meaning, since the standards or expectations they have of a particular product are continuously shifting downwards around them, and so their own desire for value and recognition must pull them towards buying 'up', or 'better', or perhaps just 'more'.

Reduced product lifespans and falling levels of product retention push us to consider purchasing what is new sooner and sooner, and the lack of potential alternatives, such as intentionally durable goods, or product-service systems where we might rent certain products from a provider, make it increasingly hard for us as individuals to distinguish what is really 'green' in a sea of brown.[22]

* * *

While our imitativeness has been of continuous interest to scholars in many areas, recent research has highlighted the fundamental role imitation plays in creating behavioural norms. While Veblen's famous theory of 'conspicuous consumption' (and 'conspicuous waste') relied heavily on his insights into this phenomenon's social and economic dynamic (which I will return to in Chapter 5), today this imitativeness can be seen to cross the boundaries we tend to place between design, production and consumption as distinct categories. It is through imitation that we learn, develop skills, gain membership of our group, avoid shame, and also gain entry into our social world.

Viewed through this lens, the relationship between design, consumption and production appears as a continuous circle of adaptation and substitution based upon imitation, a 'directed practice' whose aim is to encourage

22   Guiltnan, J. (2009) 'Creative destruction and destructive creations: Environmental ethics and planned obsolescence', *Journal of Business Ethics*, 89: 19-28.

more consumption. Discovering new models to imitate and adapt through design, and putting them into production for mass-consumption, help create the dynamic we are now all familiar with in consumerism.

As Wedgwood's story suggests, the rise of modern design coincides with increasing substitutability in production, and the requirement for specialists to imagine and create objects that are both desirable and able to be manufactured efficiently within the constraints of the factory and the market. In this brave new world of rapid, increasingly efficient mechanical substitution, ironically the vision, imagination and proposed solution of the designer become more visible and more important.

Further reading

Blaszczyk, R.L. (2000) *Imagining Consumers: Design and Innovation from Wedgwood to Corning.* Baltimore, MD: Johns Hopkins University Press.

Dolan, B. (2004) *Wedgwood: The First Tycoon.* New York: Viking.

Eaton, L. (2014) *Printed Textiles: British and American Cottons and Linens 1700–1850.* New York: Winterthur Museum, Monacelli Press.

Forty, A. (1992) *Objects of Desire: Design and Society, 1750–1980.* London: Thames & Hudson.

Hurley, S. & Chater, N. (Eds.) (2005) *Perspectives on Imitation: From Neuroscience to Social Science: Imitation, Human Development and Culture.* Volume 2 of 2. Cambridge, MA: MIT Press.

Peck, A. (Ed.) (2014) *Interwoven Globe: The Worldwide Textile Trade, 1500–1800.* New York: Metropolitan Museum of Art.

Ponti, L.L. (1990) *Gio Ponti: The Complete Works: 1923–1978.* Cambridge, MA: MIT Press.

Schwartz, H. (1996) *The Culture of the Copy: Striking Likenesses, Unreasonable Facsimiles.* New York: Free Press.

Shell, E.R. (2009) *Cheap: The High Cost of Discount Culture.* New York: Penguin Books.

Shove, E., Hand, M. Watson, M. & Ingram, J. (2007) *The Design of Everyday Life.* Oxford: Berg.

Slade, G. (2006) *Made to Break: Technology and Obsolescence in America.* Cambridge, MA: Harvard University Press.

Strasser, S., McGovern, C. & Judt, M. (Eds.) (1998) *Getting and Spending: European and American Consumer Societies in the Twentieth Century.* Cambridge: Cambridge University Press.

Styles, J. (2000) 'Product Innovation in Early Modern London', *Past and Present* 168: 124-169.

Sykas, P. (2005) *The Secret Life of Textiles.* Bolton, UK: Bolton Museums.

Uglow, J. (2002) *The Lunar Men: Five Friends whose Curiosity Changed the World.* New York: Farrar, Strauss & Giroux.

Warde, A. & Southerton, D. (Eds.) (2012) *The Habits of Consumption.* Helinski: Collegium for Advanced Studies, University of Helinski.

Wilk, R. (1994) 'Emulation, Imitation, and Global Consumerism', *Organization Environment,* 11: 314-333.

Wills, J.E. (1993) 'European Consumption and Asian Production in the Seventeenth and Eighteenth Centuries', in Brewer, J. & Porter, R. (Eds.), *Consumption and the World of Goods.* London: Routledge: 133-147.

3
Vision and ideology in design and consumption

The rise of the consumer citizen

The two stories, of the development of mass-consumption and the development of design, are not always integrated into the history of the nineteenth and twentieth centuries. This is partly because the questions we typically ask of design and of consumption can appear quite distinct. These can call on different disciplines, on the histories of design, art and architecture on the one hand, and on social, economic and cultural history, sociology and anthropology on the other.

Certainly, joining these two stories together makes a lot of sense. But this is further complicated by the technological and social forces that have contributed to modernity itself, from the advance of larger technological systems of production, transportation, communication, provision and retail, to the social, political and economic changes these brought in their train.[1]

The new technologies of the nineteenth century, such as the coming of the railway and steamship, of gas, refrigeration, the telegraph, photography and later electricity, were profoundly transformative. They helped create a dramatic increase in the size of many cities, for example by allowing the development of what we now call 'greenfield' suburbs, and the rapid importation of fresh and cheaper food and other goods into the cities. Larger urban populations of consumers also provided opportunities for more

---

1   For some valuable exceptions, see Meikle, J. (2005) *Design in the USA*. New York: Oxford University Press; and Forty, A. (1992) *Objects of Desire: Design and Society: 1750–1980*. London: Thames & Hudson.

spaces for consumption, and more varieties of shopping, including new arcades, markets and chain stores, and large department stores. The prices of mass-manufactured goods, and of many agricultural goods, fell relative to incomes, making many necessities more affordable.

From the 1870s onwards these changes provoked an increasing interest in consumption among economists and social reformers, and in the 'consumer', as a new economic version of the citizen. The older cooperative stores and organizations, which had been conceived largely as a vehicle for working class saving and security from exploitation, were now joined by new consumer organizations, many prominently involving middle class women. This growth in 'political consumerism' intersected with the development of the labour movement, including unions, and agitation for female emancipation.[2]

This renewed interest in consumption was shared by economists, social reformers, consumer groups and labour organizations. It was an expression of the fundamental tension present in all industrial societies between the promise of mass-consumption to potentially satisfy basic human needs, and the many obstacles to access created by inequalities of income and distribution, which could be harshly unfair. And if all citizens were also consumers, how could they be protected and helped in this new expanding commercial sphere?

The idea of the citizen as also a consumer emerges from this new consciousness of the centrality of mass-consumption: without a 'living wage' and better material conditions, such as cleaner and safer housing, there could be no end to poverty, disease and crime. On the other hand, protecting the consumer also had to reach back into the origins of the goods she consumed, to ensure their quality, the conditions of the labour used in their making, and fair pricing. So it is not surprising to find that early consumer organizations became involved in campaigns to ensure a minimum standard in the quality and value of goods themselves, and in trying to put pressure on makers of defective products, and producers who mistreated their workers.[3]

2   Trentmann, F. (2016) *Empire of Things: How we became a world of consumers, from the fifteenth to the twenty first century.* London: Allen Lane: 155ff.; and Hilton, M. (2002) 'The female consumer and the politics of consumption in twentieth-century Britain', *The Historical Journal*, 45.1: 103-112.

3   Sklar, K.K. (1999) 'The consumers' White Label campaign of the National Consumers' League: 1898–1918', in Strasser, S., McGovern, C. & Judt, M. (Eds.), *Getting and Spending: European and American Consumer Societies in the Twentieth Century.* Cambridge: Cambridge University Press: 17-35.

As this little humorous American poem from 1911 suggests, the consumer was often seen as a perpetual victim of commercial trickery and subterfuge:

> The milkman waters milk for me; there's garlic in my butter,
> But I'm only a consumer, and it does no good to mutter;
> I know that coal is going up and beef is getting higher,
> But I'm only a consumer, and I have no need of fire;
> While beefsteak is a luxury that wealth alone is needing,
> I'm only a consumer, and what need have I for feeding?
> My business is to pay the bill and keep in a good humor,
> And it really doesn't matter, since I'm only a consumer.
>
> The grocer sells me addled eggs; the tailor sells me shoddy,
> I'm only a consumer, and I am not anybody.
> The cobbler pegs me paper soles, the dairyman short-weights me,
> I'm only a consumer, and most everybody hates me.
> There's turnip in my pumpkin pie and ashes in my pepper,
> The world's my lazaretto, and I'm nothing but a leper;
> So lay me in my lonely grave and tread the turf down flatter.
> I'm only a consumer, and it really doesn't matter.[4]

Design entered this picture as an enabler of consumption, creating value for the consumer (and the producer), and also as a powerful communicator, persuading the consumer to buy something in an increasingly crowded field of often similar, mass-produced items. It also entered the politics of consumption, for example helping the early consumer campaigners present their ethical appeals to potential members and, on the other side of this divide, trying to persuade consumers that the products they were buying were ethically made, and of a high quality. Design also helped shape and give expression to the new environments dedicated to consumption, the shops, galleries, department stores, theatres, opera houses, parks, and housing estates, and everything else that was now for sale.

This rise of the consumer thus paralleled the rise and increasing professionalization of the designer, as a critical mediator or 'cultural intermediary' in this new world of mass-production for mass-consumption. The designer in effect became a shaper of the consumer's material, technological and social world, and of her relationships with the many objects and systems that now populated this world. As someone able to engage with what the consumer might like, the designer herself became a 'meta-consumer', able to anticipate new wants or respond to existing needs.

4   Waterman, N. (1911) 'Cheer to the consumer', in M.P. Wilder (Ed.), *The Wit and Humor of America*. 10 vols., New York: Funk & Wagnell: vol. 4, 97

Design, vision and ideology

But how was design to be understood in this new world of goods and machines? Like consumption itself, design was open to interpretation, and contestation. If design was to be considered merely the servant of the producer, then the designer could do little about the larger social problems faced by the consumer, or even about the quality and value of the goods produced. Like a downward pointing arrow on a flip-chart, the designer from this perspective seemed only to be a vehicle for solving the problems presented by the producer, to expand his markets and sell more goods.[5]

Similarly, if the consumer was simply the purchaser and user of the goods and services offered her, then her role must be limited to grateful acquiescence, passively accepting whatever the manufacturer wished upon her, her citizenship given over to him as a proxy in his determination to gain more capital and power, somewhat as the little poem above might suggest.

However, if both were understood as independent agents, able to influence the worlds of production and consumption, then the designer's vision, beliefs and values could help express the consumer's needs, and aid her in her quest for a better life, or at least one where her basic needs could be taken care of. The designer could also help the producer achieve his goal by revealing to him the desires of the consumer and how these might be fulfilled.

The designer's vision – of herself, her work and of her place in this new world – becomes critical at this point, not just because she can discover or anticipate what the consumer might want, but because she can generate innovation and interpret and 'explain' the purpose and meaning of this innovation. The designer could also engage the consumer in her vision through what might be termed a 'design ideology', a persuasive 'philosophy' that could then be expressed through the work of design itself.[6]

Wedgwood's famous cameo 'Slave Medallion' provides a useful early example of this ideological power to influence the beliefs and values of consumers through the design and production of images, objects and environments. This little medallion was produced for his Abolitionist friends in

5   See Folkmann, M.N. (2013) *The Aesthetics of Imagination in Design*. Cambridge, MA: MIT: chapter 3; and also Zurlo, F. & Cautela, C. (2014) 'Design strategies in different narratives', *Design Issues*, 30.1: 19-35.

6   See Buchanan, R. (1985) 'Declaration by design: Rhetoric, argument and demonstration in design practice', *Design Studies* 2.1: 4-22; and Buchanan, R. (2001) 'Design and the new rhetoric: Productive arts in the philosophy of culture', *Philosophy and Rhetoric*, 34.3: 183-206.

1878, and depicted a kneeling African slave in chains, praying for his freedom, with the society's appeal 'Am I not a man and a brother?' in raised capitals around the medal's rim. Although the design was not Wedgwood's own, he believed in it passionately, and gave away this medallion in multiples of thousands, bearing the cost of its manufacture himself.

With some insight, his American friend and fellow Abolitionist, Benjamin Franklin, commented that the medal would have a greater effect than 'the best written pamphlet'. Indeed, it soon became a fashionable ornament for all those horrified by the cruelties of the slave trade, and it was reproduced and sold by Wedgwood's rival potters, attempting to cash in on this new political fashion. Like a message in a bottle, or a polite eighteenth-century 'ban the bomb' badge, it was mounted in silver, stuck on hatpins and worn on silver chains by thousands of believers in the cause, as a sign of their commitment.[7]

FIGURE 3.1: WEDGWOOD SLAVE MEDALLION, MODELLED BY WILLIAM HACKWOOD, 1878

Courtesy Brooklyn Museum, New York

Such purposeful designs are often hard to comprehend without understanding their larger social and ethical contexts. Designs such as these intending to further a cause must make strong ethical arguments or claims,

7   Guyatt, M. (2000) 'The Wedgwood Slave Medallion: Values in eighteenth century design', *Journal of Design History*, 13.2: 93-105; and Margolin, S. (2002) '"And Freedom to the Slave": Antislavery ceramics, 1787–1865', in Hunter, R. (Ed.), *Ceramics in America*. London: Chipstone Foundation: 80-109.

as Wedgwood's Slave Medallion did. The designed object can find a commitment in the consumer through drawing on her intrinsic values, those 'bigger than self' values we associate with our own environmentalism, political beliefs, or sense of social justice. The designer's vision through such designs is transformed into an argument or set of beliefs that the consumer can then adopt and reproduce as her own. The intrinsic, universal appeal of the values such an object embodies, transcends the narrower 'extrinsic' ideas associated with most fashionable goods, such as a new hat or new pair of boots, which may make the consumer look 'better' in the eyes of others (hence the use of the term 'extrinsic').[8]

As this suggests, 'design ideology' is not a recent phenomenon, even if it is more obviously apparent in designs that set out to make a difference, that seek to influence how we see the world. While all advertising, and design must try to influence us in some way, and so necessarily contains at least the seeds of some rhetorical strategy, it is rare for such efforts to try to influence the 'deeper' person or citizen behind the consumer. Indeed, as with Wedgwood's medallion, the goal of this persuasion can be larger than the commercial goal of its maker, and can be shaped by a vision of what the good life itself might mean, not only for ourselves, but for a larger social and material world.

In the career, writings and designs of William Morris (1834–1896), such a world-changing vision accompanied a well-articulated design ideology, which in turn inspired many in fields distant from design and consumption itself, including manufacturers and businesses, economists and social reformers. Morris's career as a public figure also suggests how we can better frame the historical interdependence of consumption and design as two important but complementary dimensions of modernity. Beyond its role as a 'cultural intermediary' between production and consumption, design as a rhetorical practice has the capacity to influence others with its future-directed vision and ideals, and the values these signal or evoke.

8   On intrinsic communication, see Chilton P. *et al.* (2012) 'Communicating bigger-than-self problems to extrinsically-oriented audiences', WWF Publication, http://www.wwf.org.uk/wwf_articles.cfm?unewsid=5641, accessed 20 March 2012.

William Morris's gospel of work

It is difficult to talk about William Morris in such a short space, for he was a giant straddling many, seemingly contradictory fields. Although a wealthy, well-educated man and son of a stock broker, Morris chose to work with his hands as an artisan, an unusual choice in a period where manual work was widely held to be 'beneath' the dignities of the middle class. Although an accomplished poet and writer, and a successful designer of textiles, wallpaper, furniture and, later, books, Morris's engagement in making, in the work of the artisan, led him over time to become a socialist and political writer, speaker and activist. And although widely influential in this role, Morris remained a successful manufacturer and businessman, influencing many wealthy individuals and businesses in understanding and following at least an ethical portion of his visionary, utopian socialist idealism.[9]

So Morris's somewhat contradictory legacy can be seen in many diverse fields simultaneously, from poetry and literature to design and interior architecture, from socialist politics to radical economics, from utopian communalism to craft-based workshops and businesses of different sizes, including some surprisingly large manufacturers influenced by his vision. What linked these many influences together was a utopian, communitarian philosophy of work, which was essentially an ideology of design and making. This was developed in deliberate opposition to the dominant utilitarian ethic of Victorian England, of industrialism, scientism and financial capitalism.[10]

Like his first mentor, John Ruskin, Morris looked to the past and to the world of the medieval artisan to understand what good design and productive work 'should be'. It is too often assumed that this historicism was entirely romantic, ungrounded in experience. But actually, as Ruskin also well understood, all around the two men were older artisans, who knew, for example, how to make and use vegetable dyes, or construct a cabinet without any nails or glues. These ancient artisanal skills were in decline everywhere, decimated by the corrosive forces of industrialism, and the reduction of skilled labour to so many 'hands' tending the machines of the factory.

9   Kinna, R. (2000) 'William Morris: Art, work and leisure', *Journal of the History of Ideas*, 61: 493-512; and McCarthy, F. (1995) *William Morris: A Life for Our Time*. New York: Knopf.

10   Wrigley, C. (2000) 'William Morris, art and the rise of the British Labour Movement', Historian, 67: 4-10; and see Fitzpatrick, T. (2014) 'The resourceful past: William Morris, socialist romanticism and the early fiction of HG Wells', *The Wellsian: The Journal of the HG Wells Society*, 32: 36-53.

Like Ruskin, Morris also understood that the proof of the superiority of such fine craft work over the 'shoddy' products of industry lay in the objects themselves. This evidence he collected to further his own understanding and skills, and treated as a sort of material-historical argument for their superiority. These he then interpreted as a demonstration of the freedom, fulfilment and skill of the artisans themselves in their work, which he then contrasted with the slave-like conditions of the factory, where men were literally treated like machines.

As a skilled artisan, Morris differed remarkably from contemporary social and economic reformers, and even his own intellectual masters, Ruskin, Carlyle and Marx, in seeing work as a self-defining and potentially ennobling *process*, and not as the abstract but distant object of the economist's imagination. So his version of the Victorian Protestant 'gospel of work' was also distinctive, different to his middle-class or even many of his socialist peers. It was an artisan's vision of work as a hard-won source of pleasure, skill and cumulative tacit or implicit knowledge, and a lasting manifestation of human desire. It was organically connected to design as well as to making.

A dominant theme in Morris is thus the relationship between desire, which he thought naturally responded to real human needs, and the 'good work' of the artisan-designer. This was set against the slave-like realization of utilitarianism in the factory, of 'bad work', and the frustration of all good work through its manipulation by those who sought to live off it parasitically, the factory masters and owners of capital.

As one of his great admirers, the economist and historian of the labour movement, G.D.H. Cole, put it in his 1934 centenary address on Morris, Morris's great gift to humanity was his 'faith in fellowship',

> ... that faith in the power of common men to make an earthly para-
> dise, that faith that art and life will flourish together among men who
> are free, and that the quality of life and human happiness depends on
> the quality and character of the labour that men are called upon to do
> – in these things lies the substance of what Morris has to say: and the
> world has by no means learned these lessons yet.[11]

---

11   Cole, G.D.H. (1934) 'William Morris and the modern world', in *idem.*, (1938) *Persons and Periods: Studies by G.D.H. Cole*. London: 306; cited in Wrigley (2000) 'William Morris, art and the rise of the British Labour Movement': 4; and also Masquelier, C. (2016) 'Beyond capitalism and liberal democracy: On the relevance of GDH Cole's sociological critique and alternative', *Current Sociology*, 64.1: 3-21.

What distinguished Morris from most of his fellow travellers on the Left was his positive, designerly vision of what socialism meant, as it *might be lived*. For Morris, this could not be defined by abstract negatives, for example, by the absence of freedom and dignity experienced everywhere in his own day. It could not even be understood as it often is now, as certain milestones of progress in removing various obstacles to notional rights or freedoms. Rather it had to first be defined positively through a contrasting vision of what this future of freedom might look like, and what work itself could look like in such a utopia or 'earthly paradise'.

As Morris well understood, it could not be assumed that those attacking capitalism would know what to do when its bastions fell, without first undertaking this essential imaginative work of envisioning a socialist future. Work, for Morris, lay at the centre of this vision of a more just and humane future. For he well understood from his own experience that in the design and making of any object the spirit of power and dominion apparent in the factory must be avoided. Without freedom and dignity in work, valuing both its methods and results, for Morris there could be no real socialism. It was no good taking up the cruel methods of the factory masters and pretending that because the workers now 'owned' the means of production collectively (as would happen later in Russia) that they would somehow be happy and free. This would become just another form of the same tyranny, as George Orwell and others later would argue.[12]

Revolutionary also was Morris's belief that the artist's and artisan's skills could be learnt by all, and that therefore all arts and crafts were equally valuable. This idea of the potential '*universality of creativity*' was a message that was taken up by many, from young men learning bookbinding or wood-carving after reading his essays or hearing him speak, to those homemakers who would buy his company's embroidery kits and work at making their own fire stands or furnishing covers. Indeed, he inspired literally thousands of individuals to take up some form of making, in art, design or craft, across the world. For Morris, the practice of art, design and making was transformative, a work that brought the worker not only material, but also ethical and spiritual rewards.

This principle from Morris of universal creativity is still enshrined in tertiary design courses the world over. These often assume, after the

---

12   See Breton, R. (2002) 'Work perfect: William Morris and the gospel of work', *Utopian Studies*, 13.1: 43-56; and Evans, T.H. (1988) 'Folklore as utopia: English medievalists and the ideology of revivalism', *Western Folklore*, 47.4: 245-268.

Bauhaus – one of the more surprising legacies of Morris – that everyone has a creative potential that can be further developed. Creativity, for Morris, was free to all, and good work, once encouraged, was repaid in the development of skill, of pleasure in the use of what was made, and in the creation and experience of beauty, both for the maker as well as for the user. As a visitor to Morris's workshop at Merton Abbey heard from one of his workmen: 'Mr Morris believes in us men using our brains as well as our hands and does not want to turn us into machines'.[13]

FIGURE 3.2: PRINTING CHINTZES, MORRIS AND CO., MERTON ABBEY, C. 1890

From Morris and Co. (1911) A Brief Sketch of the Morris Movement and of the Firm Founded by William Morris...

A third important principle in Morris's design philosophy which alerts us to his vision was his use of nature, of environment, as a deliberate contrast to the world of the machine and its enslavement of men. After Ruskin, nature for Morris was the frame of human existence, and it was his own age's tragedy that this could not be recognized or seen. He rejected entirely the utilitarian idea that nature was simply a series of resources to be exploited by labour and the machine. Indeed, a number of writers have emphasized an ethos of

13   McCarthy, F. (1995) *William Morris*. New York: Knopf: 453; cited in Wrigley (2000) 'William Morris, art and the rise of the British Labour Movement': 6. See also Crawford, A. (1997) 'Ideas and objects: The Arts and Crafts movement in Britain', *Design Issues*, 13.1: 15-26.

'post-production' and sustainability to be found in Morris's writings, while others have traced the origins of the modern garden as an extension of the home, and also the influential 'garden city' movement, to his ideas.[14]

Morris's ideas, idealistic as they might appear today, were influential not only among those attracted directly to his work, some of whom came to share his vision, but also to many craftsmen and women and occasionally quite substantial businesses, who took up his ideals and adopted at least some of his ideas. Certainly, his influence can be seen in a number of manufacturers – from textile workers and small-scale metalworkers to luxury textile manufacturers like Arthur H. Lee, who as a young man was clearly and deeply influenced by Morris.

The case of A.H. Lee and Sons (1885–1970), maker of fine furnishing woollen textiles, is a particularly pertinent and interesting example. After starting a smaller company at Warrington in the 1880s, very much influenced by Morris's ideals, Arthur Lee built a much larger 'Tapestry Works' at Birkenhead, which at one point employed around 500 people, and included its own dye works, hand-looms, wood-block print rooms, as well as a substantial tapestry department, after which the works themselves were locally known ('Lee's Tapestry Works').

Lee ran this business following many of the ideals Morris had recommended. He treated his mainly female workers well by the standards of the time, giving them annual holidays in cottages he owned in Wales. His embroidery kits and the firm's popular historical 'Period Guide' to furnishing (c. 1929) and many other publications recall the style and content of the various publications of Morris and Co.[15]

14 See Delveaux, M. (2006) '"O me! O me! How I love the earth": William Morris's *News from Nowhere* and the birth of sustainable society', *Contemporary Justice Review*, 8.2: 131-146; Kinna, R. (2006) 'William Morris and the problem of Englishness', *European Journal of Political Theory* 5: 85-98; and McCarthy, F. (1995) *William Morris*. New York: Knopf: 162-5.

15 On small-scale manufacturing, see Crawford, A. (2002) 'W.A.S. Benson, machinery and the Arts and Crafts movement in Britain', *The Journal of Decorative and Propaganda Arts*, 24: 94-117; and on Lee's very substantial business, my essay: Crocker, R. (2012) 'Vistas on the past: Tapestries and the period style interior (c. 1900–1940)', *Interspaces*. Melbourne University, http://artinstitute.unimelb.edu.au/publications/Interspaces, accessed 1 May 2015.

Shaping the ideal home through design

In Wedgwood's cameo Slave Medallion and later in Morris's designs and uto-pian ideas about work, we can see how the intrinsic values and goals of the designer can be made manifest through their various productions and writ-ings, and how their vision can then be taken up by others, and transmitted into the world of goods, of fashion, consumption and everyday life.

As a designer Morris was a champion of design's role in realizing the ideal of the 'happy home' – not the utopian modernist home of subsequent design movements, or the orderliness and decorative profusion of the ideal Victorian home of the middle class, but of a comfortable, aesthetically satis-fying, simple (by Victorian standards) 'homely' home, for Morris a domestic world full of love and fellowship, a 'sufficient' home, anchored in its own earth, landscape or gardens.

Through frequent historical, natural and regional references, this ideal home's furniture, furnishings and interior spaces could express a living rela-tionship to place, nature, history and culture. The 'true' home, for Morris, was a refuge from the speed and violence of industrialism, its substitution of machines for people, and its devaluation of skill, of place, memory and culture.[16]

This vision was taken up with enthusiasm by many of Morris's contempo-raries. Here, for example, is the artist, Gwen Raverat, tongue-in-cheek, recall-ing the home of one of her favourite uncles, a relative of Charles Darwin, who lived his life according to the ideals Morris and Ruskin had provided:

> Uncle Richard had adored Ruskin, and worshipped Morris ... In fact, Uncle Richard had done everything that an enlightened person, flour-ishing in the middle of the nineteenth century, ought to do: taught at the Working Men's College, organised great country walks, admired Nature ... The old house at Kensington Square had a very strong flavour of its own. It was a peculiar kind of earthly paradise earthly, not celes-tial. It was a tapestry, worked in rich, bright colours to a complex pat-tern, a Morris tapestry, not a medieval one. The food was delicious, the beds were soft, the rhythm ran smoothly, everyone was kind and good and true and happy; and it seemed as if evil could never come near.[17]

16   Muthesius, S. (1988) 'Why do we buy old furniture? Aspects of the authentic antique in Britain 1870–1910', *Art History*, 11: 231-54; and Crocker, R. (2012) 'Vistas on the past'.
17   Raverat, G. (1952) *Period Piece: A Cambridge Childhood*. London: Faber: 126-7. On Svenkst Tenn and Frank's relationship with the company, see Overy, P.

Morris's vision of design was hugely influential because it was an enabling and generous vision, a vision that promised a peculiarly domestic happiness. Its expression can be found in the work of many homemakers, from Australia to America up until the Second World War, and also, in various guises, in many subsequent design movements, including most famously Art Nouveau. Liberty's of London is also a legacy of his ideas, as are many smaller luxury manufacturers, such as Svenkst Tenn, the Swedish company, founded by Estrid Ericson, and long associated with the great Austrian designer, Josef Frank.

His influence can be seen, too, in the inter-war private press movement he himself began with his own Kelmscott Press, and in the romantic fantasy literature that became so popular in the inter-war period and has survived to this day, much of it influenced by his poems and utopian fantasies. J.R.R. Tolkien's *Lord of the Rings* is one of many significant works that has been traced back to the influence of his utopian writings and poetry, in Tolkien's case, transfigured by the horrors of the author's experience of the First World War.[18]

These larger influences of Morris's design ideology derive in part from his direct engagement with the citizen-consumer as a potential designer and maker in her own right. He tried to demystify and encourage a better understanding of design and making as a source of pleasure and life-long engagement, and not just as a source of consumption. So he tried where possible to engage consumers of his own and other products into learning to make things themselves, to learn a craft skill and become in part the author of their own material world. This was the natural outcome of his gospel of work: if work was to be liberating rather than enslaving, there was no better way of understanding this than through direct experience.

Morris was an extraordinary evangelist of the personal and social value of creativity, learning by doing, and making. As well as selling his embroidery kits, he convinced many to take up some form of craft or art as a hobby or lifetime pursuit. This in turn became an established fashion. My maternal grandfather, for instance, spent happy hours making furniture in his shed, while my grandmother would carve decorations into the tables and chairs

(1998) 'Josef Frank, architect and designer: An alternative vision of the modern home', *Journal of Design History*, 11.3: 253-9.

18   See Delveaux, M. (2006) '"O me! O me! How I love the earth": William Morris's *News from Nowhere* and the birth of sustainable society', *Contemporary Justice Review*, 8.2: 131-146; and Gaunt, J. (2003) *Tolkien and the Great War: The Threshold of Middle Earth*. London: HarperCollins.

he made, an ideal of collaborative creativity and use that Morris would have approved of. This emphasis on 'Do-It-Yourself' too has a lengthy history which is still alive today.

In rejecting the slavery of the factory and the determining role of the machine in the world of work, Morris was also rejecting price as the only or ultimate determinant of value. Just as one person's work could not be exactly replaced by another's, so one skill could manifest differently in the hands of others, making one object which would attract a higher price than another. This made Morris no friend of the substitution on which the factory system depended, or the idea that 'time is money', and the capitalist's rule of surplus value, which was to be extracted from the labour of the worker.

As this little portrait suggests, the vision of a designer, freed from the controlling direction of the distant manufacturer and retailer, can have a powerful, transformative effect even in domains that seem unconnected with design. This is not, even in Morris's case, because of the user's belief in a philosophy as such, but because the works Morris produced, in poetry, story, cloth, wood and paint, could speak his vision directly to his audience, and these each took from it what they could hear, whether in the USA, Australia or distant Japan. From this perspective, design was a form of rhetoric, a poetic language that could travel the world, across all linguistic, national, ethnic and class boundaries.[19]

Vision and ideology in design is transformative because it reveals what *might* exist, and this can be influential in shaping beliefs and evoking intrinsic values in others. In every area Morris touched, this shaping of belief and evocation of values can be seen, from A.H. Lee's industry-scale but still hand-made tapestry works to humble furniture makers in regional America or Australia, producing copies of what they would be proud to acknowledge as 'Morris chairs', many years after their originator's death.

Inside the 'design factory'

Morris's story alerts us again to how value and meaning in objects or images are never entirely based on their utility or price, but also on our own beliefs

19   See Nakayama, S. (1996) 'The Impact of William Morris in Japan, 1904 to the present', *Journal of Design History*, 9.4: 273-283; and Kaplan, W. (2004) *The Arts and Crafts Movement in Europe and America: Design for the Modern World 1880–1920.* London: Thames & Hudson.

and desires when these encounter a particular object or environment. The value we perceive in a designed object is thus 'relational'; it exists in us and not just in the object or its design. While price might influence us to buy or not to buy, the value we attribute to this object may be comparative, contextual, dependent on our experience, and the circumstances of our needs; it may also embody our deeper beliefs and the values we hold dear, as the above makes clear.[20]

I became interested in the creation of value through design some years ago when trying to understand the relationship between craft and design in post-war industry. I was especially interested in Italy, because of that country's relatively late industrialization, significant role in the history of modern design and the rich variety of small-scale, often artisanal producers, who still survive in northern Italy.

The values and principles Morris followed would perhaps not have been so foreign in the social world of the artisan of northern Italy, especially in the inter-war and post-war years. In many of these artisanal producers we can recognize a belief in the liberating potential of skilled making, accompanied often by strong political ideas about the value of this often unique work, a political vision, like Morris's too, often set deliberately against the 'parasitism' of the urban bankers and professional classes.

In this social world also the artisan's family and home-life was often implicitly understood as the preeminent model for the 'good life', towards whose greater fulfilment the design of the object created in the workshop was intended, something that we can also see in Morris's various business ventures. In this world machinery arrived late, as an aid to manufacture, as indeed it had been in Morris's own workshops, and not the instrument of a distant, profit-seeking factory owner.[21]

In 1998 I visited a number of smaller manufacturers in northern Italy to try to better understand this long-term relationship between craft, small-scale artisan-directed manufacture, and modern, and now international, Italian design. I visited several small-scale producers of stainless steel goods for the

---

20   See Boradkar, P. (2010) *Designing Things: A Critical Introduction to the Culture of Objects*. Oxford: Berg: chapter 2; and see Bettiol, M. & Micelli, S. (2013) 'The hidden side of design: The relevance of artisanship', *Design Issues*, 30.1: 7-18.

21   Sparke, P. (1999) 'Nature, craft, domesticity, and the culture of consumption: The feminine face of design in Italy, 1945–70', *Modern Italy*, 4.1: 59-78; and also Lees-Maffei, G., & Sandino, L. (2004) 'Dangerous liaisons: Relationships between design, craft and art', *Journal of the History of Design*, 17.3: 207-219.

home, and also Alessi, one of the most successful, and largest of these still family-run producers.

Even in this much larger, successful producer I was struck by the survival of decidedly artisanal values. For example, at one point I found myself standing next to a big laser cutting machine, watching large sheets of stainless steel being precision cut on the factory floor. But next to this I was surprised to find a man laboriously hand-soldering a coffee pot, to a design that looked as though it had been first produced in the 1940s. On asking the production manager why this man was hand-soldering the pot, when all around us were large soldering machines, I was told that the pot had been designed by Alberto Alessi's father, Carlo himself, and the 'integrity' of the design required that it be made in this same, original, way.[22]

This impression of surviving artisanal values was reinforced by a subsequent visit to Alessi's Museum, where I became intrigued by the long history of the company, and the objects on display, including a number of their iconic designs. After some hours in the museum, my experience on the factory floor no longer seemed strange: again and again I found 'design-led' projects that large manufacturers would not have invested in, being either too hard to manufacture or too experimental in design. The Alessi 'design factory', at least in 1998, seemed a surviving extension of an ancient artisan's world, one that Morris himself might well have recognized.

The success of Alessi, and of the other Italian 'design companies', has often been explained in the ahistorical terms of 'post-Fordism', where the object is no longer designed and mass-produced in response to a universally defined need, but as a product that need only appeal to a certain niche and elite market, in an otherwise overcrowded world. While Henry Ford had perfected the system required to produce standardized and affordable goods to conquer a mass-market with typically similar needs, this argument goes, post-Fordist manufacturing, involving 'flexible specialization', evolved to respond through smaller volumes targeting different user groups. However, the problem with this theory is that this style of manufacture is not new, but

22   See De Lucchi, M. (1992) 'The world of industry and furniture design in Italy', in Castiglioni, A. & de Lucchi, M. (Eds.), *Elegant Techniques*. Milan: Electa: 52-59; and Goodman, E. (1989) 'Introduction: The political economy of the small firm in Italy', in E. Goodman *et al.* (Eds.), *Small Firms and Industrial Districts in Italy*. London: Routledge: 1-30.

has been apparent in fashion and in many other 'bespoke' forms of design and making, for centuries.[23]

Despite their size and global success, Alessi revealed their commitment to this older, artisanal model in many ways. They were less interested, for example, in creating sales through advertisements 'pushing' their products onto the market as mass-manufacturers commonly do. Instead, they emphasized the history of their company and its familial and artisanal roots, using what advertisers might call 'pulling' techniques, for example 'double branding' with individual designers, whose names they would promote to underline their commitment to design.

The meaning of the goods they sold was also repeatedly tied to the pleasures of the home and table, of friends and family, and to the everyday rituals of conviviality. This identifiable northern Italian family life appealed particularly to northern European and American audiences, an idealized vision of the home in some respects echoing Morris's earlier vision of a 'homely' home of family and fellowship. Elaborated in books referencing the anthropology and psychology of eating, cooking, drinking and the various rituals of daily life, Alessi's vision spoke to their audience's nostalgia and romantic desires, and flattered their taste, enticing them as the promise of a week's holiday in sunny Italy might.[24]

Alessi's use of psychology and anthropology in their publications in this period is an important component of this design ideology, explaining how objects could become beloved companions in our lives, recognizable tools for conviviality and everyday pleasures. In Alessi, as in many of the other Italian design-led firms, we can see a self-conscious return to an artisanal vision of design and consumption as potentially synergetic, providing a more satisfying and long-lived relationship between the consumer and her possessions, based on the home as the ultimate anchor of culture, locality and relationship. This idealization of design for the home, echoing Morris,

23   See Amin, A. (1994) 'Post-Fordism: Models, fantasies, and phantoms of transition', in Amin, A. (Ed.), *Post-Fordism*: A Reader. Oxford: Blackwell; and also Binkley, S. (2004) 'Everybody's life is like a spiral: Narrating Post-Fordism in the Lifestyle Movement of the 1970s', *Cultural Studies*, 4.1: 71-96.

24   See Mendini, A. (1979) *Paesaggio Casalingo*. Milan: Domus; and Alessi, A. (1991) 'Towards an awareness of the things we buy', in Polinoro, L. (Ed.), *Rebus Sic...* Crusinallo, Italy: Alessi: 5-10.

was pitched against the apparent meaninglessness and rapid substitutability of mass-produced goods in the global marketplace.[25]

* * *

Two imagined worlds of desire, then, must collide in the process of creating a more engaging design for the consumer within a particular time and place: the designer's vision, often accompanied by a moral stance expressed in an ideology or argument that reflects the intention of the design; and the consumer's associative understanding, and expectation that this vision might indeed, finally, change her life for the better, delivering the good life promised by consumption itself.

Buying such a consciously designed object involves us in a form of personal commitment and even sacrifice: we have 'agreed' with the designer's stance by agreeing to buy and use the object. Beyond the object's simple utility, the designed object can represent a value to us beyond the money we have paid for it. This explains why we are often willing to pay so much more for a well-designed product, whether a pair of designer shoes or an Alessi kettle; their qualities, we hope, will not only 'say something' about us to others, but also something to, and of, ourselves.

Set on a moving platform of continuous social and technological change, however, these commitments can also never entirely fall out of step with the lives of our peers. Like them, we too will fall for the 'push' messages advertising creates, demanding that we too catch up with the 'latest and the best'. In this way, however much we might value some things over others, we also become trapped in the norms created around us, by the more invasive social and technological systems of persuasion and provision that now surround us. It is to these we need to turn next to understand how both design and consumption can become 'locked in' to unsustainable means of satisfying our everyday needs.

25   See especially Muratovski, G. (2012) 'The importance of research and strategy in design and branding: Conversation with Dana Arnett', in Muratovski, G. (Ed.), *Design for Business: AGIDEAS Research*. Melbourne: AGIDEAs Press: 16-25; and Norman, D. (2004) *Emotional Design: Why we love (or hate) everyday things*. New York: Basic Books.

Further reading

Alessi, A. (2000) *The Dream Factory: Alessi since 1921*. Milan: Electa for Alessi.

Bennett, P. & Miles, R. (Eds.) (2010) *William Morris in the Twenty First Century*. Oxford, Bern: Peter Lang.

Boradkar, P. (2010) *Designing Things: A Critical Introduction to the Culture of Objects*. Oxford: Berg.

Burdek, B.E. (2005) Design: History, Theory and Practice of Product Design. Basel: Birkhauser.

Castiglioni, A. & de Lucchi, M. (Eds.) (1992) *Elegant Techniques: Italian Furniture Design 1980–1992*. Milan: Electa.

Coates, D. (2003) *Watches Tell More Than Time: Product Design, Information and the Quest for Elegance*. New York: McGraw Hill.

Goodman, E., Bamford, J. & Saynor, P. (Eds.) (1989) *Small Firms and Industrial Districts in Italy*. London: Routledge.

Hart, I. (2010) *Arts and Crafts Objects*. Manchester: Manchester University Press.

Holmes, J. (1993) *John Bowlby and Attachment Theory: Makers of Modern Psychotherapy*. London: Routledge.

Kaplan, W. (2004) *The Arts and Crafts Movement in Europe and America: Design for the Modern World 1880–1920*. London: Thames & Hudson.

McCarthy, F. (1995) *William Morris: A Life for Our Time*. New York: Knopf.

McCracken, G.D. (2005) *Culture and Consumption II: Markets, Meaning and Brand Management*. Bloomington, IN: Indiana University Press.

Miller, D. (2010) *Stuff*. Cambridge: Polity Press.

Miller, D. (1998) *A Theory of Shopping*. Ithaca, NY: Cornell University Press.

Outka, E. (2009). *Consuming Traditions: Modernity, Modernism, and the Commodified Authentic*. Oxford: Oxford University Press.

Parry, L. (2005) *Textiles of the Arts and Crafts Movement*. 2nd edn, London: Thames & Hudson.

Scarzella, P. (1987) *Steel and Style: The Story of Alessi Household Ware*. Milan: Arcadia.

Sparke, P. (1988) *Italian Design: 1780 to the Present*. London: Thames & Hudson.

Sparke, P. (2012) *An Introduction to Design and Culture*. 3rd edn, London: Routledge.

Verbeek, P.P. (2005) *What Things Do: Philosophical Reflections on Agency, Technology and Design*. Philadelphia, PA: Pennsylvania University Press.

4
Enabling systems in consumption

Systems and their sunk-cost effects

While consumerism might begin in the mind with some image of the 'good life', or at least an apparently better one, and design might work to imagine and express this image in material form, most consumption is made possible through various dominant systems of provision. Such enabling systems – transportation, communication, entertainment, retail, manufacturing, and the provision of water, gas, electricity and waste services – remain in the background of everyday life, often unnoticed until they develop problems, or fail.

These technological systems are a remarkable feature of industrialism, and have played a key role, not only in the expansion of cities over the twentieth century, but also in the expansion and acceleration of consumption itself. The exponential growth of system-enabled consumption since the 1950s has also led directly to an expansion of global greenhouse gas emissions. For this reason, these systems have become the focus of considerable effort to reduce their larger impacts on the environment.[1]

Design both enables and expresses our dependence on these systems: much design work is now associated with creating a large variety of human interfaces for these systems, from architectural interfaces supporting services like power and water, to the cars, carparks, service stations, and all the other parts of our present transport system, and the mobile phones, laptops, tablets and other devices we use to communicate and access information.

---

[1] See Nye, D.E. (1997) 'Shaping communication networks: Telegraph, telephone, computer', *Social Research*, 64.3: 1,067-1,091; and Hughes, T.P. (2004) *Human-Built World: How to Think about Technology and Culture*. Chicago, IL: Chicago University Press.

Once technological systems – for example, road networks or electricity networks – have become 'essential' services, they tend to forcibly include or 'lock in' the majority of consumers to their own form of service provision. Alternative means of providing the same service, where they still exist, become difficult to access, or are marginalized and reduced in relative value.

Developing and deploying most technological systems is costly, involving massive 'sunk costs', or irrecoverable investments, sometimes running into billions of dollars over many years. For road-based transport, for example, these sunk costs might include road construction and maintenance, car manufacturing, fuelling systems and related industries. An effect of these sunk costs is a resistance to change: to return to public transit would seem to many users to be a 'backward step', even if a better one for the environment.[2]

Sunk costs encourage commitment to the maintenance and use of particular systems, and so foster the belief that a given system is the *best and only way* in which a service might be provided. The 'way we do things now' is regarded as essential and normal, and possible alternatives, at least until they have been seen in action, will appear to have multiple, identifiable disadvantages. The system's own disadvantages, such as its negative environmental or social effects, are judged to be comparatively negligible, and their impact will be mentally discounted. The system's more positive social and economic benefits are frequently enumerated, valued and often praised.[3]

One of the paradoxes of system thinking is that it requires us to step outside the system itself to understand it as a whole, and also to be able to understand it as a human and historical construct. Systems are developed and designed not by individuals but by large numbers of people over considerable periods of time. The vision and ideology that originally inspired the system can also disappear from view, and the system itself can become normalized – an expected regime in everyday life.

For instance, after the Second World War the car came to be seen as a key component in 'modernizing' every society and economy in the West, following a model supplied by 1930s America, the dominant Western power. Post-war reconstruction in Europe involved remaking many bombed cities

2   See Geels, F.W. (2014) 'Regime resistance against low-carbon transitions: Introducing politics and power into the multi-level perspective', *Theory, Culture & Society*, 31.5: 21-40.

3   See Kelly, T. (2004) 'Sunk costs, rationality and acting for the sake of the past', *Nous*, 38.1: 60-85; Janssen, M.A., Kohler, T.A. & Scheffer, K. (2003) 'Sunk-cost effects and vulnerability to collapse in ancient societies', *Current Anthropology*, 44.5: 722-8.

into 'car-friendly' ones. The numbers of cars on European roads grew rapidly, and many older cities were changed and extended following this 'progressive' model, a trend reinforced by the construction of car parks and the demolition of older buildings and precincts.[4]

The 1950s also saw a reduction in the relative price of oil, favouring an exponential increase in the consumption of energy and resources for new industries like plastics, chemical and electronics, and of course car manufacture. The car was a key component of this economic recovery, and became a vector for economic transformation, modernizing production and consumption in many related domains, from shopping and residential suburban housing to leisure, tourism and entertainment.

Because of its multiple 'modernizing' effects, and its initial employment of large numbers of semi-skilled workers, manufacturing cars and making the city 'car-friendly' became a key component of post-war planning. The role of Modernism as an ideology driving this car-driven modernization is often overlooked. The car was a vital component of 'the city of the future' planned by so many Modernist masters, including, most famously, Le Corbusier. The car was his favoured means of transport and his villas are all designed with room for a car underneath, or beside them. Le Corbusier's influential plans for the 'Radiant City' involved sweeping roadways between tall buildings set in generous parks, with few pedestrians in sight.

In the Modernist interior, the same vision of efficiency and spatial control was applied, with another type of war on the past in evidence – the war against memory, decoration and inefficiency. Modernism promoted the development and introduction of many new appliances in the home: of built-in kitchens and new bathrooms, refrigerators, washing machines, vacuum cleaners and, later, record players and TVs. New man-made materials, chemicals, drugs and electronics, as well as new and more efficient, rational ways of growing, preparing, storing and cooking foods, were all to be used to modernize the home as well as the world outside.[5]

There were two important consequences of this Modernist vision and its ideology. Firstly, their technologically driven future of peace, prosperity

4   Lundin, P. (2008) 'Mediators of modernity: Planning experts and the making of the "car-friendly" European city', in Hard, M. & Misa, T.J. (Eds.), *Urban Machinery: Inside Modern European Cities*. Cambridge, MA: MIT Press: 257-279.

5   Pavitt, J. (2008) 'Design and the democratic ideal', in Crowley, D. & Pavitt, J. (Eds.), *Cold War Modern: 1945–1970*. London: V&A Museum: 73-93; and also Oldenziel, R. & Zachmann, K. (Eds.) (2009) *Cold War Kitchen: Americanization, Technology and European Users*. Cambridge, MA: MIT Press.

and leisure required the universal consumption of modern, more hygienic, rationally planned and efficient homes, cars and other labour-saving devices. Secondly, this utopia could only be realized by destroying the older pedestrian-centred city of 'the past'.

Paradoxically, Modernism created an ideology ideally suited to consumerism, by justifying both the widespread destruction of what already existed as 'not good enough', and by idealizing its replacement, which of course would necessarily change, in time, since it was tied to scientific and technological advancement. So despite its seemingly noble democratic idealism, the Modernist vision became the petri dish for cultivating a new and accelerated form of universal consumerism.

The freedom of the road

The story of the rise of the automobile to social and spatial dominance as *the modern means of transport* is suggestive of how the Modernist vision of the 'future' took hold. It is also the story of the destruction, in many cities, of public transit and of hundreds of older precincts, most of which had been built to a more human scale. It became necessary in this reordering of the urban environment to discipline and regulate pedestrian movement, since making cities 'car-friendly' undermined the freedom and mobility of pedestrians in the same or adjacent spaces. Making the world safe for cars also required the transfer and dedication of larger and larger amounts of land for this purpose.

The earlier determination that cars themselves should be restricted, because of the danger they posed to pedestrians and horses, was soon reversed. In the 1930s, the first golden age of motoring, regulations aiming to separate two clearly incompatible means of transport were applied everywhere in Europe and America. In more and more jurisdictions, pedestrians were fined for crossing the road without looking, or for walking on the roadway. Special lights and markings were introduced to separate them from cars when they crossed. In Britain there was such public resentment of these measures, that even the 'Belisha Beacons' (named after the then Minister of Transport), marking the first pedestrian crossings, were vandalized at night.[6]

6   Moran, J. (2006) 'Crossing the road in Britain, 1931–1976', *The History Journal* 49: 477-496; and Hass-Klau, C. (1990) *The Pedestrian and the City*. London: Belhaven Press.

It is hard now to imagine an urban world dominated by pedestrians, but old photographs from the 1900s reveal the dimensions of the changes brought by modernity: horse-drawn carts, pedestrians and bicycles can be seen jostling side by side in the streets. Indeed, before Henry Ford's innovations became more universal, most cars were intended for the wealthy. Only visionaries could imagine then that cars would one day largely replace the train and tram in many cities.

The rich clearly had an unquenchable love for the motorcar. It embodied, in one object, speed and freedom of movement, the capacity to travel large distances, and the privileges of individualized travel. Also apparent in the first 20 or so years of the car's rise to prominence was the resentment many pedestrians felt towards drivers, with many literary sources suggesting a prejudice against cars as violent and intrusive vehicles of privilege.[7]

FIGURE 4.1: MADISON SQUARE, NEW YORK (C. 1907)

Photographer unknown, E. Chickering & Co., Courtesy Library of Congress, Panoramic Photographs Collection

In Kenneth Grahame's famous children's tale, *The Wind in the Willows* (1908), for example, something of this early tension can be seen. Toad is a wealthy young 'man', and becomes obsessed with the power, speed and freedom he finds in the motorcar. He buys a series of expensive cars, crashing them all, before eventually being sent to jail for stealing a particularly alluring one. Toad's obsession is contrasted with the traditional freedom and pleasure of walking along country roads, enjoyed by his 'sensible' friends, Water Rat and Mole.

Even though written at the dawn of the motoring age, the depiction of Toad and his obsession with the car is suggestive of the very different world experienced by the majority. It seems no accident that Toad's obsession with the car in the story replaces an earlier romantic obsession with

7   See Jeremiah, D. (2010) 'Motoring and the British countryside', *Rural History*, 21.2: 233-250.

a horse-drawn gypsy caravan. Toad is a parody of the male upper-class motorist of the 1900s, whose aim was to enjoy the 'open road' without responsibility for the impact of his activities on others, or on the country-side itself.[8]

While seemingly nostalgic, Grahame believed that walking was the means of mobility through which the world could be most authentically experienced – a belief he shared with many of his generation. The most poetic passages in the book centre upon the animals' experience of the countryside as they walk; the birds, trees, rivers and streams all become especially vivid to the walkers' senses and sensibility. Grahame makes it clear that the revelation of nature, to the walker, is a powerful, even spiritual experience, with which the car's noise, speed and danger, are incompatible.[9]

Another dimension of this incompatibility can be seen in the way the car's future was seen by its Modernist protagonists – for instance, in the writings of the Futurists, the apostles of motoring, speed and mechanical flight. Their poetry and manifestos were written around the same time as Grahame's tale. In Futurism the car was a symbol of power, freedom, disruptive violence, and technological superiority, which, in their young man's vision of the future, would soon sweep aside the superstitious remnants of the past. The substitution of machines for the labour that the factories required, was scarcely noticed by Marinetti, the Futurist leader, who displayed no interest in the fate of the workers who produced these machines.[10]

Marinetti repeatedly praised the excitement, power and freedom that the car and aeroplane bestowed on their human controllers, contrasting them with the slow and stupid traditions they were replacing, and celebrating their potent overthrow of the horse and all the other cultural detritus of the past.

8   Boutle, I. (2012) '"Speed lies in the lap of the English": Motor records, masculinity, and the nation, 1907–14', *Twentieth Century British History*, 23.4: 449-472.

9   Gilead, S. (1988) 'The undoing of idyll in *The Wind in the Willows*', *Children's Literature*, 16: 145-158; and Wadsworth, S. (2014) '"When the Cup has been Drained": Addiction and recovery in *Wind in the Willows*', *Children's Literature*, 42: 42-70.

10   Lothmann, T. & Schumacher, A. (2013) 'Automobility in poetry: A conceptual metaphor approach', *Spatial Practices* 17: 213-225, 228-9; and see also Adamson, W.L. (2002) 'Avant-garde modernism and Italian Fascism', *Journal of Modern Italian Studies*, 6.2: 230-248.

The dream of flight

Despite this early embrace of the car, the symbolism of the horse and the bird in flight were still strongly associated with mobility, power and speed, and so with the new machines. From the time of the First World War, the horse, especially when winged, continued to appear, as a symbol of power, in logos and advertisements, especially for cars and the provision of petrol. The image communicated the car's central promises: liberation, unprecedented motive power, extraordinary speed, and an implied social distinction.

The winged horse of ancient legend seemed especially suggestive of the speed and power of the new self-powered 'auto' mobile. By implied association, the driver became the entitled, technically competent 'warrior', who drove *his* horse, winged with mechanical power, through the land of his imagination. The pedestrian, like Toad's old animal friends, in this way became relegated to the margins, destined to become the perpetual victim of the new machines of modernity.

Mechanical flight was the car's logical extension, and so became a symbol for the new century, a century of machines, and the daring aviator its 'superman' and seer, able to survey the city and vast tracts of the earth from on high.[11] The car itself, from the 1930s onwards, became figuratively a ground-dwelling aeroplane, its 'wings' becoming embedded in the seemingly aerodynamic designs of cars from the period.

This is evident in many corporate advertisements, especially after 1950, where the victorious jet-plane and car are depicted together, as the twin bringers of modernity, and – it was implied – of a utopian future of plenty, prosperity, health and leisure. The role of ordinary people in this vision was never really addressed; the individual democratic citizen became the 'happy' and contented consumer, always served by the promise of this new technology, and never its slave, despite this suggestion in more dystopian versions of this mechanical future.[12]

11 Cordulack, S.W. (1992) 'Art Nouveau and the will to flight', *Journal of Design History*, 5.4: 257-272, and below.
12 Marchand, R. (1998) *Creating the Corporate Soul: The Rise of Public Relations and Corporate Imagery in American Big Business.* Berkeley, CA: University of California Press: 341-356.

Norman Bel Geddes' famous design for the General Motors 'Futurama' exhibition at the New York World Fair of 1939 is a realization of the Modernist aviator's dream from above. Including a complete three-dimensional city in miniature, Bel Geddes' futuristic '1960' city, General Motors' Futurama, was uncannily realistic, dominated by highways and traffic, high-rise concrete apartment and office buildings, all carefully researched from the books and drawings of other futurist visionaries, including those of Le Corbusier. It also exploited his ability as a former theatre designer; the whole city was experienced as a narrative journey lasting about 15 minutes, and the grand finale for visitors was a life-size, walk-through street intersection that they could explore before they left (illustrated).[13]

Bel Geddes' design was, by all accounts, an extraordinary creation, anticipating the kind of immersive experience that computerized simulations of architectural space provides today. It was the most popular exhibit in the metropolitan Fair that showcased products from about 4,000 exhibitors, General Motors being one of the largest and most prominent.

The 1939 exhibition represented a radical departure for General Motors, whose previous exhibitions had been based on representations of their own factory in production. The Futurama, based upon very different and theatrically derived principles, was overwhelmingly more successful and, in the end, justified the extraordinary sum (about $8 million) that General Motors spent on it. Bel Geddes' show was seen by approximately 28,000 people each day – at least half of all the Fair's visitors. It gave them a direct and awe-filled 'experience of the future'. Dramatically staged, it involved about 600 visitors at a time being seated and then moved by a conveyor belt around the whole display. In a 15-minute ride they had a view, from the air, of the city of the future, and a speaker in each seat provided an explanatory commentary.[14]

13   Marchand, R. (1992) 'The designers go to the fair II: Norman Bel Geddes, the General Motors "Futurama" and the visit to the factory transformed', *Design Issues* 8.2: 22-40.

14   Morshed, A. (2004) 'The aesthetics of ascension in Norman Bel Geddes's Futurama', *Journal of the Society of Architectural Historians*, 63.1: 74-99.

FIGURE 4.2: NORMAN BEL GEDDES, STREET INTERSECTION IN THE CITY OF TOMORROW,
'FUTURAMA' EXHIBITION FOR GENERAL MOTORS, NEW YORK WORLD'S FAIR, 1939

Photo: Richard Garrison, in Bel Geddes, *Magic Motorways* (1940), p. 7

What made Bel Geddes' utopian vision so popular was its vast scale,
extraordinarily detailed realization and meticulous planning, along with its
capture of the novel experience of flight, and the bird's-eye vision of the city
this enabled. Above all, this was a theatre designer's work, carefully choreo-
graphed as a progression or journey, its climax suddenly making the future
seem real by allowing the visitors to experience a life-size intersection from
the city of the future, which General Motors, against the designer's advice,
insisted on populating with their own, less futuristic cars.

Among the guests of honour at the exhibition were the New York City
Mayor and government dignitaries, including Robert Moses, who shared
much of Bel Geddes' vision of the future, and became the city's biggest
builder, erecting a series of roadways or 'parkways' across and beyond the
city's boundaries – something Bel Geddes also enthusiastically endorsed.
Indeed, Bel Geddes' book, *Magic Motorways* (1940) from which the above
illustration from the Futurama is taken, is suggestive of the scope and scale
of the Modernist vision underpinning his 'city of the future'. In this book Bel
Geddes argued for a national network of highways, from coast to coast, to
realize the so far half-fulfilled promise of the motorcar. The traffic problem

for Bel Geddes, as it was for General Motors and for Moses, was a 'road problem' and not a by-product of the system itself.[15]

Government planners like Moses, aided by popular books like *Magic
Motorways*, treated the 'road problem' as a public issue to be funded by
public revenue. Urged on by corporations like GM and Ford, they managed
to extract huge sums of taxpayers' money from the government to 'fix' this
problem. Transit companies struggled under an older regime that catego-
rized them as 'private' interests, and therefore by definition unable to gain
access to taxpayers' money. Consequently many went bankrupt, or were
bought out by General Motors and then quietly dismantled, in this way
opening up almost every major city in the USA to the conquest of the car.

Individualization and substitution

The model created in America in the 1930s was transferred to Europe after
the Second World War. The car became the answer to the 'problem' of transport in and between cities, with the costs of implementing this grand modernizing vision socialized and passed on to governments. Road building,
like the subsidization of car manufacturing in the 1950s, was regarded as
being 'in the public interest', a vast investment with immediate social and
economic benefits. Public support for this was almost universal: the car was
widely accepted as the bringer of modernity to the nation, along with other
major infrastructure projects.[16]

In Britain, Australia and America in the 1950s most new homes were built
complete with a garage – one of the defining domestic spaces of modernity.
The garage kept the car 'ready at hand' for taking the driver anywhere he or
she needed to go – to the local shopping centre, to school with the children, to
work or for leisure. In every developed nation the number of cars – and parking stations – increased exponentially. The consequences of these changes

---

15   Gartman, D. (2004) 'Three ages of the automobile: The cultural logics of the
     car', *Theory Culture and Society*, 21.4/5: 169-195; and also Luger, S. (1999) *Cor-
     porate Power, American Democracy and the Automobile Industry*. New York:
     Cambridge University Press.
16   Sheller, M. & Urry, J. (2000) 'The city and the car', *International Journal of Urban
     and Regional Research*, 24.2: 735-757; Crowley, D. (2008) 'Europe reconstructed,
     Europe divided', in Crowley, D. & Pavitt, J. (Eds.), *Cold War Modern: Design,
     1945–1970*. London: V&A Museum: 43-65.

were not quite as the Modernist visionaries had imagined: city life became defined by a series of islands of activity that could be reached only by car.

When Bel Geddes published his *Magic Motorways* (1940) there were about 30 million vehicles (including trucks and buses) on America's roads – probably about half all the cars in the world. By 1960, the year that the American city in Bel Geddes' Futurama was supposed to represent, the figure was approximately 130 million worldwide. There are now 1.2 billion cars and heavy vehicles on the roads of the world and the latest estimates suggest there will be two billion by about 2035. This growth is being fuelled by the export of this modernist car-centric way of life – of 'automobility' – from America and Europe to China and India, where Tata is now selling its $2,500 car to a rapidly expanding middle class.[17]

Making cars 'greener' and more energy efficient is certainly important and valuable work, but largely misdirected if these 'green' cars require fossil fuels to power them, either directly or indirectly through power plants. Increasing efficiency, as in so many other domains, simply cannot keep up with the expansion of demand; making things more efficient is to make them cheaper, which expands the scale of demand. The Jevons paradox applies, both in the consumption of raw materials and energy used in production, and in the realm of consumption.[18]

Psychologically, the car becomes an extension of the self – an outer skin representing the person and his or her social standing – and can be used on a whim, to go almost anywhere. In Jacques Tati's series of comedies, the car is consistently depicted as an enemy of traditional French urban life. The car also literally takes on the personality of its driver; Tati himself, in the role of M. Hulot, in *M. Hulot's Holiday* (1953) is exquisitely matched to a tiny, old, two-seater sports model that constantly backfires, and is clearly unreliable. This car is deliberately staged to mock the perfection and speed of the life

17   Voelker, J. (2014) '1.2 billion vehicles on world's roads now, 2 billion by 2035: Report', *Green Car Reports*, http://www.greencarreports.com/news/1093560_1-2-billion-vehicles-on-worlds-roads-now-2-billion-by-2035-report, accessed 1 May 2015; and Anon (2008) 'The Tata Nano strikes back: Does Jevons' Paradox apply to productivity too?', http://www.theoildrum.com/node/3561, accessed 1 May 2015.

18   Farber, S. & Paez, A. (2011) 'Running to stay in place: The time-use implications of automobile oriented land-use and travel', *Journal of Transport Geography*, 19: 782-793; and see Alcott, B. (2005) 'Jevons' Paradox', *Ecological Economics*, 54.1: 9-21.

embraced by aspirational families – many with perfectly functioning modern cars – who share M. Hulot's holiday at a little seaside resort.

This mocking of the social pretensions, technophilia and car-dependence of the middle class consumer of the 1950s becomes more insistent in subsequent Tati films, and is a dominant theme in *Mon Oncle* (*My Uncle*, 1958), perhaps the best known of these films in the Anglophone world. By that time, more and more space was being devoted to the car, with many cities dedicating up to half their available land for use by cars.

In Tati's later car movie, *Traffic* (1971), scene after scene show vast traffic-jammed highways, where drivers are stuck, crashed, or immobilized by their vehicles, their lives and relationships defined by their cars. In the final scene in this film, hundreds of stationary cars wait in an endless traffic jam, while the rain pours down. The movements of the cars' windscreen wipers are made to match the gestures and personalities of the drivers, in a wonderful mechanical ballet of hands and moving wipers. As Tati's films suggest, the reality of driving is very different from what is promised to the consumer.

So obvious is this incommensurability between aspiration and reality of the kind found in driving that some researchers have now created indices of 'commuter pain'. Driving under the wrong conditions is necessarily constraining, even for the wealthy, and can be extremely frustrating, forcing the cars' occupants to drive on roads choked with traffic and fumes, spending many hours locked in long and repetitive commutes. This time is wasted since it cannot be used for other more useful work. This is a constant source of disappointment for drivers, and a cause of much anger, including road rage. It is as though, as tourists on holiday, we have been promised a luxury room with a view of the sea, but instead find ourselves in a room with continuous noise and poor quality air, and no view at all.[19]

China is quickly overtaking the USA in demand for new motor vehicles, and the government's efforts at road building simply can't keep up with the rapid growth in traffic. This has resulted in China's reputation as the world capital of traffic jams, which can last several days. In one spectacular example, which now has its own Wikipedia page, a major highway suffered a traffic jam that lasted for ten days. An ingenious entrepreneur has profited from this type of situation, by providing a fleet of motorbikes to take those who

19   See Wells, P. & Dimitrios, X. (2015) 'From "freedom of the open road" to "cocooning": Understanding resistance to change in personal private automobility', *Environmental Innovation and Societal Transitions*, 16: 106-119.

are stranded in such a jam to their destinations, leaving substitute drivers in their place to then take their cars home.[20]

More seriously, the car also exposes its occupants to new kinds of danger, including crashes that can quickly kill and maim its occupants. Impacts of over 60kph are nearly always serious, in many cases leading to brain injury or death. The human body is simply not capable of tolerating such impacts. This is extremely costly, with a global annual figure of about 1.4 million deaths from crashes, with an additional five million people each year dying from air pollution.

But even these figures seem small when compared with the estimated 50 million or so who are maimed or seriously injured each year. Many developing nations have neither the health infrastructure nor the policing power to reduce the road toll to Western levels. The real social costs of car travel are thus extremely high, with over $600 billion plus lost to traffic accidents each year alone. To this we can add the gargantuan costs of air pollution, and further, the 20% of global greenhouse gas emissions that can be traced directly to motorized transport.

In order to be able to ignore these risks and dangers, as consumers we have to identify ourselves with our cars, and see them as extensions of ourselves and expressions of who *we imagine we are*. Any alternative ways and means of achieving the same ends have to be marginalized, devalued or made to seem so inconvenient that they cannot be attempted. Like all sunk-cost effects, car-dependence is a self-reinforcing and seemingly self-explanatory 'regime'. It becomes a powerful ideological force locking us into conformity and locking out those who are unable, for a variety of reasons, to participate. Such a dominant sunk-cost effect becomes a fallacy, encouraging us to embrace substantial negative costs as if they were in fact beneficial, and hiding any less costly or damaging alternatives.

20   Stechyson, N. (2010, 24 August) 'Bumper to bumper, all the way to Beijing', *Globe and Mail*, https://web.archive.org/web/20100826082536/http://www.theglo-beandmail.com:80/news/world/asia-pacific/china-traffic-jam-stretching-100-kilometres-could-last-for-weeks/article1683094/; and *China Daily* (2011) 'Jam busing service on the road in many cities', http://www.chinadaily.com.cn/bizchina/2011-01/08/content_11812546.htm, accessed 1 May 2015.

Learning from pedestrians

Various attempts, usually initiated by health authorities or voluntary groups, to encourage more walking, more cycling, and more 'incidental exercise', are often undermined through the very efficiencies of the road system. Making the roadways 'efficient' for cars has made them impossible to cross, in this way subverting the pedestrian networks that have characterized the city since ancient times.

As in Bel Geddes' visionary 'city of the future', in which he separated pedestrians from all traffic, pedestrians have become increasingly restricted in their movements and marginalized – particularly so in those cities where the vision of modernity has been most fully realized. It is as though the original *service* cars provide has been lost to view, since the product that provides that service has become its only surviving representation. The service itself – that of urban transportation – has been eclipsed from our sight by the tool we use to access it; this is a prime example of the deception, and self-deception, consumerism entails and design helps realize.[21]

Pedestrians are often referred to as 'vulnerable road users', and for good reason. They are more likely than vehicle occupants to suffer serious injury from vehicle crashes, and in many countries this likelihood increases due to the perils created by poor or non-existent infrastructure. Even in developed nations, pedestrians fare badly compared with occupants of vehicles, because they are typically young, elderly, disabled, or poor. They also typically spend much longer in hospital recovering from their injuries if they survive.

My personal experience of this began about 20 years ago, when I became involved in a pedestrian advocacy group. Our small group focused our efforts on persuading government authorities to reduce speed limits in zones likely to attract pedestrian activity, to increase the number of pedestrian crossings, and to put more financial resources into community-based education and information campaigns.[22]

We found ready allies among police, fire and ambulance service personnel, who had direct experience of many serious crashes involving

21   See Ayres, R.U. (1999) 'Products as service carriers: Should we kill the messenger or send it back?', Paper for United Nations University: Zero Emissions Forum, available from http://archive.unu.edu/zef/publications_e/ZEF_EN_1999_01_D.pdf, accessed 16 November 2015.

22   Collins, D., Bean, C. & Kearns, R. (2009) '"Mind that Child": Childhood, traffic and walking in automobilized space', in Conley, J. & McLaren, A.T. (Eds.), *Car Troubles*. Farnham: Ashgate: 127-146.

pedestrians, and support from school principals, health professionals and injury prevention specialists. Our most outspoken supporter, however, was a local Anglican priest who declared he was 'sick of burying young people'. But, despite our best efforts, we struggled to stir the sympathies of the traffic engineers and transport department officials.

I was somewhat baffled by this, since I knew these men to be professional in their approach and generally well-meaning. But our experience is suggestive of how sunk-cost effects work, and how they develop their own momentum and ideology within a regime – sometimes many years after the regime itself was created. Trained to optimize the circulation of vehicular traffic, there was little reason for these experts to be particularly interested in pedestrians. These 'vulnerable' road users seemed marginal to their duties, and did not behave in the predictable, more rational way expected of most licensed drivers.

Over a period of about ten years, our little group encountered from these professionals three distinct kinds of opposition to our ambitions. Firstly, they questioned our legitimacy, and saw us as ignorant and emotionally involved outsiders, intruding into their area of expertise. They believed that the world was safer for pedestrians than it had ever been, and so refused to acknowledge or accept any need for radical change.

On our side, we could find little evidence to support this optimism, since pedestrians are typically counted only in certain locations and periods, and so there was no reliable 'base-line' or exposure figure to indicate numbers of pedestrians at any one time, relative to the number of drivers. This suggested to us that their figures were misleading, hiding a long-term decline in the numbers of walkers on our streets, something that had begun in earnest in the 1950s.[23]

Secondly, the regulations and policies they followed took little account of pedestrians, who seemed by definition to be in the wrong place, especially when injured. This was also reflected in the way the police reported accidents involving pedestrians, who were assumed to be a contributing cause, just by being on the road. If they were young, the parents were assumed to be at fault, and if they were old, their carers were.

Finally, the engineers could see no economic value in pedestrian activity, since their training was centred at that time (in the 1990s) on the circulation of vehicular traffic. They could state immediately the economic value

23   See 'Pedestrians: ACRS Policy Position', *Australian College of Road Safety* (2015), at http://acrs.org.au/about-us/policies/safe-road-users/pedestrians/, accessed 1 December 2015.

of their highway system, but had little idea of the value of pedestrian access most shopkeepers can immediately recognize: people have to get out of cars, and walk, to engage with others and spend money.[24]

While the regulatory context might differ from nation to nation, the plight of pedestrians in the car-dependent city is suggestive of how control becomes aligned to the interests of an established regime, and how rules and regulations will reinforce this regime and, in the process, marginalize groups that cannot conform.

Our traffic engineers could not recognize most of the negative effects of the regime. In their response to us they displayed what psychologists call 'motivated reasoning'; that is, reasoning employed to ensure that the argument presented can be reformulated or restructured to fit an expected outcome or conclusion.[25]

For example, we discovered that our traffic engineers were reluctant to reduce urban speed limits that might better protect pedestrians, because they believed it was unnecessary and would decrease the system's efficiency and increase the trip times for drivers. The case was then put that drivers 'did not want' any lowering of speed limits, and it was a regressive step 'for the economy'. 'Efficiency' was their north star in this thinking. When about five years later the government finally lowered urban speed limits, there was no discernible impact on the economy, and very few of the outraged drivers they had predicted.

Such public 'debates' always seem to take a similar, rather torturous course: the resisters are usually motivated by their commitment to the established regime, and the benefits they derive from it. Their 'rational optimism' foregrounds the economic risks involved in change, and devalues the evidence supporting their opponents' arguments – in this case the data that demonstrated that the rate of injury and death would in fact be lower at lower speeds – something that turned out to be true.[26]

* * *

24   See Litman, T. (2011) 'The economic value of walkability', Victoria Transport Policy Institute, Canada.

25   See Jain, S.P. & Maheshwaran, D. (2000) 'Motivated reasoning: A depth-of-processing perspective', *Journal of Consumer Research*, 26.4: 358-371.

26   Woolley, J.E. *et al.* (2002) 'Impacts of lower speed limits in South Australia', *IATSS Research*, 26.2: 6-17.

Fast-food companies, soft-drink bottlers, tobacco producers, coal-fired power stations, offshore dirty manufacturers, and industrialized chemical agriculture companies are among those who typically develop their own versions of such motivated arguments, or sunk-cost fallacies. Many of these companies have become industry giants in their own right, if not monopolies. Their sunk costs are necessarily enormous, spanning decades of development and expansion, and the beliefs and assumptions supporting their business, their sunk-cost effects, become particularly persuasive.

Typically, their arguments too will include a denial of any observed negative influences of their activities, and an over-valuation of the benefits of these activities. In their own defence they will demand proof that their products or processes are dangerous, leaving it up to their opponents to present this proof, and then quarrelling with the evidence when it is finally produced. In the meantime we must all suffer the system's environmental and social impacts.

In this way, technological systems of provision such as road transportation develop their own momentum, locking in a vast army of users and stakeholders, and excluding those who might not be able to access the monopoly service they offer. Those locked in to the system in turn become part of the 'data' proving the argument that the system should be funded, maintained and further enhanced. The fact that the system is bad for the environment will be hard to discern, since its existence has been naturalized and normalized: it is now an 'essential' part of everyday life.

Further reading

Amato, J. (2004) *On Foot: A History of Walking*. New York: New York University Press.

Beatley, T. (2012) *Green Cities of Europe: Global Lessons on Green Urbanism*. Washington, DC: Island Press.

Cohen, M.J. (2012) 'The future of automobile society: A socio-technical transitions perspective', *Technology Analysis and Strategic Management*, 24.4: 377-390.

Conley, J. & McLaren, A.T. (Eds.) (2009) *Car Troubles: Critical Studies of Automobility and Auto-Mobility*. Farnham, UK: Ashgate.

Farber, S. &. Paez, A. (2011) 'Running to stay in place: The time-use implications of automobile oriented land-use and travel', *Journal of Transport Geography*, 19: 782-793.

Freund, P. & Martin, J. (1993) *The Ecology of the Automobile*. Toronto, Canada: Black Rose.

Hass-Klau, C. (1990) *The Pedestrian and the City*. London: Belhaven Press.

Hillman, J., Adams, J. & Whitelegg, J. (1990) *One False Move: A Study of Children's Independent Mobility*. London: PSI.

Marchand, R. (1985) *Advertising the American Dream*. Oakland, CA: University of California Press.

McCracken, G.D. (2005) *Culture and Consumption II: Markets, Meaning and Brand Management*. Bloomington, IN: Indiana University Press: 53-90.

Meikle, J. (2010) *Twentieth Century Limited: Industrial Design in America, 1925–1939*. 3rd edn, Philadelphia, PA: Temple University Press.

Merriman, P. (2009) 'Automobility and the geographies of the car', *Geography Compass*, 3.2: 586-599.

Morrison, K.A. & Minnis, J. (2013) *Carscapes: The Motor Car, Architecture, and Landscape in England*. London: Yale University Press.

Nieuwenhuis, P. & Wells, P. (2003) *The Automotive Industry and the Environment*. Cambridge: Woodhead.

Patterson, M. (2000) 'Car culture and global environmental politics', *Review of International Studies*, 26.2: 253-270.

Soderstrom, M. (2010) *The Walkable City: From Haussmann's Boulevards to Jane Jacobs's Streets and Beyond*. Montreal, Canada: Vehicule Books.

Tolley, R.S. (Ed.) (2003) *Sustainable Transport: Planning for Walking and Cycling in Urban Environments*. London: Woodhead.

Urry, J. (2004) 'The "system" of automobility', *Theory, Culture and Society*, 21.4/5: 25-39.

Part II
The Escalation of Consumption

5
Comparison, competition and consumerism

The fifties syndrome

The economic and social changes that followed the Second World War were shaped by a widespread conviction that economic recovery and reconstruction should centre on the production of more consumer goods, with pre war American models of industrial production, distribution and retail widely adopted. Increasing productivity, enabled by cheaper energy and resources, led to the price of many goods falling relative to most incomes. This was also helped by the fact that many Western governments also subsidized education, agriculture, housing, healthcare and industrial reconstruction. This Keynesian mix of economic stimulants, trialled before the war in America, increased the purchasing power of many ordinary people, and helped generate an unprecedented 'long boom' (c. 1940–1974).

Many lower middle-class and working-class people for the first time could aspire to own their own home, new appliances, perhaps a car, and even gain access to higher education for their children. Older social divisions seemed less important after the devastation of the war, and politicians and planners were keen to avoid recreating the economic tensions that had followed the First World War.[1] Everywhere a similar, more openly democratic view of

1   See McGovern, C. (1998) 'Consumption and citizenship in the United States, 1900–1940'; and De Grazia, V. (1998) 'Changing consumption regimes in Europe, 1930–1970: Comparative perspectives on the distribution problem', in Strasser, S., McGovern, C. & Judt, M. (Eds.), *Getting and Spending: European and American Consumer Societies in the Twentieth Century*. Cambridge: Cambridge University Press: chapters 2 and 3.

economic and social life was adopted, influenced by an American model of citizenship and consumption, and a determination to create greater levels of prosperity for all.

Looking back on this period of rapid economic growth, British sociologists in the late sixties pondered an 'upward' shift in the behaviours and attitudes of many of the working class. The new 'consumer citizen' of the 1950s had begun to reveal material aspirations formerly restricted to the middle classes, and a world of barriers and social tensions that now seemed to be changing. Indeed, this apparent weakening of class consciousness and its link to consumerism was reflected in many areas, including how to best represent the consumer's interests in such prosperous times. The consumer too was influenced by the greater affordability and range of goods available, and how she saw herself and others in this new economic and social order.[2]

A widespread adoption of new 'modern' goods like automatic washing machines, refrigerators, cars and a little later, TVs, was accompanied by an increase in the influence of advertising, marketing and design. The appearance of goods, and the way they were presented, became a concern for manufacturers, retailers, advertisers and many governments. The consumer, and the production of consumer goods, now seemed not only a key to economic prosperity but also to peace and democracy during the Cold War. National and international expos and fairs became a popular means of showing off the new world of goods available to the modern democratic 'consumer citizen', and some of the larger American ones travelled the world, combining corporate and government sponsorship, and expert design.[3]

An emphasis on policies supporting the production, distribution and sale of consumer goods was linked to a new democratic emphasis on freedom of choice, and an adequate provision of opportunities for all citizens, including education and employment. Building a more meritocratic democracy on the American model, where skill and educational attainment were the

---

2   For example, Goldthorpe, J.H. *et al.* (1969) 'The affluent worker and the thesis of embourgeoisment: Some preliminary findings', *Sociology*, 1.1: 11-31; and Gurney, P. (2005) 'The battle of the consumer in postwar Britain', *Journal of Modern History*, 77.4: 956-987.

3   Macdonald, G. (2004) 'Selling the American Dream: MOMA, industrial design and post-war France', *Journal of Design History*, 17.4: 397-412; Masey, J. & Morgan, C.L. (2008) *Cold War Confrontations: US Exhibitions and their Role in the Cultural Cold War*. Baden: Lars Muller.

main markers of social advancement and professional status, consumption became the means through which the consumer could reveal their social position and express their individual character.

The early James Bond films, for example, are suggestive of this cultural shift. With a commitment only to the nation and 'Her Majesty's Secret Service', the first Bond, played by Sean Connery, seems a kind of British social chameleon, displaying his status and character through purposeful, 'professional', albeit violent confrontations, while relaxing and enjoying the traditional upper-class luxuries Ian Fleming scattered through his novels. From sports cars to casinos and luxury hotels, populated not only by upper-class Englishmen, but exotic and beautiful women, glamour and seemingly easy access to luxury made this world more alluring.

As a perceptive critic notes, Bond himself was both a throwback to earlier upper-class adventure heroes of the kind that would entertain middle-class boys in the 1930s (heroes of London's so called upper-class 'Clubland'), and a heroic embodiment of the new meritocratic, techno-cratic professionalism of the post-war era. Sean Connery's own modest Scottish background hinted at the greater social mobility this promised, a path of self-advancement through knowledge and skill, and a more 'open' consumer-democracy.[4]

Social background and once more rigid class, religious and cultural divisions were deliberately downplayed and made to seem less important in this new era of Cold War democracy, just as they had in many wartime newsreels and films. This superficial egalitarianism was also evident in popular music. For many, the rise of the Beatles seemed to prove that class barriers were no longer so important. In contrast to the previous generation's local class loyalties and collective sense of identity, a style-conscious individualism was everywhere on display, where the individual's work and interests, likes and dislikes, seemed to trump older social and economic barriers.

4   Laucht, C. (2013) 'Britannia rules the atom: The James Bond phenomenon and postwar British nuclear culture', *Journal of Popular Culture*, 46.2: 358-377; and Chapman, J. (2005) 'Bond and Britishness', in Comentale, E.P., Watt, S. & Willman, S. (Eds.), *Ian Fleming & James Bond: The Cultural Politics of 007*. Bloomington, IN: Indiana University Press: 129-43.

The newcomers

This new meritocratic democracy in Western Europe, rebuilt partly with American money on a hybrid European and American model of mass-consumption, required both a greater social mobility and a greater emphasis on corporate professionalization and consumerism. Higher education was critical in this social transformation, since it promised to create the larger numbers of professionals required for this social transformation. So from the 1950s governments expanded their higher education systems, building many new universities and technical colleges.

In retrospect, it seems not surprising that many of the more serious political conflicts of the 1960s and 1970s centred on higher education, and on the meritocratic promise bestowed on education itself as a road to social advancement. Although most students were not necessarily attacking the class structure, access to greater social and economic mobility was now assumed to be a right, of sorts, for all. As a result, this new, much larger student cohort was especially sensitive to any signs that the class system might be alive and well.[5]

Popular culture, dominated by TV, film and pop music, reflected and represented the ideals of this new more mobile, technocratic consumer democracy. Advertisements, films and TV shows in the 1960s and 1970s all contain a rather conflicted ambiguity around class and social position, using advertised products as tokens of both personal advancement and individual difference.

For example, the Benson and Hedges cigarette ads on TV in Australia during the sixties and seventies used the same slogan again and again (in over 100 different ads), 'When only the best will do... and isn't that all the time?' Making use of a determinedly middle-class English actor, Stuart Wagstaff, the message on the golden packet was clear: smoking these cigarettes could provide you with a new freedom to enjoy 'the good things' in life, regardless of your background or present situation.

These changes can be seen particularly in fashion. 'Swinging London' in many ways epitomized this new mobility, meritocracy and emphasis on a superficial equality, to be marked out only by personality, credentials, skills and individual achievement. This is also reflected in many English romantic

---

5   Benson and Hedges ads, noted in article on Stuart Wagstaff (2015), https://en.wikipedia.org/wiki/Stuart_Wagstaff, accessed 1 May 2015; and see Mercer, B. (2011) 'The paperback revolution: Mass-circulation books and the cultural origins of 1968 in Western Europe', *Journal of the History of Ideas*, 72.4: 613-636; and Marwick, A. (1998) *The Sixties*. Oxford: 272-287.

and comedy films of the era, whose main social message was often that even 'ordinary' boys and girls, from working class backgrounds, could 'make it', given a bit of luck, some style, and sufficient courage.[6]

Georges Perec's experimental novella, *Things: A Story of the Sixties* (1965), which uses a remarkable ethnographic language in its portrayal of 'things' and people, paints an interesting picture of these social changes, and the rising expectations they entailed. Dominated by the minutiae of 'things', of lists of desired or undesired furnishing, furniture, clothing, shoes and accessories, the book's young protagonists are twenty-something part-time 'market researchers', a new and ambiguous para-profession attached to the booming post-war advertising business.

Jérôme and Sylvie and their circle of young workmates and friends in Paris are part of a new generation of 'young executives', 'technocrats on the way, but only halfway, to success.' With few exceptions, they and their friends all 'came from the lower middle classes, whose values, they felt, were for them no longer adequate.' Desiring the visible comfort, luxury and greater per-fection of the upper middle classes, their world was one of aspiration and frustration, with the 'things' of the title the main focus point of their hopes, dreams, and 'careers', incomplete and insecure as they are.[7]

Devoted browsers, they are forever desiring the greater comforts and luxu-ries of the life they can see growing around them, and forever frustrated by their lack of income. They find their apartment and kitchen too small and a source of constant frustration. They live vicariously, through the magazines, movies, restaurants, and shops, and the many new things they would most like to pos-sess, from English shoes to genuine antique furniture. It is no accident that Perec has made them 'researchers' in 'consumer motivation', part of a growing army of new specialists servicing this new and expanding consumerism.

The older world of class and location, of the politics of Left and Right, of growing up to train or study followed by a settled career, of having a clear purpose in life, has melted away for Perec's consumerist newcomers. Theirs is a new form of aimless pursuit, an 'unhappiness' born of unful-filled, and unfulfillable desire. They have an itch for material advancement, but one without any goal apart from an admired 'lifestyle' and its apparent

6   See Mercer, B. (2011) 'The paperback revolution; and Metzger, R. (2012) *London in the Sixties*. London: Thames & Hudson.

7   Perec, G. (1990 [1965]) *Things: A Story of the Sixties, and A Man Asleep, Two Novels by Georges Perec*. Translated and introduced by D. Bellos, Boston, MA: Godine: 41, 50, 63; and Becker, H. (2001) 'Georges Perec's Experiments in Social Description', *Ethnography*, 2.1: 63-76.

enjoyments. This necessarily makes them unhappy: they 'wanted life's enjoyment, but all around them enjoyment was equated with ownership', an ownership never quite in their grasp.

Comparison and competition

Jérôme and Sylvie seem engrossed in a world of continuous choice, of self-evaluation and social comparison, in which the special things in their lives are important actors, tokens on a chessboard of their own dreamt-of social advancement. For they, like their friends, now feel the need to 'look the part': to attain the 'right' job, qualifications, car, address, clothes and other attributes that 'go with' the role they possess or they aspire to. We see them looking for special bargains, and little luxuries like English shoes, those things marked by the magazines as 'above' the everyday.[8]

Perec rightly sees the supposed 'informality' of the sixties as deeply misleading. This informality masked a more intensive social competition, and gave fashion in this period an extraordinary inventiveness, DIY creativity and dynamism. Its very informality led to a 'throwaway' culture of continuous change and adaptability, where the interior especially became an arena for performance, with more fashionable things fleetingly tried out, tried on, and then as quickly, abandoned.[9]

Through the avenue provided by choice, 'invidious' comparison and self-evaluation, design and marketing must continuously 'cue' consumerism. Comparison always has an 'upward' direction as we look 'up' to those seemingly above us to find the standard we 'should' be following. As in the Benson and Hedges advertisements referred to previously, Stuart Wagstaff played the 'gentleman', an apparently effortless winner, generously offering us the golden standard, representing a life of glamour and luxury which he seems to enjoy. Through assumed wealth he opens a window onto a world of glamour, beauty, sensuality, and luxury that suggest what might become available to us through the magic golden packet in his hand.

8   Dwyer, R. (2009) 'Making a habit of it: Positional consumption, conventional action and the standard of living', *Journal of Consumer Culture*, 9.3: 328-347; and see Garcia, S.M., Tor, A. & Gonzales, R. (2006) 'Ranks and rivals: A theory of competition', *Personality and Social Psychology Bulletin*, 32.7: 970-982.
9   Whiteley, N. (1987) 'Interior design in the 1960s: Arenas for performance', *Art History*, 10: 79-90; Metzger, R. (2012) *London in the Sixties*.

Negotiating our way 'upward' through this new world of suddenly available and affordable things takes up both time and effort. Indeed, to make sure we don't look like 'losers', we have to work towards attaining the best that we can afford, usually a copy of an admired 'authentic' luxury. This is catered for in many commercial and retail strategies, for example when luxury brands like BMW produce cheaper models to attract new customers or retain those who want to keep up with their 'betters'. The BMW 3 series are good representatives of this contemporary version of 'semi-luxury'. These are still endowed with the aura of the brand and its glamour, but at more accessible prices.

The upward direction of comparison and competition can be seen in many contexts. When we see someone, more or less like ourselves, with a new car, stylish clothes or even a particular haircut, we are made aware that we could have that too; it's a cue that reminds us of what we seem to lack, prompting us to see ourselves through the eyes of others. Frequent invidious comparison encourages self-evaluation, and helps us discover what we lack. This necessarily displaces the time and effort needed to pursue our more intrinsic goals. In encouraging us to return to comparison, we are confronted by the question of where we are on 'the ladder' relative to others, which becomes an encouragement to consume more. Like Perec's young couple, we become eaten up by what we are missing out on, what we come to believe we lack.[10]

This is not a recipe for happiness, cooperation or social cohesion. *American Psycho* (1991), by Bret Easton Ellis, is a dark parable of the psychopathic potential of this vicious circle of comparison, self-evaluation and competition encouraged by consumerism. The hyper-consumption he draws attention to is implicitly materialistic and perfectionistic: his anti-hero can never 'finally' attain everything that will secure him the winning spot in a world of continuously changing desirable objects and upwardly shifting standards. His psychopathic Wall Street broker is so obsessed with having it all – even the 'best' business card – that he feels obliged to kill those who have possessions that seem better than his own.[11]

10   See Garcia, S.M., Tor, A. & Schiff, T.M. (2013) 'The psychology of competition: A social comparison perspective', *Perspectives in Psychological Science*, 8.6: 634-650; and Kasser, T. (2008) 'Pain and insecurity, love and money', *Psychological Inquiry*, 19: 174-8.

11   Ellis, B.E., (1991) *American Psycho*. New York: Vintage; and see Malkmes, J. (2011) *American Consumer Culture and its Society: From F. Scott Fitzgerald's 1920s Modernism to Bret Easton Ellis' 1980s Blank Fiction*. Hamburg: Diplomica Verlag.

New designed goods, interiors and buildings can help us mark out our position against a moving background of rising standards and expectations. In this chase after 'the latest and the best' others always seem to have something a little better, more interesting, or more advanced, than we do. This 'chase and flight' applies not only to individuals, but also to corporations and public institutions, and in fact any group influenced by the same values; they will try to mark out their higher standing, perhaps with an iconic building, a new office, or just a new executive chair, and get rid of what seems 'old' and not good enough.

Comparison in consumption is necessarily escalatory. It generates a sense of urgency that will motivate us to go out and buy something a little better. Its grip is firm because it awakens our fears of social descent and scarcity. It also locks out cooperation, which becomes impossible between 'rivals'. It leads us to move from admiring and purchasing an object that performs a useful function, such as a car, to looking over our shoulder to see whether others might have an even better car, noting where our car sits in a hierarchy of other cars, and wondering if we too should now upgrade.

Cars are especially powerful among positional goods. Marketers and designers carefully position each brand and model within a particular range against the design, price and technical features of its rivals. Most manufacturers aim for a price point at or slightly above what the consumer in their target group can afford, so that in making a sacrifice to purchase the car, the buyer also makes a commitment to the product. The risk the buyer takes in this commitment is balanced by the protection offered by the brand, which appears to guarantee the lasting value of the product, that it will deliver what it promises.[12]

The brand and its associated promotional material, the product's design and associated packaging and advertisements, like a story or myth must both reveal and conceal what the product is, and what it is for. So in the advertisement the branded car becomes a magical vehicle of personal freedom and mobility, with the brand its overarching symbol and myth. The brand lives on in our minds, and unlike the dependent product, the car, can remain untarnished by any association with dubious business practices associated with a particular CEO, occasional mechanical problems or unethical environmental stories. Rather like a politician suddenly elevated

---

12   Binkley, S. (2009) 'The civilizing brand: Shifting shame thresholds and the dissemination of consumer lifestyles', *European Journal of Cultural Studies*, 12: 21-39; Schembri, S.W. *et al.* (2010) 'Brand consumption and narrative of the self', *Psychology and Marketing*, 27.6: 623-638.

to the Presidency, the aura of authority and perfection in a long-lived brand can blind us to any weakness in its line of products.

Advertising also ensures that the prospective buyer is only allowed to see a 'perfect' car, often gliding through a pristine natural environment, and not the one more typically grubby, perhaps dinted, struggling through heavy traffic. Car showrooms now involve the magic touch of architecture, which can further glamorize the brand and elevate its value in the eyes of the consumer. The showroom becomes the 'brand palace', designed like the older department stores to dazzle and impress all who enter. The men and women who staff it have to look beautiful or at least very well dressed. But the 'king' or ruler of this new store is the brand itself, with these people its attendant servants.[13]

Managing product value

This strategic representation of the product as an alluring and desirable representative of the brand is necessarily deceptive, and an important strategy for stimulating consumerism. The new car is no longer just a useful vehicle from a real factory somewhere, but *the magic vehicle* of our aspirations, a dream and a promise of mobility, self-expression, and reputational bliss. As consumers we have sacrificed hard-earned money to buy this product, its value for us keyed to its high price, and this leads us also to accept that its possession can elevate us in the eyes of others.

The designers and marketers must carefully manage our attachment and the value we now attribute to their car. For in a world of rapidly changing products and rising expectations, the best is never enough; there will always be something better, and sooner than we think. We might like to imagine that the fat, balding man in the expensive sports car next to us at the traffic lights is 'compensating' for something that is missing in his life, but the truth is that we have all been led to chase a similar compensatory dream. We are driven to jump through the hoops of a delusive quest for the perfect experience, by a system of deception in which we ourselves are complicit.

The value we attribute to many of our possessions soon declines, usually in relation to what is visible and available, to what others possess, and to the

13   Litman, T. (2009), 'Mobility as positional good: Implications for transport policy and planning', in J. Conley and A.T. Mclaren (Eds.), *Car Troubles: Critical Studies of Automobility and Auto-Mobility*. Farnham, Surrey: Ashgate: 199-218.

pace of technological and stylistic change. This decline in value is termed 'hedonic adaptation', and is found in every domain, with some items slipping down the ladder of what we value more quickly than others. We are all on a moving conveyor belt, where we must spend time, energy and money to 'catch up' with others through finding and buying a 'better' product; and when we finally manage to upgrade to that 'better' product or experience, it increases our sense of commitment.[14]

While the gleam of novelty and glamour stimulates our curiosity and eventual commitment, hedonic adaptation signals the creeping dissatisfaction that comes with familiarity. It also suggests why uniqueness and interactivity are so valued in today's consumerism. For what is interactive can be continuously stimulating: swipe the screen and all is new again. Paradoxically, the main reason why phones and tablets are so readily discarded often lies in this interactivity; the latest model will always promise a slightly better form of access, and today access is a standard we all expect.

Predicting this decline in valuing what is possessed, its rate of 'discount', is always a difficult task, and one of the key issues marketers and designers have to address. The idea is to more frequently encourage an 'upgrade' to the latest model rather than a shift to another brand. Consumer deception must be managed, and managed efficiently. The waste that is a direct consequence of this is now an essential part of a whole-of-life marketing strategy; it's not just the unethical behaviour of a few corporate businesses.[15]

'Hedonic adaptation', together with rising standards, accelerates the rate of discard and upgrade in each domain, and across domains too. This underlying logic directly contradicts the arguments of some that things are getting better, and that because they are making many things smaller, lighter and more efficient, we will somehow manage to 'reduce carbon', and even waste. There is no evidence that this 'eco-modernization' will have an impact until we deal with the escalating problem of consumerism, of the routinized creation of surplus in production and excess in consumption and waste.

---

14   On the 'treadmill' theory, Diener, E., Lucas, R.E. & Scollon, C.N. (2006) 'Beyond the hedonic treadmill: Revising the adaptation theory of well-being', *American Psychologist*, 61.4: 305-314; and see Dittmar, H. (2007) 'The costs of consumer culture and the "cage within"', *Psychological Inquiry*, 18:1: 23-31.

15   Liboiron, M. (2013) 'Modern waste as strategy', *Lo Squaderno: Explorations in Space and Society*, 29: 9-12, http://www.losquaderno.professionaldreamers.net/?cat=162, accessed 1 May 2015.

The escalation in consumerism, as I have suggested, has two dimensions: a 'vertical' one, which I have just described, where someone rapidly replaces a product with a new version of the same, for example; and a horizontal one, where the new product generates replacements in visually or materially related zones, sometimes in several domains at once. In the famous example Diderot gives (in 1772), his new clothes lead to him redecorating his whole room, something he, as a pre-modern man, is clearly not happy about.

To take a more contemporary example, a woman who commits to an upgrade of her mobile phone, might have to consider replacing the phone's cover, and this might lead her to replace her handbag or briefcase, getting ready, as it were, before that next important meeting. A smart new suit may make a man feel that he needs a haircut, and this can escalate into a search for new shoes, and perhaps a new shirt and tie. In the home, a new toaster might lead to a new kettle, a new kitchen to a new stove, a new sofa to a set of chairs, and so the list goes on.

Many young couples about to be married, inspired by TV programmes like *Grand Designs*, will plan not only to buy a new house, but also to buy new furniture and other goods to make the interior 'match' the house. This consumerism encourages a horizontal as well as a vertical upgrading of possessions. A good example, shown in British artist Grayson Perry's three-part TV documentary, *All in the Best Possible Taste* (2012), is the 'solution' of a young businesswoman, who has just bought a display home in an upmarket estate. She explains to Perry that to solve her furnishing problem, she bought the entire contents of the display home along with the house.[16]

The Diderot effect is now so common it passes almost without notice. For example, one of the most common excuses on eBay to sell a second-hand stove or dishwasher in the kitchen upgrade is that the 'old' stove, perhaps six months old, now no longer 'matches' the colour or design of the new kitchen. Some even go the other way, replacing the stove to find that their new stove no longer 'fits' the old kitchen. Such stylistic and colour mismatches are a boon to retailers, and one of the great drivers generating and accelerating the pace of consumption. In the modern home and office everything must be new, clean and up to date, and this creates a forward and

16 *In the Best of Possible Taste with Grayson Perry* (2012): http://www.channel4.com/programmes/in-the-best-possible-taste-grayson-perry/, accessed 1 November 2015.

'upward' movement that encourages frequent renewals and a horizontal escalation in 'related' consumption.[17]

Space inflation

The quest for the 'right' home, and especially the 'right' interior, becomes a particularly powerful driver in consumerism. In its formal attributes, its spaces, its unifying style and scale, and also its provision of various settings for the rituals of everyday life, the home becomes an expression of lifestyle and the demands of consumerism. It mirrors its occupants and their relationships, how they think they want to live, and what they come to value and accumulate over time.

'Space inflation' is a direct result of this fascination with the home and interior. It has been especially apparent in middle-class housing in the developed world, where interior sizes have steadily increased since the Second World War. This trend can be seen to have dramatically escalated, along with the consumption of other goods, from the mid-seventies. In Australia, for example, the average size of residential dwellings has grown from around 100 square metres in the early 1950s to over 240 square metres today, the largest average size for a home in the world.

To put this in context, the average number of people living in each house now in most Australian middle class suburbs is about a third or less of what was typical in the 1950s, but their homes are now at least twice as big as the homes of their grandparents, in this earlier era. As this suggests, even if we built our new homes to be more environmentally efficient than our grandparents' homes (and some now do), and can make them can run on less power and water, such environmental gains are typically undermined through our homes' much larger size, and their more intensive consumption of power and water.[18]

17   On the Diderot Effect, see McCracken, G.D. (1988) *Culture and Consumption: New Approaches to the Symbolic Character of Consumer Goods and Activities.* Bloomington, IN: Indiana University Press: 118-129; and Wyrwa, U. (1998) 'Consumption and consumer society: A contribution to the history of ideas', in Strasser, S. *et al.* (Eds.), *Getting and Spending:* 431-2.

18   Dwyer, R. (2009) 'The McMansionization of America? Income stratification and the standard of living in Housing, 1960–2000', *Research in Social Stratification and Mobility,* 27: 285-300; and Allon, F. (2008) *Renovation Nation.* Sydney: University of New South Wales Press.

The Australian suburban house's progress from 100 square metres of relative comfort to 240 square metres has also been driven by technological innovation. This has lowered labour costs relative to the size of each building. Many new homes, for example, are now assembled to a much greater extent from factory-made parts, such as roofing and panelling systems which can be bolted or glued together. Exploiting these innovations, along with design programmes and information management systems, builders can provide their customers with 'more' for the same or less money, and more quickly, and this becomes an attractive way to sell new homes.

Rising standards in appliances, furniture and furnishing also drive change within the building industry. Insufficient storage, inadequate kitchens or bathrooms, colours that do not match, having one bedroom or bathroom too few, all become excuses not just to renovate, but to build and move into new or larger homes. Comparison with peers, advertising and lifestyle advice (in magazines and TV shows), can all persuade homemakers to upgrade or renovate if they can afford to.

While IKEA expects their customers to start looking at new kitchens after five years of use, some wealthy people now insist on upgrading their kitchen every two to three years, with these upmarket kitchens often matched by complete 'outdoor' kitchens for taking advantage of the Australian summer. Like the car, the kitchen is now getting bigger and upgrading has become more frequent.[19]

I have personally observed this obsession with upgrading in the area where I have lived over the last 25 years. When we first moved to the beachside suburb where we now live, most of the houses were large, old, cheap, and often dilapidated, and set in large gardens. But as land prices increased, from the mid-1990s, more and more of these older homes were demolished to make way for new 'Mac-Mansions', often built in pairs or threes on the original blocks. Much narrower, but taller than the houses they replaced, some of these homes are more than 350 square metres in size.[20]

19   On the 'restless kitchen' in particular, see Shove. E. *et al.* (2007) *The Design of Everyday Life*. Oxford: Berg: 21-39; and also Parrott, K.R., *et al.* (2008) 'Kitchen remodelling: Exploring the dream kitchen projects', *Housing and Society*, 35.2: 25-42.

20   See Clune, S., Morrissey, J. & Moore, T. (2012) 'Size matters: House size and thermal efficiency as policy strategies to reduce net emissions of new developments', *Energy Policy*, 48: 657-667; and see also O'Callaghan, J. (1993) *The Australian Dream: Design of the Fifties*. Sydney: Powerhouse Museum.

FIGURE 5.1: TYPICAL 1950S SUBURBAN HOUSE, ADJACENT TO 2000S HOUSE, ADELAIDE

Photo J. Gay (2015)

The accompanying photographs show the progression, since the late 1950s, from houses of 100 square metres to those of 240 or more today. The first pictured house on the left is fairly typical of the early 1960s – a now seemingly tiny suburban house set on a generous block. At this time most of these houses comprised two bedrooms, an internal bathroom and kitchen and, as an innovation, an attached garage or carport. The second house, next to it in the first photograph, is a typical project home from the 2000s, probably of around 250 square metres, again built on a generous block, but with three or four bedrooms, at least two internal bathrooms, separate toilet and laundry, and a larger, open-plan living area. In Australia this is now a typical new house, well within the reach of a home-owning majority. Most are over twice the size of the average 1960s house.

FIGURE 5.2: WEST LAKES SHORELINE, ADELAIDE: 1990S 'MAC-MANSIONS', MOST OVER 350 M^3
        IN SIZE

Photo: J. Gay (2015)

The second photo is of a group of large villas overlooking the lake not far from where we live. These homes were pioneers in their time, when this development was expanded in the 1990s, and are similar in size to the newer houses being built in many fashionable places today, including on the nearby seafront. These homes are all over 300 square metres in size, their key attraction being the expansive water views from the front rooms. They have 4 or 5 bedrooms, many have 3 bathrooms or more, and some have more than one living area. It is not uncommon for the open-plan area at the front of each house, including the kitchen, to measure 50 square metres or more – up to half the space devoted to the average 1960s house above. These are not the houses of the really wealthy, but of successful professional, middle class people.

As all this suggests, stricter building codes, 'smarter' technologies and better rating tools favoured by most governments in Australia and elsewhere, simply cannot have any real impact on reducing resource consumption triggered by this creeping space inflation. These homes, whatever green technologies we might add to them, are necessarily and inevitably more expensive to live in, to heat and cool, and also more intensive in their consumption of water.

As in many other domains, size matters, since it indicates social standing and position; making the 'big' greener, will reduce the *relative* emissions of each home per square metre, and this may look impressive on paper. However, it can do little to reduce our overall emissions. This is yet another argument against the idea that eco-efficiency alone can lower carbon – at least without addressing more seriously the competitive, comparative dynamic behind our 'consumption problem'.

* * *

Post-sixties consumerism has had the effect of turning our lives into unfinished projects which require an increasingly large cast of material actors, on a larger, more lavish stage. The 'consuming self' is now a work in progress – to be nurtured, improved and changed through various enhancements, from luxury holidays to new clothes, cars, kitchens and homes. The central myth, continuously reinforced by branding and advertising, suggests that the 'true self' will emerge from this process like a butterfly from a cocoon, but only in the right setting and with the right products at hand.[21]

21   Campbell, C. (2004) 'I shop therefore I know I am: The metaphysical basis of modern consumerism', in Ekstrom, B. & Brembeck, H. (Eds.), *Elusive Consumption*, Oxford: Berg: 27-44.

Reputation plays an increasingly important role in this process. It is no longer something to be added to through experience, and then communicated to others through a demonstration of skill or knowledge; instead it is self-created and managed, and carefully 'curated' through social media updates, and various forms of consumption itself. Social media has further internalized this chase for reputation, for it is comparative, and necessarily involves frequent self-evaluation.[22]

Continuous comparison, competition and self-evaluation reinforce a background dread or consciousness of scarcity, a fear of missing out – 'FOMO', as it is now called. We imagine that this scarcity can be undone through acquisition and accumulation, and this gives consumerism its dynamic urgency and escalatory nature. We try, and buy, to win, and to show that we *have* won, even in some very modest way, to avoid the taint of losing, and the shame this might bring.

This focus on competition is ultimately soul-destroying, and typically displaces much of what is *not* a part of the individual's well prepared story of 'getting there'. Indeed, often those things we most enjoy, or which bring us the most intrinsic benefits, such as reading a good book, making things by hand, gardening, cooking, learning to play a musical instrument, or spending 'free' time with our family and friends, get 'bumped' off the list of things 'we must do'. As the next chapter makes clear, this urgency is in part dictated by consumerism itself, and particularly the advent of computerization, the internet and social media.

Further reading

Allon, F. (2008) *Renovation Nation: Our Obsession with Home*. Sydney: University of New South Wales Press.

Benedikt, M. (2005) 'Less for less yet: On architecture's value(s) in the marketplace', in Saunders, W.S. (Ed.), *Commodification and Spectacle in Architecture: A Harvard Design Magazine Reader*. Minneapolis: Minnesota University Press: chapter 2

Claassen, R. (2008) 'The status struggle: A recognition-based interpretation of the positional economy', *Philosophy and Social Criticism*, 34: 1,021-1,049.

Dittmar, H. (2008) *Consumer Culture, Identity and Well-being*. Hove, East Sussex: Psychology Press.

22   Bishop, R. (2001) 'The pursuit of perfection: A narrative analysis of how women's magazines cover eating disorders', *Howard Journal of Communications*, 12.4: 221-240.

Heffernan, M. (2014) *A Bigger Prize: Why Competition isn't Everything and How We Do Better.* New York: Simon & Schuster.

Kasser, T. (2002) *The High Price of Materialism.* Cambridge, MA: MIT Press.

Kohn, A. (1986) *No Contest: The Case against Competition.* Boston, MA: Houghton Mifflin.

Masey, J. & Morgan, C.L. (2008) *Cold War Confrontations: US Exhibitions and their Role in the Cultural Cold War.* Baden, Switzerland: Lars Muller.

McCracken, G.D. (2008) *Transformations: Identity Construction in Contemporary Culture.* Bloomington, IN: University of Indiana Press.

Mullainathan, S. & Shafir, E. (2013) *Scarcity: The True Cost of Not Having Enough.* London: Penguin.

Nelissen, R.M.A., Van De Ven, N. & Stapel, D. (2011) 'Status concerns and financial debts in adolescents', *Social Influence*, 6.1: 39-56.

O'Callaghan, J. (Ed.) (1993) *The Australian Dream: Design of the Fifties.* Sydney: Powerhouse Museum.

Strasser, S., McGovern, C. & Judt, M. (Eds.) (1998) *Getting and Spending: American and European Consumer Societies in the Twentieth Century.* Oxford: Oxford University Press.

Sandbrook, D. (2006) *White Heat: A History of Britain in the Swinging Sixties.* London: Abacus.

Shove, E. (2003) *Comfort, Cleanliness and Convenience: The Social Organization of Normality.* Oxford: Berg.

Silverman, J. (2015) *Terms of Service: Social Media and the Price of Constant Connection.* New York: HarperCollins.

Tatzel, M. (Ed.) (2014) *Consumption and Well-Being in the Material World.* London: Springer.

Veblen, T. (2007 [1899]) *Theory of the Leisure Class.* Oxford: Oxford University Press.

6
Technology and acceleration

Founding myths

The origins of the personal computer in the late 1960s and early 1970s is now the stuff of legend. The result of many contributing developments, these are seen as coming together in an extraordinary prototype, first tested in the so-called 'Mother of All Demos' presented by the Stanford engineer, Douglas Engelbart, to the annual Californian Computer Conference in December 1968. This demonstrated all the basic elements now taken for granted in the personal computer, including the use of a mouse, the concepts of windows, of hypertext, word-processing and file retrieval, email, modems linking computers together through microwave transmission, as well as computer graphics and editing.[1]

A visionary inventor, Engelbart was driven by the idea that to solve the increasingly complex problems of the world would require collaborative solutions, drawing on information and specialists from different locations, and aided by some type of interactive 'memory machine'. Influenced by cybernetics, systems engineering and the theories of the linguist, Benjamin Lee Whorf, Engelbart intended to show how such a memory machine might work, its visionary goal being the 'augmentation' or extension of the human intellect. To this event we can trace many subsequent revolutionary developments, and the origins of Apple. Indeed, Steve Jobs bought the patent for the mouse from Engelbart's research centre.

---

[1] See his extraordinary memoir, Engelbart, D. (1988, January) 'The augmented knowledge workshop', in Goldbert, A. (Ed.), *A History of Personal Workstations*. New York: ACM: 185-248, available at: http://www.diku.dk/OLD/undervisning/2004f/516/p73-englebart.pdf, accessed 1 November 2015.

Stewart Brand was one of the only non-engineers present during this demo. A leading member of San Francisco's counterculture, he was deeply interested in Engelbart's work, and assisted him with the video-conferencing from Menlo Park, the location of Engelbart's 'Augmentation Research Centre'. Brand shared much of Engelbart's vision of 'augmenting the human intellect', even if he pictured it in more overtly political, social and psychological terms. He was devoted to the idea that 'personal' technologies such as Engelbart's computer could further liberate human life, knowledge and consciousness, and eagerly spread the news about it to his friends in the counterculture in San Francisco.[2]

The interest of Brand and his young friends in computing might seem strange at first; after all, their hippy anti-war 'neo-medievalism', communalism and 'back to nature' ethos does not seem to be the obvious, or most promising subculture in which to nurture the development of the personal computer. However, their experimental approach to life was avowedly 'do-it-yourself' when it came to technology, and their fascination with useful, individualized 'tools for living', referred to in the subtitle of Stewart Brand's *Whole Earth Catalog*, played a significant role in generating a wider interest in Englebart's ideas and work.

The *Whole Earth Catalog* is, by any account, an extraordinary creation. Part self-help encyclopaedia and part old-fashioned mail-order catalogue of sometimes unusual but useful 'tools for living', it attempted to link like-minded young people together, and make their activities, beliefs and discoveries visible to each other. According to some estimates, by the late 1970s (when this 'back to nature' movement had largely ended) up to 10 million young Americans, over the previous decade, had spent time in a commune of some kind, whether for a few months or many years. The *Whole Earth Catalog* functioned not only as a forum to share individual readers' experiences of communal living, but also as a means of attracting fellow travellers to the cause. As one devoted early user of the *Catalog* later explained:

> I was instantly enthralled. I'd never seen anything like it. We lived in a small redneck town in Virginia—people didn't think about such things as 'whole systems' and 'nomadics' and 'Zen Buddhism' . . . *The Whole Earth Catalog* changed my life. It was my doorway to Bucky Fuller, Gregory Bateson, whole systems, communes, and lots of other things

2   Turner, F. (2005) 'Where the counterculture met the new economy: The WELL and the origins of virtual community', *Technology and Culture*, 46: 485-512.

that formed a foundation to a world model I've been building ever since.[3]

Having a science background himself, Brand was fascinated by the many possible links to be made between cybernetics, systems theory, 'micro-computer' technology and the cultural change he had become so deeply involved with. In fact, his presence can be seen in most major initiatives within the counterculture in this period, from the first 'sound and light' music shows (or Trips Festivals) associated with The Grateful Dead (which he helped stage), to the communes of Haight-Ashbury, San Francisco.

His *Whole Earth Catalog: Access to Tools*, was preceded by a lesser-known 'Whole Earth Truck Store' (from 1963), which he and his wife Lois took on tour to the communes, distributing the kind of information later found in the *Catalog*, and selling 'useful tools' to the residents. This idealism echoed the 'back to the land' ethos of the early settlers, and also the tribal life of the indigenous Indians, another subject that fascinated Brand, and to which he was personally connected.[4]

To many of those influenced by the counterculture, the early microcomputer seemed especially significant, since it was precisely the kind of DIY 'personal' technology that seemed useful to communalists and those interested in developing and spreading new ideas from their own experience, whether this was the effects of taking certain drugs or easier ways of building mud-brick houses. The 'personal computer' might also be free from the direct control of the government's 'military-industrial complex', which many like Brand saw as contributing directly to the Cold War, and also the Vietnam War.

3   Gareth Branwyn's blog cited in Turner (2005) 'Where the counterculture met the new economy': 492. See also Binkley, S. (2003) 'The seers of Menlo Park: The discourse of heroic consumption in the "Whole Earth Catalog"', *Journal of Consumer Culture*, 3.3: 283-313.

4   Zimmerman, N. (2006) 'Consuming nature: The Grateful Dead's performance of an anti-commercial counterculture', *American Music*, 24.2: 194-216; and Conn, S. (2010) 'Back to the garden: Communes, the environment, and anti-urban pastoralism at the end of the sixties', *Journal of Urban History*, 36: 831-848

From augmentation to control

The idealization of 'personal' computers as tools for self-development and social liberation, for the augmentation or extension of human capability, embodied a number of significant ethical, social and psychological tensions: who, for example, was to control the information shared between computers, and to what purpose was this extension of human knowledge to be put? 'Solving problems' could not be so easily separated or extracted from the question of 'whose problems', and 'for what purpose?'[5]

The heroic individual emerging from the counterculture generally believed they understood this moral dimension, and usually assumed that no good could come of the government and the 'military industrial complex'. The personal computer seemed particularly fascinating because it could be 'personal', and not necessarily subject to the control of the wider system. This heroic individualism became entangled in the story of the spread of personal computing over the next decade; these first computers seemed boxes of self-authored solutions and tricks which the informed technologist could use for almost any purpose, free of corporate or government oversight, or the control of the 'establishment'.

This individualistic post-counterculture idealism can be seen echoed in the unlikely storyline of the first *Star Wars* movie (1977), where a gang of footloose rebels toting do-it-yourself weaponry and a patchwork of second-hand spacecraft take on an evil totalitarian empire. It is almost as if California's famous Homebrew Computer Club had designed the rebels' weaponry in an all-night workshop, while Westinghouse and the military funders of the predecessor of the internet, the ARPANET, had designed the Empire's spaceships and their ultimate weapon, the 'Death Star'. In retrospect, this seems an imaginative fictional reconstruction of the paranoid Cold War nuclear 'shield' America had built at this time, appropriately termed 'Mutually Assured Destruction' or MAD.

The ideology of the 'Rebels' in *Star Wars* was self-consciously democratic, inclusive, spiritually engaged, collaborative and wedded to a romantic American pastoral idealism, not so distinct from that of Brand and his communalist friends. The 'Jedi Knights' with their 'Force' (and later, the 'Ewoks' with their vaguely indigenous culture), were on the side of authentic

---

5   See Bardini, T. & Friedewald, M. (2002) 'Chronicle of the death of a laboratory: Douglas Engelbart and the failure of the Knowledge Workshop', *History of Technology*, 23: 191-212.

democracy and the environment, and against centralized 'big' technology, and the corporate control and militarism of the 'empire'. The 'Death Star', as a potent symbol of America's 'military industrial complex', could only be defeated by a liberated, authentic individualism, rooted in a self-organized community, preferably somewhere out in the natural environment.[6]

Personal computers initially seemed important since they promised to augment their users' mental powers in all kinds of ways. For those influenced by the counterculture, this was a personal journey, part of a heroic stance taken 'against the establishment'. Their stance again underlines the moral commitment involved in consumption: in this case, having powerful tools for living a liberated lifestyle helped define a distinctive 'rebel' social, ethical and political stance, as did the clothes, long hair, use of drugs, amplified folk and rock music, and other markers of counterculture fashion.

This self-conscious ethical stance against the 'military-industrial' corporate mainstream was later appropriated in Apple's famous '1984' ad for the Macintosh. In many ways this advertisement attempts to recover the exciting mood, if not the founding myth, of Engelbart's original computer, seen through the eyes of the younger 'techy' followers of the counterculture. Here the 'grey' world of 'big brother' corporate computing is literally smashed open – by a young woman wielding a sledgehammer – to reveal the new 'alternative' Macintosh, a 'personal' tool for some yet to be determined mental and cultural journey towards liberation.

FIGURE 6.1: APPLE MACINTOSH 512 KB

Courtesy Cité des Sciences et de l'Industrie, Paris

6   Meyer, D.S. (1992) 'Star Wars, *Star Wars*, and American Political Culture', *Journal of Popular Culture*, 26.2: 99-115.

The 1984 ad was also an outstanding example of what became later known as the 'rebel sell' – appropriating the 'heroic individualism' and 'alternative lifestyle' of the counterculture to further nurture a more 'personal' consumerism. The idealism of 'doing your own thing' could now be materialized and used to 'personalize' your tools, clothes and other items on *any* chosen path to self-discovery and liberation. The product's brand furthered this process of personalization and internalization, since the brand lived on as a story embedded in the product, guaranteeing its unique individuality and authenticity, and now adopted by its owner.[7]

However, 'the Empire' could not be so easily defeated. Computing, as the story of *Star Wars* suggests, was not only developing towards an open collaborative or communal model of information distribution and sharing, as envisaged by Stewart Brand and his friends, but also continued to grow from its Cold War origins into more typical applications of larger automation and information retrieval systems. The 'Death Star' in the real world, inevitably, survived and prospered, with larger and larger volumes of data held, analysed and exploited for a variety of government, military and commercial purposes.

The larger computer, as a tool for automation and control, added efficiency, precision, power and speed to everything it touched, including weaponry. This led to a series of revolutionary changes in information systems, and an increasing substitution of machines or robots for labour. Jet travel and container shipping, for example, were first computerized in the 1970s, allowing the development of the unprecedented coordination, connectivity and efficiency we are now familiar with, and dramatically lowering the costs of these services.[8]

7   Stein, S. (2002) 'The "1984" Macintosh ad: Cinematic icons and constitutive rhetoric in the launch of a new machine', *Quarterly Journal of Speech*, 88.2: 169-192; and see Binkley, S. (2004) 'Everybody's life is like a spiral: Narrating Post-Fordism in the Lifestyle Movement of the 1970s', *Cultural Studies: Critical Methodologies*, 4.1: 71-96.

8   See Schor, J.S. (2005) 'Prices and quantities: Unsustainable consumption and the global economy', *Ecological Economics*, 55.3: 309-320; and Higham, J, *et al.* (2014) 'Climate change, tourist air travel and radical emissions reduction', *Journal of Cleaner Production*, 10: 1-12.

The high cost of optimization

Since the 1970s in most corporate businesses the efficiency gains of computerization have benefitted the 'bottom line', but too often at the expense of their now reduced workforces and the environment in which these companies are operating. It would be nice to say that this can be fixed by more emphasis on the environmental, social and financial 'triple bottom line' of sustainable business, and on increasing the 'dematerialization' of material demands made possible by technological innovation. However, in most cases any 'decoupling' of material flows from economic activity and financial gains tend to be offset by overall increases in consumption. This is due to consumer demand: as Stanley Jevons discovered, greater efficiencies in production will encourage more consumption.[9]

In many domains the energy and materials 'saved' through innovation and efficiency gains have led to a higher turnover, and even the production of two or more times more goods – in this way creating a long environmental 'tail' that outweighs any gains from lower emissions per unit produced. This follows a logic most easily seen in Walmart or IKEA: the $500 TV may be redesigned for Walmart using cheaper componentry and then mass-produced for under $100; the $400 bookcase may be redesigned in chipboard and foil for self-assembly in IKEA for less than $100. Aided by computer-aided design, and computer-enabled distribution and payment systems, this formula expands markets and builds 'growth' in the companies concerned, but at an aggregated environmental and social cost.

Other corporations have also discovered similar advantages in over-production itself. This is the result of the computer's ability to scale up, automate, and speed processes, and is especially apparent in textiles and plastics. Why order 10,000 items if you can order 100,000 at substantially less cost per unit? You can then sell what you cannot sell into the same market at cost, in this way generating more sales later, and edging out your 'weaker' rivals. In fashion, many clothes are now produced using this formula. They will be worn only a few times and then given away. Charities, indeed, cannot keep up with the waste this strategy generates, and they are forced to pay to bury the massive volumes of the prematurely wasted goods they cannot sell.[10]

---

9   Alcott, B. (2005) 'Jevons' Paradox', *Ecological Economics*, 54.1: 9-21; and especially Polimeni, J.M. & Polimeni, R.I. (2006) 'Jevons' Paradox and the myth of technological liberation', *Ecological Complexity*, 3.4: 344-353.

10 See Birtwistle, G. & Moore, C.M. (2007) 'Fashion clothing: Where does it all end up?', *International Journal of Retail & Distribution Management*, 35.3: 210-216.

The environmental 'externalities' created by such large volumes and low prices have become a massive problem that governments are yet to address. These products are necessarily inferior to their more expensive originals and will not last as long, and yet most will use up similar or greater amounts of energy and material to manufacture. The paradox is that the manufacturers and retailers of these goods *benefit more* if they do not last as long or fail after a relatively short space of time, since this generates repeat custom, and also 'trains' the consumer to return to the shops more often, to buy again. Because of their low cost and lower quality these cheaper goods are also often abandoned or thrown away rather than repaired, and indeed most cannot be repaired.

In electronic products this system results in the process of using of glues rather than screws for internal componentry, so that most computers, laptops, phones and tablets now can only be partially dismantled, at least without breaking or melting their plastic casings. In China, India and West Africa there are now many poor villages and towns dedicated to this dangerous recycling work, taking apart products that have not been designed to be taken apart, and certainly not by human hands.

The dramatic increases in overall volumes of cheap, affordable goods, manufactured and distributed around the world through the agency of computerization, is mirrored in a dramatic increase in overall volumes of difficult wastes, many of them, like e-wastes, complex goods put together without reference to their environmental afterlife. The now infamous photographs of young dead seabirds fed brightly coloured plastics by their doting parents, or those taken by marine scientists showing micro-plastics glowing brightly inside the bodies of plankton in the oceans, can be directly linked to this reckless consumer-driven 'post-cautionary' system of production. It is 'post-cautionary' rather than precautionary, since its long-term effects have been deliberately ignored.[11]

Global waste figures linked to this expansive consumerism are extremely depressing, but they confirm the facile thinking involved in imagining that somehow we do not have to change how we make and use what we produce. To start with, our annual production of urban waste is now at the staggering figure of 7–10 billion tonnes, and at present rates is set to double within ten years. We also generate 8–10 billion tonnes of industrial and agricultural

---

11   See Jambeck, J.R. *et al.* (2015) 'Plastic waste inputs from land into the ocean', *Science*, 347.6223: 768-771; and see especially Liboiron, M. (2015/6) 'Redefining pollution and action: The matter of plastics', *Journal of Material Culture*, 21.1: 1-24.

wastes each year. These figures equate to volumes larger than those produced by many cities.[12]

A revolution in time

Just as new computer-based technologies have dramatically increased the speed and efficiency of production, distribution and consumption, they have also transformed and increased the speed of our interactions and activities. Greater mobility, continuous connectedness, instant communication and information retrieval, have as dramatically transformed our social and psychological life over the last 30 years, much of this in ways that we are still struggling to understand and come to terms with.

In a series of illuminating essays, the sociologist Hartmut Rosa describes this dynamic transformation in terms of three interacting forms of acceleration, the technological, the social and the experiential. Relevant to our argument here, Rosa explains the 'cultural engine' of the third form acceleration takes as a 'eudaemonic impulse', or a quest for the good life, which I suggest also animates contemporary consumerism.

Rosa also emphasizes that the consequences of our high-speed society are inherently contradictory, in that for convenience and excitement most of us often want boring or difficult things to go faster, but at the same time we want to slow down to enjoy some things, which tend to be more closely keyed into the capacities of our senses. This opposing impulse towards the slower he terms 'de-synchronization', and notes that this has accompanied the accelerating dynamic of modernity for a century or more.[13]

Wanting to escape the effects of acceleration is partly the result of an increase in perceived time-scarcity; the 'fast' now seems to dominate most of our time, forcing us to concentrate on what is immediately before us, on

12   See Wilson, D.C. *et al.* (Eds.) (2015) *Global Waste Management Outlook*. UNEP and ISWA, https://www.iswa.org/fileadmin/galleries/Publications/ISWA_Reports/GWMO_summary_web.pdf, accessed 1 January 2016; and also Hardesty, B.D. & Wilcox, C. (2015, 13 February) 'Eight million tonnes of plastic are going into the oceans each year', *The Conversation*, http://the-conversation.com/eight-million-tonnes-of-plastic-are-going-into-the-ocean-each-year-37521, accessed 1 March 2015.

13   Rosa, H. (2003) 'Social acceleration: Ethical and political consequences of a de-synchronized high speed society', *Constellations*, 10.1: 3-33; and see Rosa, H. & Scheuerman, W.E. (Eds.) (2009) *High-Speed Society: Social Acceleration, Power and Modernity*. Philadelphia, PA: Pennsylvania University Press.

the screen. Forced to concentrate, we can suffer from too many simultaneous choices and demands. Emailing, for instance, is now the curse of many institutions and corporations, taking up hours of valuable time, and flooding workplace screens with 'low grade' information, much of it not related to work itself. This takes time from more important tasks, so that many are now forced to 'catch up' with what needs to be done outside of their work times. Social media, texting and messaging can be similarly demanding.

This continuous time pressure can also have a dramatic impact on our relationship to others and to place, that is, where we are presently situated. Since we can *choose* with whom to engage with online, perhaps texting or messaging distant friends, we can now also *choose* to use this constant connection as a means for disengaging with those nearest us. In this way we can disconnect from place and others, sometimes to protect ourselves from engaging with others we perhaps do not know, fear or feel uncomfortable with. This can cocoon us, turning our phones or devices into social avoidance machines.

Having conquered time and space by going online, we now have to live with the consequences. Whether we are at work and find ourselves checking the weather or our emails, checking the news, or a new movie, in our pockets there is now a constant opportunity to go online, and get lost in the virtual, and to spend hours in a state of online distraction. This can become a source of addictive dependence, making us increasingly reliant on technology for social contact.

The power of this dependence can be seen in experiments involving 'media fasts', where devices are removed from individuals, for a few hours or days. In one experiment 1,000 college students gave up all media for 24 hours. It quickly became evident how seriously addicted most of these young people were. Many could not even make it to the 24 hour mark, and they began to display the kind of symptoms of stress found in people trying to give up smoking, complaining especially of their loneliness and sense of abandonment without their more familiar access to others.[14]

This combination of social dependence, continuous connectivity and potential distraction, helps explain an almost universal increase in reported time-scarcity. The problem is partly due to the fact that more and more now cannot escape their work, the barriers between work and home life having been progressively eroded. Our minds also become more divided, between

14   Moeller, S., Powers, E. & Roberts, J. (2012) '"The world unplugged" and "24 hours without media": Media literacy to develop self-awareness regarding Media', *Comunicar*, 20.39: 45-52; and see also Barley, S.R. *et al.* (2011) 'E-mail as a source and symbol of stress', *Organization Science*, 22.4: 887-906.

here and there, now and then, online and offline. This helps create the subjective experience of life itself moving faster, with the present time seeming 'contracted'. For we now find we can only focus on what is immediately in front of us, within a much narrower horizon of time, where the longer-term tends to fade from view, and the more demanding present takes precedence.

Just as our present moment has 'contracted', so our memory is being affected. For since memory relies on place, or rather on the places we have experienced or imagined, we now have fewer stable reference points to which we can connect our memories. Instead we experience a continuous sequence of images that weave in and out of the 'real' and proximate, in time, and on a daily basis. This dilutes the solidity and fixed points in the environment on which we traditionally relied to develop memories and also proximate ties, that is with the community on which we once relied.[15]

The sheer vastness of the online world, and its endless succession of images, and its role as a seemingly permanent repository of seemingly reliable information, can also undermine even our need to remember. Now we just have to look up something on Wikipedia, rather than more laboriously find this information and evaluate it for ourselves. By automatically archiving everything, our need to remember, to select, reflect upon and then make use of what we can remember, is receding and declining. The online is thus not only placeless, and thus more difficult to remember in and of itself, but is also full of records we can rely on that we do not have to remember.

Given this vast volume of information available to us, we also require search engines to filter and prioritize what we have found. This has led to a reinforcing momentum apparent in most searches that is easily exploited by interested parties: the interests we express through our search will always throw up linked images, sites and advertisements. For example, look for a new car, or a place to stay somewhere, and you will have pop-up ads for these products for months in your subsequent searches.[16]

15   See Lübbe, H. (2009) 'The contraction of the present', in Rosa, H. & Scheuerman, W.R. (Eds.), *High-Speed Society: Social Acceleration, Power and Modernity*. Philadelphia, PA: Pennsylvania University Press: 159-178; and Pocock, B., Skinner, N. & Williams, P. (2012) *Time Bomb: Work, Rest and Play in Australia Today*. Sydney: New South.

16   Frost-Arnold, K. (2014) 'Trustworthiness and truth: The epistemic pitfalls of internet accountability', *Episteme*, 11.1: 63-81; and see Brulle, R., Carmichael, J. & Jenkins, J. (2012) 'Shifting public opinion on climate change: An empirical assessment of factors influencing concern over climate change in the US, 2002–2010', *Climatic Change*, 114.2: 169-188·

Look up 'climate change scepticism' and you will find thousands of blog-gers and other sites dedicated to this 'information'. Indeed, you may never need to check what you have found, or to see real science news relating to climate change. From now on, it is likely that all your information about climate change will become 'filtered' by your own views, and when you stumble upon science news, you will go back to your favourite blogger to 'interpret' what you have read. This reinforcement can foster prejudice, misinformation and misrepresentation, becoming a boon for purveyors of conspiracy theories, misinformation and lies. There is no truth filter on the Internet.

From the digital to the 'physible'

Technology, as Engelhart and Brand understood it, might 'co-evolve' with us, changing ourselves and augmenting our understanding as it develops, but it is also shaped in turn by the goals we set it, and the purposes we have in mind. Indeed, most technological devices have a clearly defined goal, a set of 'rules' that determine how we use the device and for what purpose. Often likened to a script, these goal-determined rules can affect our behav iour and understanding, and often in ways that have unintended social and environmental outcomes.[17]

A good example of this is 3D printing, which at first sight has the hallmarks of a 'disruptive technology'. Enthusiasts declare that the impact of 3D print-ing will be as transformative as the computer was, freeing the designer and manufacturer of many former constraints, and reducing the skills required in many forms of designing, making and manufacturing. Many have also claimed various large benefits, only partially substantiated, for the environ-ment. They even claim that 3D printing will lead to a re-localization or de-globalization of whole industries, and in this way help bring production and consumption back into a notionally more beneficial realignment.

Leaving our doubts to one side, 3D printing has produced some significant results. It has democratized and accelerated design and making, and cre-ated a very flexible means of one-off or small-batch production, influencing

17   Verbeek, P.-P. (2006) 'Materializing morality: Design ethics and technological mediation', *Science, Technology and Human Values*, 31.3: 361-380; and Verbeek, P.-P., & Slob, A. (Eds.) (2006) *User Behaviour and Technology Development*. London: Springer.

the work of artists, designers and craftspeople in many domains. One of my former design students supported his family while he studied by selling his 3D printed jewellery online. Virtual 3D print shops like Shapeways provide services to a large range of customers, from the barely competent amateur to the professional designer-maker.[18]

FIGURE 6.2: MAKERBOT THING-O-MATIC WITH BLUE RABBIT

Photo courtesy Makerbot Industries

18   See Berman, B. (2012) '3-D printing: The new industrial revolution', *Business Horizons*, 55: 155-162; but also Birtchnell, T. & Urry, J. (2013) '3D, SF and the future', *Futures*, 50: 25-34.

3D printing is able to democratize and accelerate creative activities, and this has dramatic implications especially for the design professions. 3D printing is now widely used in industry, in making one-off or small-batch car parts, for example, or customizing shoes and other consumer goods. In China and northern Europe, manufacturers are starting to make small buildings on scaled-up 3D printers.

As if to signal this machine's coming of age, one of the most important jobs for at least one staff member at Shapeways is to police their customers' designs. This reminds us of an ethical issue also found in the current use of drones and robots. The presence of a design online in a digital form, termed by some a 'physible', can encourage a form of accelerated 'personal' production, where the dream of a newly empowered user can be made real in minutes. In the hands of some, this is not necessarily a desirable capability. In one recent case, for example, someone was arrested for producing a child sex toy on a 'personal' 3D printer; in another, a young 'libertarian' released, on the Internet, the 'physible' for a homemade gun.[19]

While DIY 3D printing has empowered many to engage more directly and creatively in new technology, it has also put the capacity for instant designing and making into the hands of people with stupid or dangerous ideas. Like many other great innovations, it has also accelerated the waste making capacity of the consumer to a new level: what you imagine you want, you can make instantly, and then use and discard, without the kind of constraints or responsibilities a professional engineer or designer must follow.

3D printing waste, at least in theory, takes up much less volume than waste from conventional forms of making, since it is an 'additive' form of manufacturing – that is, is based on adding material to material, and not cutting material away, as we might in making a table out of wood. In theory also its wastes can be recycled. However, outside of a professionally managed factory, it is unlikely that this will result in the 'saving' of waste we might expect. As recyclers of plastics will tell you, anything that contains resins or plastics is unlikely to be recyclable more than a few times; and someone whose skill level on a 3D printer is not high might make 10 versions of a favourite game avatar before getting it right. As with other 'recyclable' materials, there is no real obligation on users to recycle what they discard.

19   Johnson, J.L. (2013) 'Print, lock and load: 3-D printers, creation of guns, and the potential threat to Fourth Amendment Rights', *University of Illinois Journal of Law, Technology and Policy*, 2: 337-361.

Indeed, there is also a growing awareness among experts of the health hazards involved in working with 3D printers – from the airborne dust particles released in the process, to the more insidious impact of plasticizers in the feedstocks used. As in the case of nanoparticles and micro-plastics, a game of forensic and regulatory catch-up has begun, but this may not be sufficiently quick to save those already affected, or those who will be affected in the near future.[20]

Whatever advantages 3D printing might have in so many industrial applications, as a 'personal' product it has a number of risks that derive directly from its status as an affordable consumer product and home-based activity. Being so cheap it will generate more dangers and more waste than most have anticipated, and the waste will in turn become an environmental hazard, joining other human-made wastes in their complexity and potential toxicity. Like other post-cautionary products, this waste has not been anticipated, and is often not noticed until after it has become widespread and its associated problems are reported.

Indeed, 3D printers are merely the latest in a long line of post-cautionary products, whose attractive functionality and potential profitability is considered justification enough to move from concept to production. The irony is that computerization itself has empowered us to be forewarned, to see the more complex environmental relationships that each product can potentially bring into the world, before we hit the 'produce' button. Instead, we continue to make cheap, throwaway, waste-making products that damage not only the environment but our health, in the naïve belief that this will be justified (for some) 'in the end'.

* * *

Computerization embodies many of our oldest and most noble dreams of extending or augmenting our intelligence, and of saving the world, or at least making it a better place. These dreams are certainly not entirely dead, but have been captured and diverted by commerce for its own ends. The 'Death Star' has certainly not yet been disabled or defeated as it was in the movie.

Although providing many notable benefits, instead of furthering environmental efficiencies and reducing energy and material use, computers have

20   Stephens, B. *et al.* (2013) 'Ultrafine particle emissions from desktop 3D printers', *Atmospheric Environment*, 79: 334-339. On technophilia, see Mosco, V. (1999) 'Cyber-Monopoly: A web of techno-myths', *Science as Culture*: 8.1: 5-22.

enhanced, accelerated and multiplied the production of cheaper, more short-lived goods and services, often at severe environmental and social costs. The information overload provided by computerization is now skilfully exploited to enhance and expand consumerism, seemingly without any knowledge or awareness of its direct consequences.

Computerization and social acceleration also results in us having less undistracted, unscheduled and reflective time, and less time for engaging with, or doing, what we most enjoy. The tapestry of our virtual world is threaded with commercial links and incentives to consume, and consume again. However authentic we think we might seem online, and whatever we might say, we are being manipulated to 'try and buy'. And this consumerism is not just about some ideal 'dematerialized' software, or some unproblematic range of eco-products and apps, but about physical objects, many of which are short-lived, with their own emissions and other noticeable impacts on the environment.

In fact, there is little substantial evidence that we are trading material consumption for purely virtual consumption; rather there is considerable evidence that in many circumstances a 're-materialization' is also taking place, as in my example of the 3D printing, where we can remake our favourite objects, again and again. While doing so might be cheaper than getting someone else to do it, and might be fun and challenging, it necessarily also has a material, environmental impact. In short, whatever benefits we might have gained from computerization and the online world, its deep entanglement in commodification, and in the encouragement and facilitation of consumerism, ensures that a 'low carbon future' is not yet one of them, at least without our serious attention and determined intervention into the world of consumption itself.

Further reading

Binkley, S. (2007) *Getting Loose: Lifestyle Consumption in the 1970s*. Durham, NC: Duke University Press.

Brand, S. (1987) *The Media Lab: Inventing the Future at MIT*. New York: Viking.

Carr, N. (2010) *The Shallows: How the Internet is Changing the Way we Read, Think and Remember*. London: Atlantic Books.

Carr, N. (2015) *The Glass Cage: Where Automation is Taking Us*. New York: Norton.

Floridi, L. (2014) *The Fourth Revolution: How the Infosphere is Reshaping Human Reality*. Oxford: Oxford University Press.

Kasser, T. (2002) *The High Price of Materialism*. Cambridge, MA: MIT Press.

Kirk, A.G. (2007) *Counterculture Green: The Whole Earth Catalog and American Environmentalism*. Lawrence, KS: University Press of Kansas.

Polimeni, J.M. *et al.* (2007) *The Jevons Paradox and the Myth of Resource Efficiency Improvements*. London: Earthscan.

Rosa, H. & Scheuerman, W.E. (Eds.) (2009) *High-Speed Society: Social Acceleration, Power and Modernity*. Philadelphia, PA: Pennsylvania University Press.

Sennett, R. (1998) *The Corrosion of Character*. New York: Norton.

Sennett, R. (2007) *The Culture of the New Capitalism*. New Haven: Yale University Press.

Silverman, J. (2015) *Terms of Service: Social Media and the Price of Constant Connection*. New York: Harper.

Slade, G. (2006) *Made to Break: Technology and Obsolescence in America*. Cambridge, MA: Harvard University Press.

Taylor, A. (2014) *The People's Platform: Taking Back Power and Culture in the Digital Age*. New York: Metropolitan Books.

Tomlinson, J. (2007) *The Culture of Speed: The Coming of Immediacy*. London: Sage.

Turkle, S. (2012) *Alone Together: Why We Expect More from Technology and Less from Each Other*. New York: Basic Books.

Turner, F. (2006) *From Counterculture to Cyberculture: Stewart Brand, the Whole Earth Network, and the Rise of Digital Utopianism*. Chicago: University of Chicago Press.

Turow, J. (2011) *The Daily You: How the New Advertising Industry is Defining Your Identity and Your Worth*. New Haven, CT: Yale University Press.

Wu, T. (2010) *The Master Switch: The Rise and Fall of Information Empires*. New York: Vintage.

7
The consumption of nature

From the gardens of childhood

For seven years of my childhood my parents worked in India. The house we lived in was a colonial-era bungalow with very thick walls and high ceilings, set in a garden within a high-walled compound. While we were in Delhi, I spent much of my time in this garden. Climbing trees, digging ditches in the flowerbeds to make rivers for little 'boats', crawling among the towering canna lilies, or playing cricket and badminton on the lawn with my brother and cousin, are among my most enduring memories.

In the 1950s, Delhi – the seat of India's newly independent government – was a city of around two million, divided between Old Delhi and the sedate, formally laid out British 'garden city' of Lutyens' capital, New Delhi, where we lived. On many weekends during the cooler months my father would take us three boys out on car trips to where we could go walking, just outside Delhi, in what he called the 'jungle', an untidy landscape of thorn bushes and taller flowering trees, teeming with wildlife.[1]

Over our heads circled kites and many smaller kestrels, their shrill whistles filling the air. Running past us on the ground were small lizards, rabbits and chipmunks, and we regularly saw jackals and foxes, troops of monkeys, and various kinds of deer. In the trees there was a cacophony of birds of all sizes and varieties, including parrots, hoopoes and finches. To reach this dusty wilderness we drove down narrow roads rutted with bullock cart

---

[1]   See Jaffrey, M. (2005) *Climbing the Mango Tree*. London: Random House – a memoir of a Delhi childhood from about 15 years earlier.

tracks, and past a handful of ancient mud-walled villages, through a landscape that had changed little since the days of the Mughals.

Now, when I revisit Delhi, a city of around 25 (or more) million, I find myself wondering if this is indeed the same city we lived in. I am struck not only by its vastly increased population, the pollution and traffic, but by its sheer physical spread, and the resulting destruction of most of the wilderness and agricultural land that once surrounded it. Cars, buses and trucks have conquered much of the available public space, and all but the most persistent animals and birds have been driven out.[2]

The only wild animals left in this now vast city are those best able to avoid human beings and the scavengers – sparrows, minahs, pigeons, crows and kites and some chipmunks and monkeys – all living off the crumbs of civilization. The 'jungle' we used to visit, near the tomb of the Mughal ruler, Humayun (1508–1556), then an overgrown ruin, is now a public monument in a park not far from the centre of modern Delhi. The jungle where we once walked has been devoured by the city, along with all its neighbouring fields and villages.

Since 1960, Delhi has grown over ten times, and the population of India has tripled, from 400 million to over 1.2 billion. From a country made up largely of villages and fields, of peasants, artisans, traders and labourers, over the last half century India has become a vast industrial, urbanized giant, a close second to China in the scale of its transformation. And, as in China, its environment has suffered accordingly.[3]

The remorseless expansion of population, industry, roads and chemical-intensive agriculture and, of course, the poaching of many animals and birds, have all played their role in the destruction of India's wildlife – a phenomenon duplicated all over the world. Naturalists describe this as a 'great extinction', or even a 'holocaust' – always most marked wherever development has worked its grim magic.

2   See Dalrymple, W. (2011) *City of Djinns: A Year in Delhi*. New York: HarperCollins; and Guha, R. (2007) *India after Gandhi: The History of the World's Largest Democracy*. New York: HarperCollins.
3   Litchfield, C. (2013) 'Telling the truth about animals and environments: Media and pro-environmental behaviour', in Crocker, R. & Lehmann, S. (Eds), *Motivating Change*. London: Routledge: 158-177; and see the 'Red List' produced by the IUCN, at http://www.iucnredlist.org, accessed 1 May 2015.

This erasure of so many animals – seen as collateral damage to development and industrialization – is soon forgotten in a world of apparently more pressing priorities. Vast numbers of apes and monkeys, rare dolphins, elephants, deer, and large cats, as well as many birds and smaller animals, have experienced this holocaust, and mostly within my lifetime. Unfortunately, it is now only the iconic animals, like gorillas, tigers and elephants, which draw our attention, and occasionally our charity.

When I was a child in Delhi, the world's total population was around three billion. It is now around seven billion. In the 1950s only a very small, and wealthy, percentage of the population could engage in what we might now recognize as consumerism, and the materials available – the 'stuff' that everything was made from – made this earlier form of consumerism quite distinct from our own. Throwaway packaging was nearly all paper, card or tin, and vastly fewer items were 'made to break'. But during the next two decades this began to change, and the belief that a modern, scientific, industrial economy would solve all the problems of the past began to dominate.

In the West, this led to an unquestioning belief in the value of an economy based on the increasing production of consumer goods, an overuse of chemical fertilizers, pesticides and drugs in agriculture, large-scale energy infrastructure schemes, rational, but often socially and environmentally disastrous planning regimes, and a continuous expansion in both suburban housing and road building. It was widely believed that creating more goods would result in higher standards of living, and in this way would generate prosperity within each nation.

Rachel Carson's *Silent Spring* (1962) was among the first of many books to show the direct link between the growing faith in the commercialized application of science underlying this new 'modern' society and its deadly impact on the environment. The silence of the birds became a potent image for a generation that witnessed this environmental transformation.[4]

4   Lockwood, A. (2012) 'The affective legacy of Silent Spring', *Environmental Humanities*, 1: 123-140; and Lytle, M.H. (2007) *The Gentle Subversive: Rachel Carson, Silent Spring, and the Rise of the Environmental Movement*. Oxford: Oxford University Press.

Understanding 'nature'

As my own experience suggests, each of us comes to understand 'nature' and environment quite differently, depending on our memories, experiences and cultural backgrounds. My father, who was brought up in the dry, rolling hills of South Australia's Mid-North, loved and even pined for this country while he was in Europe. On the other hand, I have met Europeans who come to Australia and can't bear the brightness of the sun, the aggressive cacophony (and behaviour) of the parrots and other birds, and the heat or dryness of the landscape.[5]

The power of our ideas about nature is remarkable, since nature helps to order in our minds a constellation of other related concepts. Acting as a cognitive frame, nature links together associated ideas, which then find expression in our speech. This apparent hold 'nature' has over us is very ancient. However, while we seem to be drawn to nature and natural environments, and intuitively prefer certain types of natural environment to built ones, our understanding of what 'nature' might mean, and the value we attribute to a particular environment or part of nature, can vary considerably between individuals and cultures.[6]

It is not uncommon, therefore, in an environmental quarrel today, to find two opposing sides each claiming to be defending a particular environment, such as a forest or river. For example, both environmentalists and loggers in Tasmania have argued for their divergent cases – conservation or continued but selective logging – from their love of the forest and their special knowledge of this environment. The same environment can thus be interpreted differently, and dramatically so.

I have an example of this from my local neighbourhood: a linear park, created on either side of a small creek that runs down to the beach near where I live, has been a bone of contention between a riding club and the local residents' association for some time. For many years now, the government agency that manages the land and the creek has been slowly improving the

5   See Schultz, P. (2000) 'Empathizing with nature: The effects of perspective taking on concern for environmental issues', *Journal of Social Issues*, 56.3: 391-406; and see also Nye, D.E. (2003) 'Technology, nature and American origin stories', *Environmental History*, 8: 7-24.

6   Lakoff, G. (2010) 'Why it matters how we frame the environment', *Environmental Communication*, 4.1: 70-81; and Corbett, J.B. (2006) *Communicating Nature: How we Create and Understand Environmental Messages*. Washington, DC: Island Press.

area, by creating a series of wetlands to attract birds and other wildlife along its length, making it an attractive park for walkers and cyclists. The policy has been actively supported by most residents, and the government agency's improvements are widely appreciated.

However, for many years, members of the riding club have been allowed to use the final stretch of this parkland, before it reaches the sea, to pasture their horses. Local children have learned to ride there during this period, and the horses are popular with some residents, who, over time, have become used to the idea that these horses 'belong' there. The residents' association, however, rightly claims that the manure from the horses affects the water quality and pollutes the beach, and is delaying the completion of the plan for a series of wetlands to run along the final stretch of the creek. On their side, the riding club points out that, upstream, factories and workshops are having a worse effect on the water quality, and that fixing that problem should be the government authority's priority.

FIGURE 7.1: HORSES ON TORRENS CREEK RESERVE, HENLEY BEACH (ADELAIDE), SOUTH AUSTRALIA

Photo: J. Gay (2015)

FIGURE 7.2: WETLAND, TORRENS CREEK RESERVE, FULHAM (ADELAIDE), SOUTH AUSTRALIA
Photo: J. Gay (2015)

In addition to the larger influences that frame our understanding of nature and environment, our own activities and interests can shape how we see a particular natural environment, what we believe should happen to it, or how it should be used or managed. Most locals, for example, want pollution to be eradicated, and believe that water quality should be improved. Most approve of the programme of wetland development, but then differences emerge, since many have a sentimental attachment to the horses.[7]

What gives these types of conflict their depth and heat is our own sense of what is 'right', and what is at stake, and the danger of losing what we hold dear – place and nature, however these are understood. All this can bring many tensions to the surface within a community. How we value, or fail to value, nature – or at least an identified part of the natural environment – can even become a defining moment in our membership of the broader community: if we seem to fail to value a particular environment, we are communicating, at least to some, that we do not care. And how we value nature, increasingly

7   See Shmueli, D.F. (2008) 'Framing in geographical analysis of environmental conflicts: Theory, methodology and three case studies', *Geoforum*, 39.6: 2,048-2,061; and Robertson, M.M. & Wainwright, J.D. (2013) 'The value of nature to the state', *Annals of the Association of American Geographers*, 103.4: 890-905.

cast in the distancing language of economics, can also create tensions and conflicts over what might seem an 'obvious' environmental issue.

Nature's role as a cognitive frame has many dimensions, and can become a powerful moral compass. If someone violates a part of nature for no purpose, even those who otherwise view the environment with seeming disinterest can become shocked and upset. In Australia, for example, if someone cruelly mistreats or kills kangaroos, wombats, horses, dogs or other iconic animals or birds, the incident will be on the news for days, and the suspected culprit subject to torrents of media-fanned indignation. In practice, as a nation we seem to have much less regard for the many farm animals we kill for food, or for those driven out of their habitats by development.

This love of particular animals and birds, trees and flowers, and the places and landscapes associated with them, has been well documented. It is found in most people, even where cultural and individual differences are quite marked. It has also been found to have a positive influence on our health and well-being. For instance, having access to views of gardens and other landscapes has been linked to shorter recovery times for patients in hospitals, and to greater productivity and reduced absenteeism at work. And a direct experience of such natural environments seems to be a vital factor in our development as children.[8]

Nature as idea

As a concept, nature appears at the birth of religion, philosophy and culture, as well as in the early history of science. To the Greeks, nature ('phusis') was a vital concept in philosophy, literature, poetry, science and medicine. In the Christian Middle Ages a belief in 'natura' as divine creation, a Latin translation of the Greek term, peppers most works from this era, often as a theological category suggesting bodily or material existence, as distinct from the all-important spiritual world.

From the Renaissance onwards, Greek and Latin texts about nature and science were rediscovered and typically recast into Christian terms. One response to this revival of interest in 'natural philosophy' came to be summarized in the popular notion, used especially by scientists and theologians

8   See Ulrich, R.S. (1986) 'Human responses to vegetation and landscapes', *Landscape and Urban Planning*, 13: 29-44; and Louv, R. (2005) *Last Child in the Woods: Saving our Children from Nature-Deficit Disorder*. New York: Algonquin.

during the seventeenth century, that nature as divine creation was like a 'book' to be explored through the tools of the intellect, just as the 'book of God', the Bible, was to be understood through skilful study.

This famous theory of the 'two books' helped justify and position early science or 'natural philosophy' within a larger religious frame, as the 'pious' exercise of practical reason. By tracing the 'footmarks' of God in his creation, early scientists like Robert Boyle and Isaac Newton could draw upon a powerful argument that justified and positioned their experiments and theoretical works within an acceptable religious context.[9]

Modern science thus has its roots in this final shift in Western conceptions of nature. By reemphasizing the divine origin of nature as a field created for human benefit, and as a reflection of divine wisdom that might be better understood, the early scientists created a mental space in which they could learn from the object itself, rather than merely through the writings of the ancients, as their medieval predecessors had done. This shift also reflects the search for pattern and meaning in nature, where mathematics and direct observation played increasingly important roles, inspiring many a gentleman to dabble in what was then called 'natural philosophy'.[10]

The study of nature, for the first time, could be both generalized and particularized, and understood in evidential, objective terms. It could be separated from people as a series of objects to puzzle over, whether composed of even smaller parts or 'atoms', or seen in the solar system itself, which became an immensely popular focus of polite study in the eighteenth century. Atomism was especially attractive, long before there was any evidence for it; it provided a tool for imagining the structure of matter as regulated, patterned and legible, with God for Newton, Boyle and their fellow natural philosophers, setting the world in motion 'in the beginning', rather like a giant clock.

Early modern science was, of course, also closely linked to the expanding world of trade, which revealed many new plants, animals and other natural phenomena to the scientist, doctor, merchant and landowner. These exotic things could be examined, and experimented with, sometimes for considerable personal profit. In much early correspondence there is an apparent concern for understanding exotic plants and animals and their potential uses.

9   Harrison, P. (2006) '"The 'Book of Nature" and early modern science', in van Berkel, K. & Vanderjagt, A. (Eds.), *The Book of Nature in Early Modern and Modern History*. Leuven, Belgium: Peeters: 1-26.

10 Merchant, C. (2006) 'The Scientific Revolution and the Death of Nature', Isis, 97.3: 513-533; and Crocker, R. (Ed.) (2001) *Religion, Reason and Nature in Early Modern Europe*. Dordrecht: Kluwer: introduction.

The conquest of nature

The modern use of the term 'environment' in many ways embodies this earlier dichotomy in our understanding of nature, as a series of objects for examination, and as things to be 'discovered' and transformed into something of greater value. The term 'environment' thus reflects our preference for objectification, optimization or maximisation and, eventually, wastage and destruction. 'Environment' is thus inflected with a Western tendency to turn nature into substitutable objects to be controlled for our benefit, and systems of objects, also 'out there', for intellectual discovery and commercial use.

The result of this has been unimaginable destruction. The story of the early 'Atlantic system', where Europeans traded slaves for the plantation-grown products of the Americas, is well enough known, but examples of its wanton destructiveness can still shock us. Whole populations of native people were destroyed, and ecosystems uprooted or seriously damaged to make room for plantations of sugar, cotton or coffee, and the other foundational commodities of modern trade.[11]

More recently, the globalization of Western manufacturing since the late 1970s has spread across the world the same kind of problems that triggered the development of the environmental movement in the USA and Europe during the sixties. Rivers may no longer catch fire in the developed world, but similar, deadly pollution is in evidence in Asia, as earlier models of low cost, rapid resource extraction and manufacture, of make-use-and-waste, take hold in distant and less regulated lands.[12]

Globalization has also added its own immense momentum to these problems. Without the escalatory engine of consumerism, population growth should only have doubled our environmental load over the last 50 years or so, but an exponential global growth of consumption, and the consequent 'great acceleration' in greenhouse gas emissions, have multiplied and extended earlier problems into more and more domains, especially since the 1980s. The vast scale, range, accelerated speed and technical

11   Hobhouse, H. (1999) *Seeds of Change: Six Plants that Transformed Mankind.* Rev. edn, London: Macmillan.
12   Schor, J.S. (2005) 'Prices and quantities: Unsustainable consumption and the global economy', Ecological Economics, 55.3: 309-320; and see also Hobhouse, H. (1999) *Seeds of Change: Six Plants that Transformed Mankind.* Rev. edn, London: Macmillan.

sophistication of our systems has turned the double quest of science into an ongoing 'conquest' of nature that spares no creature or place.[13]

Every culture, on attaining prosperity, also brings to the global table its own idea of what morsels from the environment are the most desirable. Rare minerals, plants, insects, birds and animals are now caught up in an insatiable race to market. For example, three-quarters of the population of central African elephants have been lost since 1985, because of the global, mostly Asian, demand for ivory, and there are grave fears that their southern and eastern cousins will suffer the same fate. Demand for the supposed 'medical' virtues of rhinoceros horn has led to a similar devastation of this animal. In the last decade alone, there has been a 5,000% increase in poaching rhinos, and their horns are now worth more per gram than gold or cocaine.[14]

This is today's turbo-charged version of what happened to whales in the nineteenth century. It is estimated that numbers of African elephants and rhinos in the wild are down to fewer than 20,000 and 30,000, respectively, which equates to a decline of over 90% since before the Second World War. It is unlikely that these species, along with many other similarly desirable creatures, will survive this trend. Despite all the goodwill of international organizations and governments, it seems nothing can resist the global vortex of consumerist demand. Ivory and rhino horn, like tiger parts, are traditional luxuries in Asia, and were once reserved for the wealthy, and so remain among the most desirable, and markers of wealth and power in these societies.

The momentum of this demand, enhanced by the scale, speed, and technological reach of 'harvesting' corporations or interested traders – whether 'legal' or 'illegal' – continually confounds the best laid plans of governments and intergovernmental agencies. African elephants, for example, are threatened on multiple fronts, from an illegal trade, ending in the shops of South East Asia, from local corruption, and from the activities of 'businessmen', who, like perverse Wall Street traders, stockpile large quantities of ivory, banking upon the elephant's eventual demise. At the heart of this destruction of one of the earth's most beautiful animals lies the self-deception and moral cynicism

13   See Luke, T.W. (1998) 'The (un)wise (ab)use of nature: Environmentalism as globalized consumerism', *Alternatives: Global, Local, Political*, 23.2: 175-212.

14   Dao, T.V., Dang, N.V. & Hall, C.M. (2016) 'The marketplace management of illegal elixirs: Illicit consumption of rhino horn', *Consumption, Markets and Culture*, 19.3: 1-17.

of consumerism, and its willingness to value what makes us feel 'better' today, while overlooking the consequences of our actions tomorrow.[15]

Telling stories about nature

The global acceleration of the exploitation of all kinds of resources – whether legal or illegal – to meet a continuously expanding demand, now sits within a radically different moral, political and technological landscape from that of the sixties. We might now understand and see the interconnectedness of our world much more deeply than we ever could before, but we still can't reign in the risks involved in applied science and technology in a post-cautionary manner.

Indeed, scientific advances and technological development have grown exponentially, in every area, since 1950, and have dramatically changed how we collectively understand nature and environment, and also their relationship to our bodies and minds. These changes, in turn, are steadily percolating through the systems of governance and trade we have inherited from the past. For some, this creates grounds for hope, but for others, increased, and also legitimate, anxiety.

Firstly, the scientific knowledge of what makes us distinctly human, and sets us apart from animals and other creatures, has changed profoundly over the last 50 years. Only religious fundamentalists subscribe now to the idea that other mammals are entirely or categorically 'inferior' to human beings. The old stories, quite simply, no longer work. The more we subject our bodies and minds, and those of our animal relatives, to scientific scrutiny, the more similarities, along with more differences, we find, in language, intelligence, memory and emotion. Animals like the gorilla and the chimpanzee now appear to be more like us and we appear more like them.

The once seemingly objective and scientific – and biblically endorsed – view that other creatures are 'inferior', and have been placed in the world for human benefit, has been largely dismantled, and cannot easily be remade, except by censoring science itself. This has set the stage for a conflict between religious fundamentalists and scientists in a wide range of educational, political and legal arenas, not just in America but also explosively in the Middle East and South East Asia. Vegetarianism, once the moral stance

15   Bennett, E.L. (2014) 'Legal ivory trade in a corrupt world and its impact on African elephant populations', *Conservation Biology*, 29.1: 54-60.

of a small minority, is now being urged on us by scientists concerned about the greenhouse gas emissions and environmental destruction caused by large-scale industrialized meat production.[16]

Secondly, dramatic urbanization and population growth, and technological development, have changed our more subjective experience and understanding of 'nature'. In contrast with the world of my childhood, where most of us experienced the environment as a more or less unproblematic, unchanging background to our lives, it is now possible to live an entire human life within a predominantly urban environment, much of it indoors, with children's play restricted to electronic media and occasional chaperoned outings to sports or leisure centres.

For many young people, the result is a lack of daily contact and familiarity with the natural environment, giving rise to a rather divided attitude. On the one hand, they are taught that nature is to be cherished, as something pristine and beautiful, and of long-term value to all, but on the other that nature is something to be afraid of, since it is 'dirty', unpredictable and full of unknown diseases – alien dangers that cannot be controlled and might invade either body or mind at any moment following exposure.[17]

These contradictory views of nature, manipulated and magnified by the media, could once be filtered by experience: we could go out and discover for ourselves that nature could be beautiful and also dangerous; or we could swim in rivers or seas and find that dangers there could be avoided if we had sufficient knowledge and skill.

Now there are many barriers to spending time in almost any form of natural environment. Buildings, roads and cars, dominate the urban environment and in many newer cities there is a scarcity of parks and natural spaces. For many, the media is the only source of their knowledge of nature. The interiors of the buildings where they study, live and work are filled with screens and incitements to buy, all presenting sometimes very distorted and foreshortened views of 'nature'.[18]

16   Ravetz, J. (2004) 'The post normal science of precaution', *Futures*, 36: 347-357; and Petersen, D. (2012) *The Moral Lives of Animals*. London: Bloomsbury.
17   Dickinson, E. (2014), 'Ecocultural schizophrenia: Dialectical environmental discourses and practices', *Communication, Culture and Critique*, 7: 612-631; and Louv, R. (2005) *Last Child in the Woods: Saving our Children from Nature-Deficit Disorder*. New York: Algonquin.
18   Litchfield, C. (2013) 'Telling the truth about animals and environments: MEDIA and pro-environmental behaviour', in Crocker, R. & Lehmann, S. (Eds.), *Motivating Change*. London: Routledge: chapter 8.

Thirdly, as this suggests, how we experience nature is now managed by a series of tightly coordinated spheres of commercial interest. Although physically separated from any direct experience of natural environments, we are fed a rich diet of pictures and images of nature, most often to stimulate our interest in a particular product or experience. A film or photograph of a pristine forest or river will be used to raise the value of an object or service, whether this is a box of chocolates, a tourist destination, or a new car. 'Pure' nature still represents the 'most real' experience we can attain.

For example, the New Zealand's tourist ministry's extremely successful campaign, '100 per cent Pure', which has run for over ten years, has imaginatively transformed the whole nation into a pristine landscape of unpolluted 'nature' – unaffected, somehow, by the large scale agricultural industries that dominate much of the country, or by the reality of a colonial past which involved the extinction of a number of its native species. Instead, the whole nation has become synonymous with a pristine green beauty, an Edenic Europe in the Pacific.[19]

Wherever the ground is prepared for tourism, there is an inevitable transformation of 'pristine' spaces. Safety fences, walkways, viewing ramps, parking lots and special 'visitor centres' spring up everywhere, adjacent to the world's 'beauty spots'. We are now expected to experience wilderness from the safety of our cars, or at least have our safe cars not too far away. This is evident in national parks in Australia, America and anywhere in the world where there is a designated natural 'destination' for people to visit and 'consume'. Couples and families will park as close as possible to where they can sit or walk in a forest or nature reserve; they keep their car 'ready at hand', just in case some danger should surprise them.

Nature as perfection

Advertisers and marketers are quick to recognize that nature, as frame, image and memory, retains a power over us that can stimulate deeper, longer-lasting commitments. As a result, the natural has become something

19   Reis, A.C. (2012), 'Experiences of commodified nature: Performances and narratives of nature-based tourists on Stewart Island, New Zealand', *Tourist Studies*, 21.3: 305-324; and Morgan, N., Pritchard, A. & Piggott, R. (2002) 'New Zealand, 100% pure: The creation of a powerful niche destination brand', *Journal of Brand Management*, 9.4/5: 335-354.

of a psychic guarantee, helping reduce our fears and anxieties as consumers. However, it can also be exploited to arouse our deeper fears – also to make us buy. Using this or that product, we are told, will eliminate nasty, but natural odours; using a toothbrush regularly (and then throwing it away) will eliminate dangerous germs; using this 'natural' medicine will reduce our chances of a heart attack or stroke. The car itself will protect us from the danger of other cars and the scary, unpredictable world outside, just as guns will protect us from wild bears, and from other people with guns.[20]

This co-opting of nature to entertain, persuade and sell draws on a deep inner interconnectedness: we might no longer have the time to learn about, and engage with nature 'out there', but we will always be interested enough to pause, and look, and then move on – most likely with a suitably 'natural' product on our shopping list. We will watch a half-hour programme about the snow leopard, which probably took two to three years to shoot, and feel enriched by the experience, but still know little about the animals and birds in our street. We might watch someone cutting down an old tree to make room for a new house, but fail to recognize that such 'unwanted' things are as much a part of 'pristine' nature as the beauty spots we visit, and also worthy of care.

As all this suggests, 'nature' remains an ultimate argument for purchasing something. In design, marketing and advertising nature has moral weight, and is closely associated with our more intrinsic values and beliefs. If a product is 'natural', it seems to assert a truth, a purity, and a material value elevated above other 'man-made' goods, even if they are similar, cheaper, and more effective. Nature is one of the ultimate sources of 'value signalling'. Science, of course, is then drawn into this formula to 'prove' or demonstrate the truth of the claims being made.

Our local Sunday newspaper, for example, contains a series of lift-out sections, which reflect the typical domains of consumerism as so many aspects of an elusive, imagined 'good life'. Along with the real estate, interior design, travel, and fashion sections, is a lifestyle supplement called, appropriately, *Body and Soul*. It focuses largely on health, beauty and self-improvement – through exercise, diet, relationships, sex, attitudes, and goals. Its ten pages are filled with advertisements for 'natural' cures, exercise regimes, self-help

20   Rollins, W. (2006) 'Reflections on a spare tire: SUVs and postmodern environmental consciousness', *Environmental History*, 11: 684-723; and Parguel, B., Benoit-Moreau, F.,& Russell, C.A. (2015) 'Can evoking nature in advertising mislead consumers? The power of "executional greenwashing"', *International Journal of Advertising*, 34.1: 107-134.

programmes and special diets, many of which are then endorsed in its articles, with resident experts always at hand to answer any queries.[21]

On every page there are strange juxtapositions of articles and advertisements; for example, an article about foods that are supposed to be good for cancer prevention might be placed next to a half-page advertisement for a product claiming to increase the size of your breasts 'naturally'. Although the contrast can be amusing, the unifying subtext here is to remind the paper's readers of what they lack, or how they *fail* to meet the higher standards suggested by the articles and the latest 'research'.

Most readers are led to conclude that their diet is rarely an approved one, and that they can always benefit from some supplements or additional products. Their face, legs, bottom or breasts might be unattractive to others, at least in comparison with those of the models in the advertisements. In the article this will be explained in terms of a failure to take the right exercise, the right diet, or the right supplements. Perhaps you have some bad habits that should be eliminated or, best of all, some persistent, embarrassing problem like bad breath. In this way, your happiness and health are made to seem to depend on the products or services promoted.[22]

Such advice presents a series of visual cues to remind us of our distance from the 'perfect' life described, which of course is the most natural. What is presented reminds us continuously of how far we have to go to 'get there'. Whether we think we need to reduce weight, retard ageing, rid ourselves of bad habits, cure chronic conditions, or heal our relationships, there is a solution for us, and if we are not sure what to do, we can write to the experts themselves for advice.

Typical 'green' marketing like this can also be used to mask what is an otherwise environmentally damaging or unethical product. Airlines and car hire companies, for example, advertise travel, and then allow you to 'offset' your considerable footprint, while you travel; this assuages your sense of guilt, which is stimulated through the same advertising. Similarly, 'charity

---

21   See News Corporation's explanation of this lift-out's value to potential advertisers: http://www.newscorpaustralia.com/brand/bodysoul, accessed 1 September 2015.

22   Dittmar, H. (2007) 'The costs of consumer culture and the "cage within": The impact of the material "good life" and "body perfect" ideals on individuals' identity and well-being', *Psychological Inquiry*, 18:1: 23-31; and Bishop, R. (2001) 'The pursuit of perfection: A narrative analysis of how women's magazines cover eating disorders', *Howard Journal of Communications*, 12.4: 221-240

water' campaigns claim a certain percentage of the price of a plastic bottle of water or soft drink will be given to a water-related charity in Africa.

The moral weight that comes with the names of these charities also helps to pull the soft-drink companies involved up the steps of an ethical ladder. It also helps them sell more products into their market – a 'win-win' for their business. The problem for the consumer remains the truth: that while buying such a product might assuage our feelings of guilt, and even help those distant villagers, buying water in a plastic bottle will add more waste to the world, and increase our environmental woes. This style of campaign simply becomes an ethical lever to stimulate consumerism.[23]

Natural Zombies

Nature, for many, has become a restorative image, seen on a page or screen heavily edited and managed by commercial interests. Children, for example, are more familiar with the names and logos of leading brands than with birds, trees and flowers, even those just outside their own windows. Since most adults aged under 50, in the developed world, have been brought up in a similar but less intensely populated media landscape, they too are deeply affected by what Richard Louv terms a 'nature-deficit syndrome'.

We are all vulnerable to advertising and corporate greenwashing because, like children, we attribute 'life' and personality, even a unique and authentic character, to products we like or regularly engage with. This artificial 'vitalization' of products in our minds is one of the main goals of advertising, branding and design. By bringing the alien, mass-manufactured object to 'life' in our minds, what is by nature dead can then be 'resurrected' through branding and design – rather like a zombie in a movie. It becomes 'real' and something that we can believe in, to the point where we are even ready to spend money on it.[24]

23   See Crocker, R. (2013) 'Ethicalization and greenwashing: Business, sustainability and design', *Design for Business: AGIDEAS Research*, vol. 2. Bristol: Intellect: 162-175.

24   Hill, J.A. (2011) 'Endangered childhoods: How consumerism is impacting child and youth identity', *Media, Culture and Society*, 33: 347-362; and also Avis, M. & Aitken, R. (2015) 'Intertwined: Brand personification, brand personality and brand relationships in historical perspective', *Journal of Historical Research in Marketing*, 7.2: 208-231.

Brands, especially, are metaphorical zombies – magically created and empowered spirits or anima. Like ancient daemons or spirits, they can project images of their own abilities and perfections into our minds. We become possessed by our favourite brands. They take up residence in our minds and seduce us through their remorseless idealism and perfectionism, through which they promise to bestow on us certain desirable characteristics or traits: beauty, sexiness, fame or social elevation.

A skin product might be 'number one in France', and therefore takes on the intriguing qualities of beautiful French women, and the long history of French dedication to the 'science' and art of beauty; we might wistfully think for a moment of our visit to Paris, or our wish to go there. The real message in such advertisements, however, is to remind us of what we lack, and their carefully positioned promise, of course, to remove or erase this deficit.

Freedom, or escape, from guilt or shame is another potent motive for consumption, emphasized in other studies of advertising and branding. Green products make us feel less responsible as individuals for the environmental damage consumerism entails, or at least this is their promise. Hybrid cars, for example, are often promoted using images that suggest they are environmentally 'invisible'. Advertisers, making largely unsubstantiated claims, allege these cars prevent the damage we would otherwise cause to the environment by driving normal cars.[25]

Unfortunately, the evidence shows again and again that there is no such escape. Environmental impacts derive from social practices that cross the boundaries of our lives, and the categories we value. So building a 'low carbon' green house, or buying a green car, will make very little difference to our overall 'footprint' if our neighbours have 'high carbon' homes, if our electricity service is from an old coal-fired power station, or if we have to commute long distances to work. The problem is a collective and global one, and individual choice in consumption might be well intentioned, but cannot provide a real solution.

* * *

'Natural' branding, marketing and advertising neatly sum up the alienation and dislocation from nature we have come to experience and expect over the last 50 years or so. Increasing numbers of people are now living in a

25   Li, X. (2013) 'A comparative analysis of hybrid car advertisements in the USA and China: Desire, globalization, and environment', *Environmental Communication*, 7.4: 512-528.

hybrid, mobile, urbanized, 'switched on' world, where the natural environment has been largely excluded from everyday life – an exclusion that is continuously reinforced through the media. In this brave new world, nature and environment have become unfamiliar, and thus more easily manipulated for commercial advantage.

This dislocation begins in the distracting, competitive, seemingly urgent deception of consumerism, and its technically enabled ability to mask or hide both our own more positive capabilities, and those of now 'distant' others. Instead, we are asked to find and then buy something 'better' than what we already have. This has become a reckless pursuit threatening to destroy the natural world for ourselves, its pretended benefactors, and also for those other creatures who must live in it as we do, but unprotected by our technologies.

In the next, final part of this book, I turn back to the question of sustainability, and what we might mean by this term. I start by asking if it is indeed possible to live a life of fulfilment as a consumer without consuming so much and damaging the environment. I make the case below, from past experience, that it is, but will require a radically different understanding of the goal of consumption itself. This I argue we have rather lost sight of in the quest for 'greener' forms of consumption. I then look at how we might move progressively towards this 'new' more sustainable form of consumption in psychological and material terms.

Further reading

Corbett, J.B. (2006) *Communicating Nature: How We Create and Understand Environmental Messages*. Washington, DC: Island Press.

Egan, M. (2007) *Barry Commoner and the Science of Survival: The Remaking of American Environmentalism*. Cambridge, MA: MIT Press.

Evernden, N. (1992) *The Social Creation of Nature*. Baltimore, MD: Johns Hopkins University Press.

Dauvergne, P. (2008) *The Shadows of Consumption: Consequences for the Global Environment*. Cambridge, MA: MIT Press.

Glacken, C.J. (1967) *Traces on the Rhodian Shore: Nature and Culture in Western Thought from Ancient Times to the End of the Eighteenth Century*. Berkeley, CA: California University Press.

Hobhouse, H. (1999) *Seeds of Change: Six Plants that Transformed Mankind*. Rev. edn, London: Macmillan.

Kaplan, R. & Kaplan, S. (1989) *The Experience of Nature: A Psychological Perspective*. Cambridge: Cambridge University Press.

Louv, R. (2005) *Last Child in the Woods: Saving Our Children from Nature-Deficit Disorder.* New York: Algonquin.

Lytle, M.H. (2007) *The Gentle Subversive: Rachel Carson, Silent Spring, and the Rise of the Environmental Movement.* Oxford: Oxford University Press.

Merchant, C. (2003) *Reinventing Eden: The Fate of Nature in Western Civilization.* 2nd rev. edn, London: Routledge.

Mitchell, J.R. (2000) *Something New under the Sun: An Environmental History of the Twentieth-Century World.* New York: Norton.

Petersen, D. (2012) *The Moral Lives of Animals.* London: Bloomsbury.

Plumwood, V. (2002) *Environmental Culture: The Ecological Crisis of Reason.* London: Psychology Press.

Simmons, I.G. (2007) *Global Environmental History: 10,000 BC to AD 2000.* Edinburgh: Edinburgh University Press.

Soper, K. (1995) *What is Nature?* Oxford: Blackwell.

Steffen, W. Crutzen, P.J. & McNeil, J.R. (2007) 'The Anthropocene: Are humans now overwhelming the great forces of nature?', *Ambio*, 36.8: 614-621.

Thiele, L.P. (2011) *Indra's Net and the Midas Touch.* Cambridge, MA: MIT Press.

Tuan, Y.-F. (1974) *Topophilia: A Study of Environmental Perception, Attitudes and Values.* New York: Columbia University Press.

Wilson, E.O. (1984) *Biophilia.* Cambridge: Cambridge University Press.

Part III
Towards sustainable consumption

8
Learning from the past

What is 'sustainable consumption'?

It has become increasingly obvious that we must now move towards not only more 'eco-efficient' or 'low-carbon' products and systems, but also towards more sustainable consumption practices. As I have argued, the Jevons paradox is alive and well: technological innovations or improvements introduced to increase efficiencies and reduce emissions are often found to be implicated in 'vertical' or 'horizontal' increases in overall consumption.

It may be possible to argue against such a paradox in specific instances, but the trends we see around us confirm this frequently observed link between greater efficiency, lower prices and increases in consumption. In a well-documented example from the Netherlands, a nationwide switch to energy efficient lightbulbs resulted in an overall reduction in power consumption, but at much less than the predicted rate. Subsequent research found that with such cheaper lighting now made available, many residents had increased the number of lights in their homes, and left lights on for longer since the initiative had effectively reduced their power bills.[1]

This type of unintended effect underlines again the importance of treating the consumption problem as a complex issue that crosses many domains. Consumer behaviour is driven by a range of social, economic, geographical and technological influences, including rising standards, social norms, advertising and marketing, larger political contexts, household income level and financial circumstances, positional anxieties, and personal time

[1] Verbeek, P.-P., & Slob, A. (Eds.) (2006) *User Behaviour and Technology Development: Shaping Sustainable Relations between Consumers and Technologies.* London: Springer: Introduction.

pressures. None of these can be changed by a single magic economic bullet, or media reminders to consumers to choose more wisely.

This makes the notion of 'sustainable consumption' both particularly relevant and problematic. Derived from the idea of 'sustainable development', first presented in the famous Brundtland Commission Report, *Our Common Future*, in 1987, 'sustainable consumption' is typically defined along these lines:

> the use of services and related products which respond to basic needs and bring a better quality of life while minimising the use of natural resources and toxic materials as well as the emissions of waste and pollutants over the life-cycle so as not to jeopardise the needs of future generations.[2]

Like the notion of 'sustainable development', 'sustainable consumption' is an attempt to kill two proverbial birds with one stone, to both eradicate poverty and reduce emissions. In the face of massive, globally encompassing social and economic change, including continuing population growth, rapid urbanization, political instability and the unfolding catastrophe of climate change, this seems a most challenging undertaking. 'Sustainable consumption' must somehow offer us a pathway between the costs of an embedded overconsumption in the developed world, and the dangers of failing to satisfy basic needs in the developing world.

As this would suggest, the notion of 'sustainable consumption' can invite debate about which strategies might have the most effect in both domains – reducing emissions while also enabling greater equity of access. Intellectually, it also challenges the long-held assumption that our material 'needs' are somehow elastic, relative to context, and therefore not amenable to serious enquiry. Like many terms born of compromise, it can appear contradictory and is open to interpretation.[3]

Talk of 'sustainable consumption', especially when it is applied to individuals, also inevitably strays into the thickets of ethics, and the question of needs and social and cultural equity: when is enough truly enough? What are our real needs, and should distant others be forced to pay such a high

2   Cited in Lorek, S. & Fuchs, D. (2013) 'Strong sustainable consumption governance: A precondition for a degrowth path?' *Journal of Cleaner Production*, 38: 37.

3   See Beder, S. (2006) *Environmental Principles and Policies: An Interdisciplinary Introduction*. London: Earthscan: chapter 1; and Seyfang, G. (2009) *The New Economics of Sustainable Consumption*. London: Palgrave Macmillan: chapters 1–2.

environmental and social price for our wants, as is happening now, as climate change progresses? Should we be engineering a reduction in 'growth' when growth seems so necessary to help those in the developing world escape poverty?

Enabling the good life

Once we have recognized that, beyond certain basic needs, the accumulation of goods cannot satisfy our more intrinsic needs, how these intrinsic needs might be better understood and satisfied becomes an important topic in itself. This has led to a growing interest in 'alternative consumption' practices, including those emphasizing a reduction in consumption or various forms of 'collective consumption'. For similar reasons there is also a developing interest in the consumption practices of the past, and in critically revisiting discourses on 'thrift' and moderation, many of which date back two centuries or more.[4]

Most of these studies focussing on a reduction in consumption begin from a recognition that many human needs cannot be satisfied by economic acts alone, even if the provision of goods and services might *enable* their satisfaction. While it is undeniable that food, water and shelter are essential human needs, so are education, work, security and community, each of which is hard to reduce to simple economic terms. The Nobel laureate, economist Amartya Sen, has been particularly significant in offering a useful way of reconsidering this problem.

In Sen's seminal essay on 'The Living Standard' (1984), he questioned the common economic measurement of the 'standard of living' in terms of goods of 'utility or opulence', arguing instead that a more credible universal standard should be based upon the degree to which an individual, anywhere, can enjoy the capacity to 'function without deficiency'. Such deficiencies are not mysterious: a denial of access to education, housing, healthcare, basic nourishment and other minimal requirements create 'deficiencies' that necessarily prevent the development of our ability to function fully as human beings and realize our capabilities.[5]

4   See Evans, D. (2011) 'Thrifty, green or frugal: Reflections on sustainable consumption in a changing economic climate', *Geoforum*, 42: 550-557.
5   On Sen and the application of his thought, see Alkire, S. (2005) 'Why the capability approach?' *Journal of Human Development*, 6.1: 115-135.

The value of Sen's perspective lies in its definition of needs in terms of the realization of our capabilities, and its linkage of these needs to the more fundamental one of access, and equity of access. This refocuses the economic discussion more positively on what might be called life's 'satisfiers', such as gaining an education, rather than more narrowly on their material enablers, such as how to pay for a schoolteacher. While the second is obviously important, the goal of universal education must first be prioritized and agreed to, before the second can be contemplated.

Sen also dispenses with the myth that somehow our capabilities can be realized through individual effort alone. Apart from a lack of evidence for this, this belief becomes a diversion in a lot of policy discourse, as we struggle to fit the prejudices of our (usually) comfortable Western audience to the realities of material deficiencies that still restrict and damage a billion or more human lives across the world.

For Sen, our lives are built on a range of basic services, relationships and exchanges, only some of which attain financial visibility. For example, living in a traditional family compound somewhere in an 'undeveloped' village in South East Asia, we might not technically own or pay for our own home. However, we might have a relatively high standard of living through the communal support and relationships we enjoy by living in such an arrangement. Many everyday 'services' which we would pay for in a city like New York, such as childminding, cooking, help with maintenance and repairs, we may not need to pay for as individuals in communal settings like this.[6]

Without such background traditional institutions and relationships, individual access to education, housing or healthcare can become expensive and difficult to obtain, and this can make it harder for the individual to attain their capabilities, even if other indicators of economic progress might seem very positive. For example, GDP might be high in the USA or Australia, but if someone was living in a disadvantaged group in a poor neighbourhood in these nations, this person might have less access to the enablers of a good life than the person in the village just described, who in fact may be living on a quarter of the income of even the poorest in a 'rich' country.

6   Jackson, T. (2006) 'Consuming paradise? Towards a social and cultural psychology of sustainable consumption', in Jackson (Ed.), *The Earthscan Reader in Sustainable Consumption*. London: Earthscan: 367-395.

Rather like the distinction made by Erich Fromm between 'having' and 'being', many of life's satisfiers cannot be individually possessed or owned, but must be experienced through the presence and participation of others. As this suggests, needs might indeed be 'elastic', but their satisfaction is often less to do with money than with the presence of others, and the incentives our relationships, interests and activities supply us with.

For instance, recent research on thrift suggests that some report being happier when they spend less, and more carefully. The reasons for this seem to be that being more conscious in spending yields a greater sense of personal control, and a sense of ongoing progress towards some defined goal. It may also involve dislodging spending and consuming from the central importance bestowed on them by the media, and privileging other activities, interests and relationships. And it may also involve a greater awareness of the background sacrifices involved in much individual consumption today, such as working long hours, and accumulating debt.[7]

For many, 'thrift' or 'frugality' now suggest a more conscious attempt to reduce consumption, to simplify one's life. However, there are many, and were many more, for whom greater care or caution in consumption was normal, a habitual standard. This style of consumption, once typical in the generation that grew up in Europe and America between the two wars, has been described recently in the useful term 'custodial consumption'. This suggests a greater spirit of stewardship in possession, an attachment that does not so easily foresee a future where the possession is wasted and replaced by the 'next best thing'.[8]

From a time-based perspective, *custodial* consumers (my preferred term) consumers display a 'stewardship' towards their possessions, and resist throwing them away. This resistance is based on a conscious reduction in the kind of 'discounting' of the future benefit of what is possessed that characterizes much everyday consumption. For example, we might now buy a car with the assumption that we will have to trade it in in about five years

7   Chancellor, J. & Lyubomirsky, S. (2014) 'Money for happiness; The hedonic benefits of thrift', in Tatzel, M. (Ed.), *Consumption and Well-Being in the Material World*. London: Springer: 13-48; and Podkalicka, A. & Tang, L. (2014) 'Deploying diverse approaches to an integrated study of thrift', *Continuum*, 28.3: 422-437.

8   Cherrier, H. (2010) 'Custodian behavior: A material expression of anti-consumerism', *Consumption, Markets and Culture*, 13.3: 259-272; and see Lane, R. & Watson, M. (2012) 'Stewardship of things: The radical potential of product stewardship for re-framing responsibilities and relationships to products and materials', *Geoforum*, 43: 1,254-1,265.

20

for another better one. The custodial consumer rejects this assumption of future waste-making. For the custodial consumer the possession is good in itself and therefore worth keeping, maintaining, and even repairing.

My father's books

I was made to consider this distinction, between custodial consumption and everyday consumerism, personally, some years ago, shortly after my father died. The day after his funeral, like many grieving relatives, my brother and I had the difficult task of sorting through his possessions. He had left an old house full of books, a collection of classical (vinyl) records, some antique furniture, artworks and clothes. There were also piles of old letters and smaller decorative items, often gifts or mementos collected during a very long life of work and travel.

A significant task was to sort through his collection of around four thousand books. Even though I had seen them many times, in passing, I had never gone through them in detail. Books that followed the course of his own life, including biographies, histories and studies relating to the countries in which he had worked, dominated the collection. To these he had added several hundred on the history and geography of his family's home state of South Australia, mostly accumulated over the last 30 years of his life. There was also a quite extensive collection of books on the early history of travel and exploration, an interest he had maintained throughout his life.[9]

However, what I found most intriguing was a much smaller number of books from his student days at Oxford, when he largely supported himself and must have had very little money. They were pocket editions of classics like Gilbert White's *Natural History of Selbourne*, and Johnson's *Lives of the Poets*. Inside their covers he had scribbled little notes recording his reflections on them, each note carefully dated, and some of these notes separated by ten years or more, as he had returned to them.

9   See Crocker, W.R. (1981) *Travelling Back: Memoirs*. Melbourne: Macmillan: chapter 3.

FIGURE 8.1: H.O. LOCK (1925), DORSET. LONDON: A & C BLACK, FRONTISPIECE

Photo: M. Russell (2016)

There were also several books on Dorset, the English county his great grandparents had come from. Most had been published in the first decade of the twentieth century, a time when this region was still relatively free of modernized agriculture and the development that followed the Second World War. At that time the contrast between the 'old ways' and the new must have seemed striking. The delicate watercolours that accompanied each chapter of these books contained no images of the machines of modernity, no cars, trucks, buses or even tractors. This was not lost on my father, who spoke wistfully of his time in England as a student, and the relative absence of cars.

I found myself puzzling over these books he had bought as a young man, and thinking about them in several different ways. The conventional view might be that they were part of an attempt to become more familiar with the canon of English middle-class culture, which perhaps his own modest upbringing as a farmer's son in remote South Australia had denied him. The bookshelves of many middle class families in the inter-war period must have included classics similar to those he had bought.[10]

However, if some of these early books were typical, there were also others that were more distinctive, including Rowntree on poverty, and Mayhew on slum life in London. Coming from a modest evangelical Anglican farming family, whose bedtime reading had consisted of an illustrated volume of Bunyan's *Pilgrim's Progress*, at Balliol in Oxford he had become involved in Christian socialism and internationalism, and these books must have been important reading.

I also saw an obvious connection, which had somehow eluded me in the confusion of our clearing-up tasks: that the bulk of the library he had amassed was actually founded on this early orientation and commitment. In progressively adding to these original interests over time, accumulating many volumes of political histories and biographies I had seen so many times, he had managed to also obscure these early first steps into an interest that had dominated his life.

As a number of anthropologists have reminded us, examining an individual's possessions is akin to an archaeological dig, revealing over time a unique tapestry – a 'social cosmology' – which is gradually revealed in, and through, their collected belongings. Every significant possession has its own story, and this becomes one of sometimes many companion stories over time. In this way possessions can reveal likes and dislikes, significant experiences, places and relationships over a lifetime.[11]

Our inner lives are perhaps most directly expressed through cultural possessions like books, films, artworks, musical instruments or recordings, since these often link back to our more intrinsic goals and values. Reading, like music, is relational in its impacts; books become substitutes for their authors, their values, ideas and stories. In turn, books become markers in

---

10   See also Belk, R.W. (1990) 'The role of possessions in constructing and maintaining a sense of past', *Advances in Consumer Research*, 17: 669-676; and Crocker, R. (2015) 'The haunted interior: Memory, nostalgia and identity in the inter-war interior', In Daou, D., Huppatz, D.J. & Phuong, D.Q. (Eds.), *Unbounded: On the Interior and Interiority*. Newcastle upon Tyne: Cambridge Scholars Press: 103-127.

11   See Csikszentmihalyi, M. (1993) 'Why we need things', in Lubar, S. & Kingery, W.D. (Eds.), *History from Things: Essays on Material Culture*. Washington, DC: Smithsonian Institute: 20-29; and Miller, D. (2008) *The Comfort of Things*. Cambridge: Polity.

our own lives, and windows into other worlds, worlds we might never have seen or understood without them.

My father, like many of his generation, subscribed to what I have chosen to describe here as *custodial consumption*. I have chosen this consciously in preference to 'moderation', 'thrift' or 'frugality' since these suggest some conscious commitment to reducing or minimizing consumption, which was alien to him and never seemed necessary; his upbringing and way of life dictated an attitude towards consumption, and to waste, very different to that of the post-war generation of consumers, a sense of stewardship that too few in the developed, 'high-consuming' world now possess.[12]

My father grew up in an Edwardian 'aspirational' lower middle-class family, intensely conscious of their English and colonial origins. As a farmer's son, like his three brothers, he aspired to leave the farm, gain an education, and in this way 'make his mark' in the world. Individual ambition as moral purpose, as a religiously defined 'calling', was taken very seriously in his family, and encouraged by his parents.

Related to this, his achievements were therefore never to be marked by an accumulation of luxury goods. They were signalled instead by the painstaking and sacrificial accumulations of education and the useful skills this education provided, with reputation widely understood as the social record for such a life of effort and achievement.

Custodial consumption

This type of high-minded moral pursuit of individual and social betterment has been described many times as a defining characteristic of the Victorian and Edwardian middle classes, especially the 'lower' ones, and historians and anthropologists have observed a similar moralism and idealism in the middle class across northern Europe in this earlier period.

Money, for example, was never talked about during my father's upbringing, even when it was in short supply, and I remember him frequently telling us boys never to talk about it either. This was related to his belief that the accumulation of money was often down to luck or good fortune,

12   See Cherrier, H. (2010) 'Custodian behavior: A material expression of anti-consumerism', *Consumption, Markets and Culture*, 13.3: 259-272; and Lehtonen, T. & Pantzar, M. (2002) 'The ethos of thrift: The Promotion of bank saving in Finland during the 1950s', *Journal of Material Culture*, 7.2: 211-231.

and not possessing it was not a sign of some weakness or failure, as is so often wrongly assumed now. Instead, if ethically accumulated, money was assumed to be the reward of hard work and could do good in the world.[13]

Possessions were accumulated as occasion and need arose, when money to pay for them was available, and pride was taken in using and maintaining them in 'good repair'. Indeed, when my father was a young man in the 1920s, 'custodial consumption' was widespread. For most working people it was also unavoidable, since the necessities of life required spending a much greater proportion of one's basic income. For the middle classes who could afford to spend more, there were still many social and cultural barriers to overspending, that have since been removed.

Another major point of difference was the material context of his upbringing. Many items and foods were produced locally, or at least within the region, and it was harder for shoppers to become 'distanced' from the production of the objects of their consumption as they are now. While many objects were made in factories, more items were made locally, with the assistance of machines perhaps, but not exclusively so, as is more common today. Standard household items, such as kettles and chairs, were repaired and reused, sometimes many times over. Lives dedicated to skilled making and repairing were in evidence everywhere.[14]

Consumption occurs in and across many domains in our lives; it is deeply social but also closely integrated with our goals and sense of identity. In the past, as today, consumption often involved strongly held opinions and moral judgements, often evinced when social norms appeared to be challenged. Consumption that could be seen to contribute to a good life was highly valued, whereas consumption that seemed excessive, unreasonable, wasteful or greedy was openly condemned.

Brought up in this more frugal social world, my father remained a custodial consumer throughout his life. After he died, my brother and I found in his house very few examples of mass-produced electronic goods, appliances and gadgets, or even cheap, packaged goods that are evident in most

---

13   See especially Frykman, J. & Lofgren, O. (1987) *Culture Builders: A Historical Anthropology of Middle-Class Life*. Trans. A. Crozier, New Brunswick, NJ: Rutgers University Press: 6ff.

14   Cooper, T. (2008) 'Challenging the "refuse revolution": War, waste and the rediscovery of recycling, 1900–50', *Historical Research*, 81.214: 710-731; and Strasser, S. (2003) 'The alien past: Consumer culture in historical perspective', *Journal of Consumer Policy*, 26.4: 375-393.

homes today. In fact, to outsiders, the personal effects he left behind would have seemed Spartan indeed.

Although he was comfortably well off at the time of his death, he had relatively few clothes: I counted five suits, a formal 'dress suit', two sports coats, and perhaps a dozen shirts, along with a similarly modest variety of pyjamas and underclothes. Everything was kept and repaired until it could not be worn. He would darn his woollen socks, a skill he had learned in the army, and would have his shoes repaired whenever he could. I found a pair of old brown leather brogues that he had had made in India in the 1950s; they were so well looked after that they were still wearable.[15]

Like many elderly people, he clung to the fashions that dominated his twenties and thirties. For myself, the custodial attitude underlying his possessions was symbolized by his wristwatch, which at the time of his death must have been 70 years old, and still working. It was a small, rectangular, steel (not even stainless) pre-war Longines, in an art deco style, once fashionable among young men in the 1930s.

Increasingly, during his very long life (he died a centenarian), his custodial attitudes stood in stark contrast with those of his neighbours, many of whom I came to know during my many visits to his house. Like most middle class Australians today, they were busy working to pay off debts, renovating their homes, going out to be entertained, taking overseas holidays, and of course driving everywhere in their cars, whereas my father had always walked everywhere, whenever he could.

Much as he liked his neighbours, my father believed they lacked awareness of the risks of overspending. 'Caveat emptor' ('buyer beware') was one of his favourite sayings – something that he felt these people had somehow missed. He reflexively denigrated their timesaving takeaway or processed foods and drinks, and the waste packaging and spoiled food that ended up in their bins. Indeed, my father had a horror of packaged foods, partly because of his long relationship with farming: he saw packaged food, and especially fast food, as an insult to local farmers.

As this suggests, his custodial attitudes to consumption assumed a direct dependence between consumption and its source in production. It recognized waste as the necessary outcome of consumption, and something intimately connected to it. He also recognized that the production of valued goods is not always easy or pleasant, that it involves human labour and

15   See McCollough, J. (2012) 'Determinants of a throwaway society: A sustainable consumption issue', *Journal of Socio-Economics*, 41.1: 110-117.

sometimes considerable hard-won skill, and is never to be taken for granted. For my father, packaged food was food that had been deliberately distanced from the buyer, who was then enticed by advertising into purchasing it.[16]

This caution towards consumption, admiration for honest production, and the understanding from his own experience that these two, production and consumption, are necessarily interdependent, was also revealed in his habits with regard to waste. Each week my father's bin contained only one small plastic bag of household rubbish; cans, bottles and plastics were neatly washed and separated, even before the local council began collecting recyclable bottles, tins, plastics and paper separately. He seemed to assume that someone would want and value his old bottles and cans. Understanding waste, and how to deal with it, by burying, burning or giving it away, had been a necessary part of his upbringing.[17]

Towards the throwaway society

My father's values and beliefs were fixed long before I was born, in an Edwardian, still British imperial world that in Australia became gradually eclipsed, after the Second World War, by an era dominated by America, the first modern mass-consumer society. This new fifties world was dominated by the car, the TV and other consumer goods. In my father's earlier, now vanished pre-war world, life had been very different. The 'material flows' we now worry about might have been technically less efficient then, but for many they were sufficient for a good life. An army of men and women were engaged in informal systems of artisanal manufacture, selling (often door to door), recycling, repairing or repurposing – certainly a more 'circular economy' by our standards today. With the exception of the wealthy, most people were custodial consumers; they could not be anything else.

16   Blythman, J. (2015, 22 February) 'Inside the food industry: The surprising truth about what you eat', *The Guardian*, http://www.theguardian.com/lifeand-style/2015/feb/21/a-feast-of-engineering-whats-really-in-your-food, accessed 22 February 2015; and Blythman, J. (2015) *Swallow This: Serving up the Food Industry's Darkest Secrets*. London: Fourth Estate.

17   Cooper, T. (2006) 'Rags, bones and recycling bins', *History Today*, 56.2: 17-18; and see Clapp, J. (2002) 'The distancing of waste: Overconsumption in a global economy', in Princen, T., Maniates, M. & Conca, K. (Eds.), *Confronting Consumption*. Cambridge, MA: MIT Press: 155-175.

Like many of his generation, through his upbringing, education and values, my father did not feel comfortable with the consumerism that became the social norm during the 1950s and 1960s. He was early concerned by its impact, and soon became involved in local environmental groups. He particularly disliked the destruction of trees and natural landscapes driven by development, and the impact of industrialized monoculture on farming. This he understood as a direct attack on the values, skills and way of life of the small producers with whom he had always identified.

My father's view of consumption was once not so exceptional. Most people of my generation can remember their grandparents' homes, with many having similar custodial attitudes towards consumption and waste. Because my mother was nearly 20 years younger than my father, I also remember well her parents' home, which mirrored many of the features and tastes visible in my father's. My grandfather had been a schoolteacher, and they too possessed many books. Their custodial attitudes to consumption were very apparent to us children.[18]

My own generation, those who grew up from the 1950s onwards, were introduced to a series of influential innovations, including the car, the supermarket and the TV. These, and a series of time-saving mass-produced appliances and other items of convenience and disposability, played an important role in changing our everyday norms and expectations. My maternal grandparents' generation, and my father's, had an ethos of thrift: they were custodial consumers, in part, because they had been made aware of the risk of scarcity, having seen the suffering this could cause.

While the 1930s introduced many of the twentieth century's dominant technologies to their generation, it was only in the 1950s that these technologies became widespread outside America, more affordable, and placed in the context of greater economic security. In the 1930s the old and the new had existed side by side, as many photographs from that period attest. The horse was still widely used in agriculture, for rounding up sheep or cattle, and in towns, for delivering goods, or picking up rubbish.

Following the Second World War the car became the key consumer product of many national economies as they switched from wartime industries to the production of consumer goods. Newer, more efficient and accessible systems of provision appeared, encouraging everyone to aspire to higher

18 Mackay, H. (1997) *Generations: Baby Boomers, Their Parents and their Children.* Sydney: Macmillan: 14ff.; and see also Cross, G. (1993) *Time and Money: The Making of Consumer Culture.* London: Routledge: 128ff.

standards in the home. This became increasingly important, with the TV coming to dominate the living room, replacing the central role once played by the hearth or fire place.[19]

In the next generation – the 'baby-boomers' – other values came to the fore, often involving a deliberate jettisoning of the restraints in consumption and waste that the previous generation had so valued. These new consumerist values were affected by the experience of the Cold War and by the economic 'long boom' of the 1950s and 1960s. Particularly significant was the promise of mobility and freedom embodied in the car, and of a future that would be simultaneously more secure but perhaps more frightening, with the possibility of nuclear annihilation never far away.

For most Australians in the 1950s, as for most British people, America became the source of the modern, and of a new materialistic, consumerist vision of what modern living meant. American influence was everywhere – in the shows on TV, and in the new appliances for the home and the cars in the garage. The 1950s generation, outside America at least, was also subject to a new style of professional corporate persuasion for the first time, in PR, marketing and advertising. These advertisements trained consumers to change their habits and routines, to become more like the ideal consumers on TV.

Brought up in a pre-war society based largely on custodial consumption, my father, along with most of his generation, struggled against many of the changes they witnessed in the new society of the 1950s and 1960s, and especially the dominance of TV, its invasive advertising and the associated institutions of mass motoring and the supermarket. One of my father's greatest difficulties came in the waste making the new consumerism involved. He, and many others, could not understand the virtues of single-use throwaway products, or such 'conveniences' as teabags or instant coffee.[20]

---

19   See Twenge, J.M. & Kasser, T. (2013) 'Generational changes in materialism and work centrality, 1976–2007', *Personality and Social Psychology Bulletin*, 39.7: 883-897.

20   On discounting, see McCollough, J. (2012) 'Determinants of a throwaway society: A sustainable consumption issue', *Journal of Socio-Economics*, 41.1: 110-117.

This more rapid discounting of value in many products, as we shall see, is a particularly insidious characteristic of consumerism, since in many areas it not only generates unnecessary wastes, but also increases the number of goods we 'have to' purchase, from packets of tissues and other single-use products, to fashion items and electronic goods that we feel obliged to upgrade sooner and sooner.

* * *

What we want and what we buy tend to be shaped by prior experience and beliefs. Our consumption practices are patterned and justified to ourselves in a narrative of our own self-development, identity formation and growth, within a prevailing social and material culture. Individual consumption may be habitual and routine, but is given direction by larger goals, and these are tied to values, since we must believe in what we think we want or need. These values are slow to change: my father remained who he was, and stuck to what he valued, over a very long life.[21]

'Sustainable consumption', as this suggests, is not simply a matter of economic incentivization, or a list of 'do's and don'ts', or, as some imagine, something that will happen automatically if we manage to reduce the generation of carbon in our systems of provision through technological intervention. This is not to deny the importance of such strategies, but we must also consider consumption within the longer term development of its psychological and social contexts.

Many of my father's generation, I have suggested here, were 'custodial' consumers. This seems a useful term to capture an ethos that has now largely disappeared from the developed world. It is useful also in suggesting that it is possible to live a rich and full life without becoming caught up in the accelerated cycle of consumption, use and discard we now find all around us and imagine to be essential. To return to this older standard of 'custodial consumption' may not be entirely possible, or in some cases entirely desirable, but it suggests a little more clearly what the creation or recreation of 'sustainable consumption' must entail for everyday life, for attitudes and values.

21   See Wapner, P. (2010) 'Sacrifice in an age of comfort', in Maniates, M. & Meyer, J.M. (Eds.), *The Environmental Politics of Sacrifice*. Cambridge, MA: MIT Press: 33–59; see also the other essays in this volume, especially those by Hall, Peterson and Princen.

One other issue raised here is that of the 'creation of lack' generated by contemporary marketing and advertising, and its widespread use to artificially discount the value of what we possess. This creates a space for desire in the consumer, and for the new, but in children, and in some adults, this can occur at a very high cost. It is to this psychological dimension of the problem I will now turn.

Further reading

Brinkman, S. (2010) 'Character, personality and identity: On historical aspects of human identity', *Nordic Sociology*, 62.1: 65-85.

Csikszentmihalyi, M. & Rochberg-Halton, E. (1981) *The Meaning of Things: Domestic Symbols and the Self.* Cambridge: Cambridge University Press.

Hilton, M. (2003) *Consumerism in Twentieth Century Britain*. Cambridge: Cambridge University Press.

Frykman, J. & Lofgren, O. (1987) *Culture Builders: A Historical Anthropology of Middle-Class Life.* Trans. A. Crozier, New Brunswick, NJ: Rutgers University Press.

McCracken, G. (2005) *Culture and Consumption II: Markets, Meaning and Brand Management.* Bloomington, IN: Indiana University Press.

Miller, D. (Ed.) (2001) *Home Possessions: Material Culture behind Closed Doors.* Oxford: Berg.

Miller, D. (2008) *The Comfort of Things.* Cambridge: Polity.

Nicole. P. (2010) *Sucking Eggs: What Your Wartime Granny Could Teach You about Diet, Thrift and Going Green.* London: Vintage.

Oldenziel, R. & Zachmann, K. (Eds.) (2009) *Cold War Kitchen: Americanization, Technology and European Users.* Cambridge, MA: MIT Press.

Outka, E. (2009) *Consuming Traditions: Modernity, Modernism, and the Commodified Authentic.* Oxford: Oxford University Press.

Overy, R. (2009) *The Morbid Age: Britain and the Crisis of Civilization, 1919–1939.* London: Allen Lane.

Parr, J. (1999) *Domestic Goods: The Material, the Moral and the Economic in the Postwar Years.* Toronto: University of Toronto Press.

Pavitt, J. (Ed.) (2008) *Cold War Modern: Design 1945–1970.* London: Victoria and Albert Museum.

Ritivoi, A.D. (2002) *Yesterday's Self: Nostalgia and the Immigrant Identity*. New York: Rowman & Littlefield.

Samuel, R. (1994) *Theatres of Memory: Past and Present in Contemporary Culture.* London: Verso.

Shove, E. (2003) *Comfort, Cleanliness and Convenience: The Social Organization of Normality.* Oxford: Berg.

Strasser, S. (1999) *Waste and Want: A Social History of Trash.* New York: Henry Holt.

9
Values, goals and time

Catching up with debt

Consumerism has retrained us over time to imagine the good life as dependent on the accumulation of certain goods and experiences. Since the money required to obtain what we think we need can exceed what we have, debt becomes a significant means of extending our capacity to spend, so that we can get what we want sooner. In this way debt has become an increasingly important facilitator of consumerism.

Easily accessed debt also encourages a more rapid rate of discounting, of devaluing what we already possess, in readiness to upgrade to the latest and the best. For example, the two-year-old mobile phone we have might seem 'old' in comparison to our friend's new one, which may be larger and thinner, with a better video function. That we can so easily borrow to upgrade encourages us to devalue the 'old' item more rapidly, as this can be replaced by simply signing a new contract.

Easy credit becomes an essential part of many agreements we sign on to, and this encourages us to more readily discount what is 'old' or not quite good enough, and upgrade sooner. With many products this can even become the easiest option.[1] The manipulation of the rate of discounting

---

1   See Bernthal, M.J., Crockett, D. & Rose, R. (2005) 'Credit cards as lifestyle facilitators', *Journal of Consumer Research*, 32.1: 130-145; and on discounting, McCollough, J. (2012) 'Determinants of a throwaway society: A sustainable consumption issue', *Journal of Socio-Economics*, 41.1: 110-117; and Frederick, S. (2006) 'Valuing future life and future lives: A framework for understanding discounting', *Journal of Economic Psychology*, 27.5: 667-680.

through such offers, including product or part obsolescence, are now essential ingredients in many corporate marketing systems.

From mortgages to agreements on furniture, school fees and car repayments, life for the consumer can become a treadmill of repayments servicing multiple debt contracts. In one recent news story based on interviews with financial planners, it was revealed that some of their wealthiest clients were living pay cheque to pay cheque. Keeping up with extensive lists of obligations meant they had nothing left at the end of each fortnight. Indeed some were earning over $500,000 p.a. but were on this same treadmill.[2]

Longer working hours for these clients also contributed to more spending and more debt, as there was less time available for cooking, cleaning, childcare or social activities. Indeed, many busy successful people now pay others to fill in for them at home, whether this is hiring nannies to care for their children, cleaners to do their chores, or 'concierges' to run their errands. A lack of time also creates a demand for 'single-use' items and 'time-saving' devices, and of course encourages more eating out, which can cost large sums over a year.

Debt binds us not only to our creditors, but also to a timed series of payments. Since in many occupations the more hours we spend working can result in more pay or perhaps a bonus, the pressure from debt can add a sense of urgency to our use of time, suggesting to us the money we *could* be earning if we used our time more efficiently. By working harder and longer, so it seems, we try to 'catch up' with debt's obligations, and perhaps increase our income to repay debts faster.[3]

Time in this way becomes intimately equated with money. It becomes a commodity that we can trade for more money and perhaps a better lifestyle. Rather like a ruler against which every action must be measured, each minute and hour seems to become a unit of 'time-money'. 'Wasting' this 'time-money', even in minutes, reminds us of the money that we now lack, even if we are earning much more than many others. This consciousness of

2   Kasperkevic, J. (2015, 25 December) '$100,000 and up is not enough: eVen the rich live paycheck to paycheck', *The Guardian*, at http://www.theguardian.com/business/2015/dec/25/wealthy-americans-living-paycheck-to-paycheck-income-paying-bills, accessed 1 January 2016.
3   Bernthal, M.J., Crockett, D. & Rose, R. (2005) 'Credit cards as lifestyle facilitators', *Journal of Consumer Research*, 32.1: 130-145; and Penaloza, L. & Barnhart, M. (2011) 'Living US capitalism: The normalization of credit/debt', *Journal of Consumer Research*, 38.4: 743-762.

time-scarcity soon justifies an increasingly tighter allocation of time, and an obsessive interest in time saving routines or devices.

A good example of this comes from the introduction to Carl Honoré's *In Praise of Slowness*, where he describes how, as a harried young parent, he had considered buying some books that promised to reduce bedtime reading to his children to just 'one minute' for each story. These 'one-minute' stories had been rewritten with ultra-busy, time-poor parents in mind. When he caught himself timing his reading to his young son to see how long he was taking, he began to realize how destructive such calculations were, and how harried by this idea of time-scarcity he had become.[4]

As this suggests, the idea of 'time-saving' can lead us to devalue or discount those more important, social and creative activities that take time but seem to have no monetary value. These are nevertheless important to our well-being and those around us. Such discounting can also be transferred to the source of any 'time-wasting': these people too become a 'waste' of time-money. This turns time-money into the only recognizable measure of value, and this can have serious personal repercussions.

For example, children whose parents do not read to them can have problems learning to read at school, and this can result in other problems for them and their parents. People who don't cook end up spending money on take away food or eating out, which may not be good for the health. Friends and relatives who do not stay in touch become estranged from each other. Couples who allow no time for intimacy and enjoyment can end up quarrelling and separating. People who do not spend time with their elderly parents come to regret it later, after they have passed on.

This internalization of time-scarcity as 'time-money' creates a sense of urgency and anxiety that narrows our horizons and limits our ability to relate to others. It creates a sense of lack that is closely associated with consumerism, encouraging a restlessness that only new experiences and more things can seem to fill.

4   Honoré, C. (2006), In *Praise of Slowness: Challenging the Cult of Speed*. New York: Harper: 2-10. See also Pocock, B., Skinner, N. & Williams, P. (2012) *Time Bomb: Work, Rest and Play in Australia Today*. Sydney: New South.

The heart of the dilemma

This tendency to undervalue an individual or a relationship because they seem to take up too much time can also be traced to what is often termed 'value conflict'; time-scarcity can drive us into more and more of these types of conflict. Rather like the dilemma experienced by the father being asked to read to his children, who is also a time-stressed executive conscious of the report he must write, value conflicts typically present themselves as every-day inner conflicts, often taking their particular form from the context in which they are situated.

Since values are the guiding principles we hold to be important, and these shape our attitudes, goals and everyday behaviour, anxieties about our own security, about money and time, can come to dominate our thinking and behaviour, and lead us to draw upon some values more than others. If we just 'don't have time' for those people, then we will be unlikely to feel compassion for them, or greater understanding for their own problems.[5]

Like furniture in our little mental room, with few variations values have been found to be universal across cultures, and are always there for us to use if we can draw upon them. Compassion and selfishness, for instance, are universally experienced and recognized. However, individual identity, goals and norms, and especially the changing social contexts we live in, all tend to determine which values we will draw upon in different contexts and places.

Psychologists often distinguish between 'extrinsic' values, which refer to how others see or experience us, such as security, safety, social status or wealth, and 'intrinsic' values, those that we hold on to more intimately, such as compassion, love and care for others and for the environment. Generally speaking, intrinsic values are 'bigger than self' values, including pro-environmental ones, while extrinsic values concern the defence and advancement of the self, within our social and material world.[6]

These two groups of values, extrinsic and intrinsic, are difficult to harmonize or act on at the same time: we cannot easily worry about our money issues and think about caring for others or the environment at the same

5   See Dittmar, H. (2007) 'The costs of consumer culture and the "cage within": The impact of the material "good life" and "body perfect" ideals on individuals' identity and well-being', *Psychological Inquiry*, 18:1: 23-31.

6   See Schwartz, S.H. (1992) 'Universals in the content and structure of values: Theoretical advances and empirical tests in 20 countries', in Zanna, M.P. (Ed.), *Advances in Experimental Social Psychology*, 25. Orlando, FL: Academic Press: 1-65.

time. Conditions or situations where we are forced to, can create dilemmas or conflicts in us, as Honoré's story suggests.

Consumption is now a natural setting for multiple value conflicts and dilemmas, as our beliefs and norms can be challenged by what we find, and our self-interest can be drawn into conflict with our intrinsic values, goals and beliefs. A harried parent at a checkout, for example, may not believe in giving sweets to their child, but their self-interest may lead them to give in, rather than having to endure her screaming in front of an audience of strangers.

Our judgements about the worth and meaning of particular purchases, and about what we will not, or should not buy, typically align with our values. In everyday shopping, for example, values are engaged through a variety of 'rules' we think are important. I might tell myself: 'We should not eat so much meat', or 'I should cycle instead of driving'. The goals of these rules for consumption are assumed: 'Eating less meat will make me healthier', and 'Cycling is good for me and is better for the environment than driving'.

Rules or norms like these, justified by what we take to be facts, in this way can spill over into a sort of micro-politics of consumption, where a neighbour's new gas-guzzling SUV can really annoy us, while another person's ugly or aggressive tattoos can fill us with horror. 'Consumerism' in its early use to describe a movement defending the interests of the consumer, often referred to such moral judgements, arraying them against not only the person who seemed to spend unwisely, but also against shopkeepers or money lenders who were unfair in their dealings with us as consumers. Most environmentalists engage in a similar type of micro-politics, but one focused on the impact of consumption on the environment.[7]

However important such norms, beliefs and their associated values might seem, the social and material contexts of our lives, as I have tried to emphasize, tend to determine what we do in practice, and these too can become a powerful source of value conflict. For example, I am keen on cycling to work, but if I were working in a city where cycling is more dangerous than it is here, and distances to and from work much greater, I might consider other ways of getting to and from work, possibly driving. This option might be positively encouraged by other external factors, again beyond my control,

7   See Hobson, K. (2006) 'Bins, bulbs, and shower timers: On the "techno-ethics" of sustainable living', *Ethics, Place and Environment*, 9.3: 317-336; and Howell, R.A. (2013) 'It's not (just) "the environment, stupid!" Values, motivations, and routes to engagement of people adopting lower-carbon lifestyles', *Global Environmental Change*, 23.1: 281-290.

such as an absence of public transport. Such a new situation would present me with a practical dilemma and a new kind of value conflict.

Changing contexts can also 'prime' or evoke certain of our values over others more directly. For example, giving individuals glossy magazines full of luxury goods to look at has been found to prime their extrinsic values, even if they are known to be strongly interested in the environment and willing to engage in 'bigger than self' issues in other situations. This type of priming, as occurs in advertising and social media, tends to suppress people's more intrinsic values, even if for only short periods.

In one experiment, for example, a group of students was encouraged to join a car-pooling scheme and told that this would save them money. Another group was encouraged to take part in the same scheme, but was told it would help the environment. The experimenters had set out to deliberately prime the first group's extrinsic values, whereas the second group's pro-environmental or intrinsic values were being primed. On leaving the room, the extrinsically primed group mostly failed to recycle the paper used in the session, while the second group did.[8]

The way we frame or understand many such everyday activities has a powerful influence on the values that we engage when responding to them. 'Pro-environmental values' can be awakened or suppressed according to how the relevant issues are presented to us, and in what context. This suggests the powerful role of media and social context in shaping our attitudes and the values these must draw upon. How the story is told, in other words, can change our response, for good or ill.

A self-centred society

The values we hold dear can have a significant effect on our beliefs and goals, and these in turn can help shape our consumption practices, within the boundaries set by prevailing social and material norms and structures. Many advertisements, for example, seek to stimulate and engage extrinsic desires and values, by awakening concerns about how we look, or encouraging us to notice what we lack, or reminding us how far we have to go to gain that perfect image. By 'creating a need' in this way ads encourage us to

8   Crompton, T. (2013) 'Behaviour change: A dangerous distraction', in Crocker, R. & Lehmann, S. (Eds.), *Motivating Change*. London: Routledge: 111-126.

buy what is being promoted; but this 'need' is necessarily experienced as a lack in us, a perception reinforced in most commercial media.

However, advertising is not alone in priming our extrinsic values. Most news reports, and much government policy, also evoke extrinsic values, for example, raising our concerns for our own safety or financial security relative to that of others. By emphasizing 'user pays' and individual responsibility, governments also reinforce a public consciousness of security, safety, relative social position and economic worth – all extrinsic values. The now very dominant idea of the 'economy' as something separate from us, 'up' there, and run by those important people, has a similar effect.[9]

This ambient social priming of extrinsic values encourages consumerism, for three reasons. Firstly, consumerism promises to help us express our social and economic worth and position relative to others, and this nicely coincides with a neoliberal economic emphasis on public services being essentially commodities we pay for as 'consumers'. Secondly, neoliberal economics seems to assume that 'everyone' (except, bizarrely, the now always ethical corporation) should be self-interested, and should concentrate on bettering their own position and economic status relative to that of others. This encourages competition and comparison, and ensures that other individuals, groups and even significant institutions in the wider society, including the government itself, will be made to appear similarly self-interested.

Thirdly, as a recent British survey discovered, this framing of community and public services such as health or welfare, as forms of individual consumption, also makes us more cynical about, and distrusting of, others and established social institutions, their motivations and beliefs, and we also become less willing to participate in the public sphere. This too drives us back to consumption as to the only seemingly legitimate means of social interaction, and of individual and social expression.[10]

9   Kasser, T. *et al.* (2007) 'Some costs of American corporate capitalism: A psychological exploration of value and goal conflicts', *Psychological Inquiry*, 18.1: 1-22; Sivanatham, N. & Petit, N.C. (2010) 'Protecting the self through consumption: Status goods as affirmational commodities', *Journal of Experimental Social Psychology*, 46.3: 564-570.

10   See Crompton, T. *et al.* (2016) *Perceptions Matter: The Common Cause UK Values Survey*. London: Common Cause Foundation; and Kasser, T. *et al.* (2007) 'Some costs of American corporate capitalism: A psychological exploration of value and goal conflicts', *Psychological Inquiry*, 18.1: 1-22, and rejoinders in this same issue.

From an individual's point of view, the trouble with this society-wide, and officially legitimated, tendency to encourage a focus on social and economic self-interest, and particularly to reinforce our consciousness of scarcity, of money and 'time-money', is that it encourages the pursuit of extrinsic but not intrinsic rewards: 'We have to do this now, otherwise we might miss out.'

Extrinsic rewards are inherently less satisfying or fulfilling than intrinsic ones. Indeed, one of the major themes in many literary and artistic works over the last 300 years, and also in many religious and ethical texts, is the failure of these types of 'worldly' pursuits to yield the benefit we might have assumed. To take a contemporary example, a musician might work as a stockbroker to earn money, but might miss the enjoyment and fulfilment she once gained in music, and feel as though her life is passing her by; this self-denial for social approval or monetary gain is everywhere, but is now inflected with the language and insistence of economic necessity and consumerism.[11]

Indeed, I have come across this type of value conflict frequently as a teacher: some students will pursue their studies in design because of some hoped for future financial or status reward, while others will do so out of a real passion for the subject, and perhaps to help others or the environment. In every faculty in the university similar value conflicts are played out, with many eager young people trying to get into medicine, law or one of the professions for their supposed rewards. Pushed by the values of the 'selfish society' around them, by parents and family, fewer and fewer want to pursue the pure sciences, maths, music or the arts, since these provide no certain ticket to a financially rewarding career, and the status this brings.[12]

Consumerism, in its present neoliberal framing, reminds us of what we lack, and generates a 'discounting' of the value of what we, and others, already possess, both in social and material terms. Consumerism internalizes a materialistic perception of the world and others, where both ourselves and others are judged and understood in terms of what they possess, what they are 'worth' (in money terms) and what they therefore must lack.

11   This example comes from Ahuvia, A.C. (2005) 'Beyond the extended self: Loved objects and consumers' identity narratives', *Journal of Consumer Research*, 32: 171-184; and see also Crompton, T. *et al.* (2016), *Perceptions Matter*.

12   See Kasser, T. & Kasser, V.G. (2001) 'The dreams of people high and low in materialism', *Journal of Economic Psychology*, 22: 693-719; and Kasser, T. (2002) *The High Price of Materialism*, Cambridge, MA: MIT Press.

Consumerism thus encourages us to notice what we and others are missing out on, or what is wrong with us or them, in appearance or behaviour.

Consumerism in this way becomes the essential mental dimension of a larger social and political context, a prevailing public culture that continuously encourages and rewards self-centred values, goals and norms. This makes compassion and intrinsic values seem optional, 'spiritual' (and thus supposedly merely imaginary) or romantic (not 'realistic' like money-sense), and of course, 'bad for the economy'.

Learning to play the flute

Doing something or pursuing something outside this dominant materialistic culture of consumerism is often made to seem strange and unrewarding, even if the opposite might be true. Somewhat like smoking, the problem of consumerism's self-reinforcing dominance is deeply contextual. Smoking is a social as well as personal act, and binds smokers together, with smoking itself becoming the norm, the 'good' thing to do. When someone who has given up smoking goes to a place where everyone else is smoking, she will feel considerable anxiety, since an ambient support for *not smoking* has been removed.

In the sixties, when I was about 17 and surrounded by other smokers, I began to smoke myself. In my early twenties, after a serious bout of bronchitis, I tried to give it up, a torturous process that was extremely challenging, since nearly all my friends were smokers. Smoking was then a widely accepted social norm, rather like texting or using a mobile phone is now, and there were no 'non-smoking' areas as there are now; people smoked on trains, planes and in most social venues, including restaurants.[13]

After about two years of repeatedly failing to give up, the one thing that eventually worked for me might now seem a little eccentric, and certainly nothing a doctor would recommend. This was learning to play the flute. The two main reasons this solution worked so well for me seem instructive here.

Firstly, playing the flute forced me to engage my full attention; thinking about the music before me, and the coordinated activity of hands and

13   See Pryzbylski, A.K. *et al.* (2013) 'Motivational, emotional and behavioural correlates of fear of missing out', *Computers in Human Behaviour*, 29: 1,841-1,848; and Cheever, N.A. *et al.* (2014) 'Out of sight is not out of mind: The impact of restricting wireless mobile device use on anxiety levels among low, moderate and high users', *Computers in Human Behaviour*, 37: 290-7.

mouth left no room for thinking about cigarettes. I was also using my lungs in a new and more demanding way, which I discovered was incompatible with smoking; I soon learned that smoking made me feel dizzy and sick if I tried playing the flute afterwards.

Secondly, taking up the flute also replaced a more passive, 'external good' – a comforting social activity involving consumption – with one that required considerable thought and skill. Instead of looking over my shoulder and conforming to what others were doing and what others valued, I was pursuing my own, more intrinsic love of music. I had replaced an 'external' good, through which I was influenced by others, with a more engaging 'internal good', and one that grew more interesting, creative and challenging as I progressed.[14]

Without really understanding it at the time, I had stumbled upon a key strategy in dealing with many bad habits and minor mental addictions. By changing the context or setting, along with the intent or goal of the activity, it is possible to loosen the grip of the addictive behaviour or habit, especially if the new activity is incompatible with the old. Like smoking, practices supporting consumerism are typically habitual and contextual, and linked to a range of everyday routines and places, such as going to the shopping centre, or using social media to connect with others.

Playing a range of sports and games, for example, engaging with more gentle physical activities such as yoga or Tai Chi, or volunteering with others in a large range of activities, can help us to rediscover our own intrinsic goals and build relationships with others engaging in the same pursuits. These also leave little time for routines or practices associated with consumerism.

As to their economic value, these intrinsically rewarding activities often contribute significantly to a larger social economy – an economy of relationship and community, that unfortunately remains largely invisible in most standard economic models. However, without its volunteer army of mothers and carers, lifesavers, country firemen, ambulance drivers, emergency service crews and school sports instructors, the Australian Government, for example, would have to spend billions every year on developing the skills these people now develop in their 'spare' time.[15]

14 McKenzie-Mohr, D. *et al.* (2012) *Social Marketing to Protect the Environment: What Works.* London: Sage: Introduction.

15 See Bianchi, M. (2008) 'Time and preferences in cultural consumption', in Hutter, M. & Throsby, D. (Eds), *Value and Valuation in Art and Culture.* Cambridge: Cambridge University Press: 236-260, and Nistico, S. (2015) 'Enjoyment takes time: Some implications for choice theory', *Economics*, 9: 1-40.

To take another example, Australia's Landcare programme, a voluntary environmental association to assist with land remediation, run by and for farmers, has been very successful, not only in terms of building social capital, but in real monetary terms. Reputed to have resulted in a seven to one return on the government's original investment, this scheme brought farmers together in a series of learning networks to tackle typical Australian agricultural problems, such as rising salinity levels, pests, and soil erosion. According to one study, its most striking benefit lay in its generation of social benefit of an intrinsic character, such as the development of a sense of community, and on sharing and extending knowledge and skill.[16]

As these examples suggest, it is possible to dislodge the dominance of extrinsic goals and values in everyday life by engaging individuals in activities that are more closely associated with their intrinsic values and goals. These may not be reduced to commodities, but still have economic value, even if they do not appear in our official economic data.

As in my giving up smoking, it is not usually possible to prevent individuals engaging in activities that are addictive or bad for them without providing them with alternative and ultimately more satisfying goals and associated activities. These activities are necessarily more 'distant' from those that support consumerism and prime extrinsic values. They are often also more inherently satisfying, since these are typically associated with our intrinsic sense of identity and purpose.

Rediscovering the land

Shifting our goals and activities away from consumerism, may be more difficult now because so much of our daily life is invested in beliefs and routines associated with consumption. In every domain we are now encouraged to defer our intrinsic goals in favour of extrinsic ones, many of them tied to practices and beliefs associated with consumerism.

Breaking these ties requires a reawakening of intrinsic goals and values, and this can most easily be accomplished through a period of involvement in activities that cannot be so easily commoditized. Immersion in natural

16   Sobels, J., Curtis, A. & Lockie, S. (2001) 'The role of Landcare group networks in rural Australia: Exploring the contribution to social capital', *Journal of Rural Studies*, 17: 265-276.

environments, in pursuits that require our full attention and develop our skills, or in activities where we are helping others, tends to stimulate and engage intrinsic goals, values and related beliefs, since they are experienced as deeply rewarding in themselves.

In one interesting example from 2013, the Australian Conservation Council developed a walking tour, hosted by a group of indigenous people, the Goolarabooloo community, whose 'country' is near Broome in north-western Western Australia. The group had set up a walking trail in 1987 as a cultural awareness and educational programme to encourage their own young people to return to experience their 'country', to conserve, renew, and stay connected to their heritage, and to maintain and develop skills in hunting, fishing and other traditional activities.[17]

While the group occasionally took non-Indigenous people on this walking trail along one of their own song-lines, the 2013 'Lurajarri Trail' had a slightly different purpose, since it deliberately included a group of visitors recruited from the wider Australian community, with the explicit aim of seeing whether this walk could awaken the participants' intrinsic, pro-environmental values. Volunteers of all ages from all walks of life, the participants would accompany their indigenous guides on a nine-day walking tour, a 90 km journey over their traditional lands, along a song-line which included ancient middens of stone and shells, left by the ancestors of today's Goolarabooloo, many hundreds, and even thousands of years, earlier.

Not allowed to take mobile phones or other technological devices on this walk, the group followed their guides' path, learning to see and experience 'country' as their hosts have done, for millennia. Stopping to rest, see and understand, to cook, eat and camp, and to learn to make tools and weapons needed for hunting, most who joined this unique 'learning by doing' experience found it deeply transformative.

17   See http://www.goolarabooloo.org.au/lurujarri.html, accessed 1 November 2015; and Thornton, C. (2015) 'Not just "Stuff": Design, animism and materiality', *Proceedings of the Unmaking Waste Conference*, http://unmakingwaste2015.org/wp-content/uploads/2015/09/UMW_Session_10.pdf, accessed 1 November 2015. I am very grateful to Chris Thornton for his willingness to share this material with me, including his photographs.

FIGURE 9.1: PARTICIPANTS ON THE LURUJARRI HERITAGE TRAIL, WESTERN AUSTRALIA

Photo: C. Thornton (2013)

The participants interviewed afterwards never saw the landscape again in the same way, and most reported a heightened sense of awareness – of environment, light, sky, and air – and a greater interest in the animals and plants they encountered, as well as in other people. Most of the visitors also reported afterwards how it had changed their attitudes towards consumerism, making them more wary and sceptical of the everyday world of 'time is money' they had briefly left behind

Apart from the temporary displacement of consumerism by more engaging shared, intrinsic activities, another important aspect of walking this trail was the direct experience of the indigenous point of view. This ancient way of life is based upon a spiritual and material relationship to 'country', its landscapes and creatures. These are 'remembered' and recorded in the mind through the walk itself, rather like stages in a pilgrimage, for place and memory are necessarily and intimately linked.[18]

It goes without saying that, to indigenous people, 'country' is more than a piece of ground that might be substituted for another, but rather a

18   Sinatra, J. & Murphy, P. (Eds.) (1999) *Listen to the People, Listen to the Land.* Melbourne: Melbourne University Press; and see also Connerton, D. (2009) *How Modernity Forgets.* Cambridge: Cambridge University Press.

relationship at the heart of their own being and culture, to be reawakened, through memory and place, during such journeys. In fact, the elders of the Goolarabooloo had fought against the creation of a massive gas terminal on land near the centre of this walk – and on their song-line – during a gruelling legal contest that lasted about seven years.

Their ongoing relationship to their land is difficult for us to understand, since in most cases we can see little difference between one unoccupied stretch of land and the next, especially in that dry hot, sparsely covered country that covers much of central and northern Australia. For us it seems so readily substitutable, an abundant resource to be 'used up', to extract some greater value from. This ability to see what can be substituted is the basis of our industrial civilization, but it directly conflicts with their vision of the world, and of their 'country'.

To the indigenous person, 'land' is not a uniform product or substance with certain shared categories. It is always unique and can never be substituted or given away for money, or used for purposes that will compromise or destroy its integrity. In this indigenous world, the rock, tree, hill and river are always unique in time and place, and cannot be owned but only overseen by their custodians, which are linked to them by ancient bloodlines, songs and memories.[19]

To understand this relationship requires 'deep listening', another important component of this ancient worldview, and one that especially interested many of the visitors on the walk. Through stories of ancient heroes and animals set within this country, longstanding relationships are revealed, dependencies and obligations acknowledged, human and animal roles defined and explained, useful resources and tools discovered or made, and the unique character and integrity of every thing revealed.

'Deep listening' is a way of connecting the ancestral memory and stories associated with the land and its rocks, trees, animals, and birds, to the mind of the living indigenous person. Deep listening to stories, as both children and adults, about places, animals and birds, is also the way they can learn the practical knowledge required to survive in an often harsh and unforgiving environment, and of assimilating this ancient knowledge without recourse to writing or reading.

19   See Bentarrak, K. (1984) *Reading the Country: Introduction to Nomadology*. Perth: Freemantle Arts Centre Press; and Roe, P. (1983) *Gularabulu: Stories from the West Kimberley*. Perth: Freemantle Arts Centre Press.

Walking to 'remember' place and ancestors, and to connect with their spirits, and the deep listening that this requires, are themes running through many of the world's surviving indigenous and traditional cultures. Walking as meditation, as learning and understanding, and as connecting with the past, is still performed by walkers, monks and pilgrims in many parts of the world.

Walking also reveals insights into time and place. Time is the fourth dimension of our experience of space, and not simply a movement of divisible, substitutable objects that can be 'lost' or 'saved', or substituted for money. It is a powerful dimension of the material and also of the spiritual world.[20]

The very idea of time-scarcity we now accept as so necessary is the delusive creation of an urge to consume what we imagine we need for some personal benefit. However, the good life we aim for can never be attained through these means. We need to look again at how we have flattened time and space in this endless pursuit of consumption and profit, since we cannot live on, or within, the destruction and waste this generates, and neither can any of the other creatures we share this world with.

* * *

Discovering intrinsic values and goals outside the circle of consumerism is difficult in many contexts today, and this is why I have emphasized here the value of immersion in activities or experiences that can allow us to rediscover our intrinsic goals and values, through practices that can act as counterpoints to contemporary consumerism.

My father's method of doing this throughout his long life is perhaps instructive here: however busy he might have been, whatever he was doing, and however bad the weather might have been outside, he would take long walks every day, preferably into the country or through a park, to settle his mind and lift his spirits. Indeed, many are now coming back to recognize the value of this 'immersion' in nature, with some doctors in Britain, for example, now prescribing gardening to their depressed or inactive patients.[21]

There are many opportunities for escaping consumerism all around us, and they always have been there, if we only let ourselves find them. They can easily be configured into our daily lives, and do not have to involve an exotic trip to a 'pristine' destination. The 'cage' of consumerism can be

---

20 See Macfarlane, R. (2012) *The Old Ways: A Journey on Foot*. London: Hamish Hamilton; and Ingold, T. (2006) 'Rethinking the animate, re-animating thought', *Ethnos*, 71.1: 9-20.

21 Buck, D. (2016) *Gardens and Health: Implications for Policy and Practice*. Kings Fund: London

broken open, but this becomes much easier if the systems and infrastructures around us are reconfigured to support us in this goal. As this suggests, we need to do much more about marketing and advertising, and design, if we want to reduce our dependence on consumerism.

In the next chapter I revisit the problem of this resistant consumerist context that surrounds most of us, emphasizing again the designer's perspective, and how the designer can become involved in reconfiguring these contexts. I pursue a collaborative, 'relational' approach to this goal, placing great emphasis on the value of 'co-creation' or co-design to this end. This is an approach that involves the user and other interested parties in the design and making of the intended solution.

Further reading

Alexander, J., Crompton, T. & Shrubsole, G. (2010) *Think of Me as Evil? Opening the Ethical Debates in Advertising.* Godalming, UK: PIRC, WWF-UK.

Carr, N. (2010) *The Shallows: How the Internet is Changing the Way We Read, Think and Remember.* London: Atlantic Books.

Common Cause Foundation (2015) at http://valuesandframes.org, accessed 1 November 2015.

Connerton, D. (2009) *How Modernity Forgets.* Cambridge: Cambridge University Press.

Crocker, R. & Lehmann, S. (Eds.) (2013) *Motivating Change: Sustainable Design and Behaviour in the Built Environment.* London: Routledge.

Dauvergne, P. (2008) *The Shadows of Consumption: Consequences for the Global Environment.* Cambridge, MA: MIT Press.

Dittmar, H. (2008) *Consumer Culture, Identity and Well-being.* Hove, East Sussex: Psychology Press.

Ehrenfeld, J.H. (2008) *Sustainability by Design: A Subversive Strategy for Transforming Our Consumer Culture.* New Haven, CT: Yale University Press.

Maniates, M. & Meyer, J.M. (Eds.) (2010) *The Environmental Politics of Sacrifice.* Cambridge, MA: MIT Press.

Kasser, T. (2002) *The High Price of Materialism.* Cambridge, MA: MIT Press.

Nistico, S. (2015) 'Enjoyment takes time: Some implications for choice theory', *Economics (e-journal),* 9: 1-40.

Pantzar, M. (2010) 'Future shock: Discussing the changing temporal architecture of daily life', *Journal of Futures Studies,* 14.4: 1-22.

Pellandini-Simanyi, L. (2014) *Consumption Norms and Everyday Ethics.* London: Palgrave Macmillan.

Schor, J.B. (2010) *Plenitude: The New Economics of True Wealth.* New York: Penguin.

Seyfang, G. (2009) *The New Economics of Sustainable Consumption.* London: Palgrave Macmillan.

Verbeek, P.-P. (2005) *What Things Do: Philosophical Reflections on Agency, Technology and Design.* Philadelphia, PA: Pennsylvania University Press.

Walker, S. (2014) *Designing Sustainability: Making Radical Changes in a Material World.* London: Routledge.

10
From post-caution to precaution

The post-cautionary principle

On all fruit items in most supermarkets now there are small, round or oval, plastic or vinyl 'PLU' or 'Price Look Up' stickers. These help identify the product and its category, the country of origin, and sometimes even the grower. Although these give retailers and consumers much more information about the products being sold, this good idea is negated by its environmental nuisance factor. Hundreds of millions of these little labels are produced each year around the world. Most are unrecyclable; they don't break down, and soon become a contaminant in waste and in compost.

While more recently there have been moves to develop PLUs that do break down in the soil, these will probably take many years to overtake the very large numbers of plastic ones being produced. At present most PLU stickers, thrown into compost bins or landfill with their fruit, remain in the soil for a very long time. Like many other similar good ideas such as the microplastics now polluting the oceans, PLUs are a powerful reminder of how our linear economy of 'make, use and trash' originates. A good idea, some capital, and a commitment to avoiding any legal or copyright problems, and the world can become your market.[1]

This sums up 'post-cautionary' design and product development. It is not the result of any conscious effort or willingness to damage the environment, but the inevitable side-effect of an established system of innovation, design

1   See Campbell, K. (2012) '4 Takeaways from Seattle's composting experience', *Earthfix*, 16 February 2012, http://www.opb.org/news/article/urban-composting-programs-take-root-in-the-northwe/, accessed 1 January 2016. My original reference has been taken down.

and development, mass-production and distribution that treats the environment as 'somebody else's problem'.

In contrast to the precautionary principle – first enunciated in Hippocrates's famous dictum, 'First do no harm'– the post-cautionary 'principle' most now follow, perhaps unaware that they do so, insists that possible harm can be ignored until *after* it has become a problem. The ecologist John Paull, reflecting on a number of more egregious cases than my comparably innocuous little plastic stickers, defines the principle in these terms:

> Where there are threats of serious or irreversible damage, the lack of full scientific certainty shall be used as a reason for not implementing cost-effective measures until *after* the environmental degradation has actually occurred.[2]

I would add to this that 'full scientific certainty' usually means expecting someone in the government – and therefore paid for by the taxpayer – to trace the problem back to its source, and then to *prove* a relationship of cause and effect, in many cases a difficult and lengthy process, often complicated by the required legal intervention. Paull's definition, by negation, neatly highlights the importance of *influence* in precaution, and contrasts this with the more narrowly defined *cause and effect* relationships accepted in most post-cautionary decision-making.

While regulatory agencies in the EU and US have moved to adopt the precautionary principle to assess the risks brought to their attention simply to enable them to act more effectively, the development of most of the products they have to deal with still follow a post-cautionary logic. Indeed, post-caution still characterizes most of our interactions with the natural environment, at all scales. Paull gives the example of the recent destruction of one of the largest living hardwood trees in Australia. In Tasmania, in 2003, during a 'routine' logging operation of surrounding trees, 'El Grande' was accidentally killed in a fire set to the neighbouring forest as part of 'standard' forest clearing operations. It is very unlikely that trees like El Grande,

---

2   My emphasis; from Paull, J. (2007) 'Certified organic forests & timber: The Hippocratic opportunity', in *Proceedings of the ANZSEE Conference*. Australia New Zealand Society for Ecological Economics, 2007: 3, http://orgprints.org/11042/, accessed 1 December 2015. See also Farber, D. (2015) 'Coping with uncertainty: Cost–benefit analysis, the precautionary principle, and climate change', *Washington Law Journal*, 90: 1,659-1,688.

which stood at about 57 metres, and was about 350 years old, will ever be grown again.[3]

The post-cautionary principle is also evident in the world of everyday consumption, where many products and systems we rely on have well documented negative environmental effects. For example, road-based transportation networks and air travel are among the best documented of emission producing systems, yet replacing them is still a utopian idea. Car ownership continues to climb. There are an estimated 1.5 billion vehicles on the world's roads; this figure is set to double, and soon.[4]

The sunk-cost effects generated by car-dependence noted above, are now embedded in our work, leisure and relationships, the layout of most cities, and all trade-related activities. Greater efficiency alone cannot fix this problem: more efficient cars, trucks and jets are being added to our fleets every year, but the steady increase in the number of people driving or flying, and the additional reasons consumers will find to use these services, overwhelms most efficiency gains over time.

In the world of consumer products, a similar conundrum is apparent. To take an everyday example, dental professionals encourage us to brush our teeth every day and replace our toothbrushes every three months. According to some estimates, around 4.5 billion toothbrushes are in use at any one time; three billion, and possibly many more, are thrown away each year. Most are made from a cocktail of oil-based plastics (mostly PE or PPE), nylon and some wire, and there are few alternatives available, none of which yet enjoy dental approval, and most of which are also short lived. The toothbrush is one of many similar problematic objects available in the supermarket.

Typically, it is assumed that a plastic toothbrush, because it is technically recyclable will be recycled. But recycling a toothbrush, like recycling many other plastic products, might make us feel we are doing something, but is not really a meaningful solution. What is recycled anyway is often 'down-cycled', and cannot be recycled more than a few times; and of these many

3   See also Turnbull, P. (2016) 'Ancient indigenous forest trees', in *Companion to Tasmanian Arts, Heritage and History*. University of Tasmania, http://www.utas.edu.au/tasmanian-companion/biogs/E000040b.htm, accessed 30 January 2016.

4   Estimated from Davis, S.C., Diegel, S.W. & Boundy, R.G. (2015) *Transport Energy Data Book*, edition 34 (online). US Department of Energy, http://cta.ornl.gov/data/download34.shtml, accessed 1 November 2015.

billions of plastic objects produced, on average only 20% are in fact recycled globally.[5]

Asking questions first

The qualities that make plastic toothbrushes ideal for brushing teeth – their durability, relatively hygienic qualities, resistance to heat and chemical exposure – also makes them durable in the ground and in the sea. Walk around any developing nation with poor waste infrastructure and see for yourself: choked beaches full of this type of plastic detritus, with many of these items neatly stamped with 'recyclable' symbols.

Much of this material is supposed to be 'non-toxic', but what this means for a chemist is different to what it can mean for a bird that feeds this brightly coloured stuff to its young, or to a fish or whale that must now ingest doses of micro-plastics and plasticizers with its food. To a chemist, toxicity is generally measured against a notional *maximum*, understood in terms of the substance's 'lethal dose', whereas to an ecologist, even if she were to use such terms, the danger of a substance is based on what it does in the wild, within a network of dependent relationships, as in the case of the seabirds just mentioned.

The problem thus lies not only in choosing particular materials, but also in the logic of an inherited post-cautionary applied science, where the product is chosen for a specific purpose, but not for its potential effects on a larger ecological system. The 'burden of proof' of damage in this post-cautionary world rests on linking, in the lab, the evidential *effect* of a product, on what it *has proven to have damaged*, back to its chemical *cause*. This is evident in the history of many recent ongoing environmental issues, from micro-plastics in the sea to the use of pesticides that affect bees.[6]

5   Cooper, T. (2009) 'War on waste? The politics of waste and recycling in post-war Britain, 1950–1975', *Capitalism Nature Socialism*, 20.4: 53-72; and Oldenzeil, R. & Weber, H. (2013) 'Introduction: Recycling reconsidered', *Contemporary European History*, 22.3: 347-370.
6   Liboiron, M. (2016) 'Redefining pollution and action: The matter of plastics', *Journal of Material Culture*, 21.1: 1-24; Syberg, K. *et al.* (2015) 'Microplastics: Addressing ecological risk through lessons learned', *Environmental Toxicology and Chemistry*, 34.5: 945-53.

Like the problem of the useful toothbrush, most of the environmental problems linked to industry become 'wicked problems' when we consider what must be done with them in the larger natural systems they eventually must impact. So much time and money has gone into their development and production as useful aids in human life, finding solutions for their later and somehow unforeseen environmental impacts, seem a sort of sideshow to the main business, which is producing and selling them for their necessary service: that is, keeping our teeth clean.

The sunk costs of such products make manufacturers reluctant to kill the metaphorical 'goose that has laid the golden egg'. It is much easier to follow a process of 'redesign' typically led by marketing experts and engineers in-house, with the designers perhaps throwing in a few eco-indicators to improve the problematic product in question. The *effect* of the manufacturer's sunk costs can be seen in such examples of 'business as usual' ('BAU').

However, if we were more serious about solving such problems as a community of citizen-consumers, rather than only as a community of rival companies, we would start by asking a number of basic, but important questions. The first, obviously, is to look more closely at the problem itself: *What is the problem, and what are its real environmental and social dimensions?* Surprisingly, sunk-cost effects can prevent a company asking even this first question with sufficient honesty. The toothbrush, for example, for the toothbrush maker, will typically remain 'the solution' they are looking for. Sunk-cost effects soon become sunk-cost fallacies, arguments that justify and support the status quo, and undermine any challenging alternative ideas.[7]

The second question, therefore, which must follow this first one, is: *What service is the product supposed to accomplish for the consumer?* Even the most sub-optimal, and environmentally damaging products are attempts to provide a service of some kind to the consumer, from the plastic toys we can only use once or twice, to the plastic bags that litter our beaches. So what is a toothbrush for and is there anything else that can fulfil its tooth-cleaning service?[8]

7   Cunha, M., & Caldieraro, F. (2009) 'Sunk-cost effects on purely behavorial investments', *Cognitive Science*, 33: 105-113; and Jain, S.P. & Maheshwaran, D. (2000) 'Motivated reasoning: A depth-of-processing perspective', *Journal of Consumer Research*, 26.4: 358-371.
8   See Ayres, R.U. (1999) 'Products as service carriers: Should we kill the messenger or send it back?' Paper for United Nations University: Zero Emissions Forum, http://archive.unu.edu/zef/publications_e/ZEF_EN_1999_01_D.pdf, accessed 1 November 2015.

Most everyday products like toothbrushes or disposable razors are typically the 'faces' or vehicles for a particular use or service. This service might be talking to others at a distance, seeing moving images or listening to music, or sweeping rubbish off our streets. The *service*, whatever it is, needs first to be really well understood in its broader environmental and social contexts and potential influences.

From a social point of view, tooth-brushing exists within larger groups of activities, or routines, such as 'getting up' and 'getting ready'; from a material point of view, the toothbrush is linked in time and space to other things, toothpaste, the hot water service, the soap, the shower, etc. The use of each of these must be coordinated in time, and these in turn tend to shape behaviour towards the end or goal of the service itself: that is, cleaning teeth.

In many parts of the world tooth-cleaning has involved medicinal plants rather than brushes (which are also very ancient in origin). In India people have for centuries used fresh twigs from the Neem (*Azadirachta indica*), a large flowering tree with powerful anti-bacterial properties. Many still do, and there are close relatives of this tree all over the world, including Australia's own 'White Cedar'. Is the solution to our toothbrush problem perhaps in part a pharmaceutical one?

Unfortunately, the typical market-led approach to innovation today would see an entrepreneur discover neem oil while on holiday in India. 'Mr Neem' would then take it home, and rush another patented product to market, perhaps a mouth wash (of the kind readily available in India). But 'Mr Neem' would be ready to protect his patent from dental companies interested in his idea, extracting his own price from any deal. Meanwhile, our toothbrush mountain will continue to grow.[9]

As this suggests, the third question we must ask is: *Who can best help expand our understanding of this problem and any potential solutions?* This is not just a question about surveying consumers or dental technicians. Instead, it requires a mapping of the relationships currently involved in the product itself, its lifecycle in provision and use, and disposal. This question is concerned with *whose knowledge* can contribute to understanding the service and its provision better. This question becomes harder to ask in

---

9   On this problem, see, for example, Efferth, T. *et al.* (2016) 'Biopiracy of natural products and good bioprospecting practice', *Phytomedicine*, 23.2: 166-173. On the seabirds and problem of plastic wastes, see Wilcox, C., Van, S.E. & Hardesty, B.D. (2015) 'Threat of plastic pollution to seabirds is global, pervasive, and increasing', *Proceedings of the National Academy of Sciences of the United States of America*, 112.38: 11,899-11,904.

hierarchic organizations, when 'we already know who to ask' is the typical answer given to such a question.

In our hypothetical example of the toothbrush, tooth-brushing for dental hygiene is the service, a very ancient one, but one that is currently 'explained' only through the monopoly of a very successful product, whose birth coincided with the more widespread use of modern plastics in the 1930s. Finding other relevant stakeholders, apart from dentists, should be a priority. For example, resource experts and ecologists should be consulted, since their work is affected too; it is they who must work out what to do with our toothbrush mountain in the wild. By including these 'outsiders' in the conversation, the designer and manufacturer can begin to see the problem in a broader, more precautionary light.[10]

The aim of this is to define the problem within a network of relationships – within its own interdependent industrial, social and natural ecosystem, as it were. In this way it becomes possible to expand our understanding of the problem to the point where we can really see where the most optimal solutions might lie. The principle of precaution can alert us to the fact that the service a product provides is not a fixed and inevitable necessity; it occurs within a larger context, and sometimes can involve other, more negative outcomes we need to understand before we take our 'good idea' further.

As this suggests, the final question should be: *How can we best collaborate to produce a positive outcome?* This final question is typically left unasked, because, as I tried to explain in Chapter 5, there is a widespread assumption that collaboration is either to be avoided altogether as a 'waste of time', or is somehow 'natural' in organizations, a dangerous and largely unfounded assumption. We need to develop strategies for involving others, ensuring that they are encouraged to contribute, and that all others at the table can hear them too.[11]

10   See Pang, R. (2015) 'Raw materials in the toothbrush', *Design Life Cycle* (online) for a good summary of the historical and chemical issues, http://www.designlife-cycle.com/plastic-toothbrush/, accessed 1 December 2015.

11   Arnold, M. (2016) 'Fostering sustainability by linking co-creation and relationship management concepts', *Journal of Cleaner Production*, 98.1: 1-10.

The many uses of co-creation

One of the more positive stories in the history of computerization has been the development of more collaborative forms of decision-making which I alluded to in Chapter 6. Two distinct strands can be identified in this development: the first, starting with the work of Douglas Engelbart and others interested in the notion of shared expertise to solve complex problems and further developed in MIT's Media Lab, is a story dominated by the technologies of collaboration and communication.

The second is the development of 'user-centred' approaches to design and development, pioneered by groups of designers in Scandinavia in the 1960s, but later taken up in the USA as 'participatory design' and 'universal design'. These now have many names, such as 'user-centred design' and 'co-design', each with their own distinct histories and emphases, but in common they place the user at the centre of the design and development process.

More recently, 'co-creation' has been rediscovered in business as a way of developing products with the user's involvement, and there is now a large literature that explains how potential users might be coaxed into helping companies develop their 'next big thing'. Here I am more interested in the use of co-creation as a *co-production* strategy, as a way of involving end-users and other stakeholders in the collaborative design in response to a defined need. From this perspective, 'co-creation' is an act of 'collective creativity', but in this case has the goal of greater sustainability.[12]

Depending on the problem to be addressed and the domain in which this productive collaboration or 'co-creation' is to be used, relevant end-users or stakeholders, including experts, can come from many walks of life. In one collaborative research project in which I was involved, the end-users were children – three groups of patients in a large hospital with specialized treatment needs – and the experts were mainly nurses, with a handful of specialists and ward doctors.

The goal of this project was based upon a widely recognized need: to improve communication between hospital staff and the children in their care. The central problem here was that most children arrive in hospitals feeling scared and often unable to understand the medical staff's technical

12   Sanders, E. & Stappers, P. (2008) 'Co-creation and the new landscapes of design', *CoDesign*, 4.1: 5-18; and Fuad-Luke, A. (2009) *Design Activism: Beautiful Strangeness for a Sustainable World*. London: Earthscan: chapter 5.

explanations. Most hospitals still rely on textual information for patients, and this is of little help if their patients cannot read, or have limited skill in English.[13]

In this project, the designer, our then PhD student, Belinda Paulovich, developed and trialled a series of visual tools to aid better communication between hospital staff and patients in three selected treatment domains, chosen because of the great differences between them. Asthma patients came in large numbers and had to be attended to very quickly, and information had to be made easier for both parents and children to understand; children requiring rehabilitation after injury needed to know about their own treatment journeys, and 'where to next' within the hospital; children suffering from gastro-intestinal problems had to know more about their own bodies, and the impact that diet and routine could have on their health.

Belinda developed these aids in an iterative process of co-creation and 'action research' on site, where children, doctors and nurses were observed, and the latter interviewed as essential intermediaries to the children. This was necessary because of the difficulties in interviewing the children themselves, many of whom were experiencing trauma and anxiety. As intermediaries, the nurses were given checklists to fill out, following every interaction with their child patients, and this provided a data set that could then be used to more fully understand the communication problems in each clinical setting.[14]

The project soon revealed that the main benefit of design-led co-creation lies in its iterative, collaborative, user-centred character: Belinda could repeatedly try out her prototype communication tools on the three groups of children, with the nurses acting as intermediaries. These tools could be progressively refined and improved until it was clear that they were indeed working, enabling the communication required. Co-creation in this case helped Belinda to cut through the problems that typically beset professional hierarchical workplaces like hospitals, where information tends to be

13   Baker, S.C. & Watson, B.M. (2015) 'Understanding the health communication process advancing the research agenda to improve health care interactions and patient care', *Journal of Language and Social Psychology*, 34.6: 687-701.

14   Paulovich, B. (2015) 'Design to improve the health education experience: Using participatory design methods in hospitals with clinicians and patients', *Visible Language*, 49.1: 108-123. I am very grateful to Belinda Paulovich for sharing this information, and her design, with me.

infused with technical jargon, and power relations tend to get in the way of necessary change.[15]

FIGURE 10.1: SAMPLE CARD, FRONT AND BACK, FROM SET OF CARDS

Designed by Belinda Paulovich (2015)

 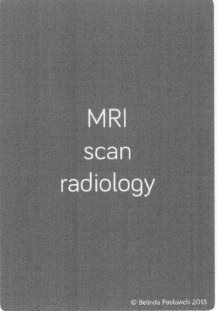

Co-creation is valuable to designers interested in solving entrenched problems like these, because it has the capacity to cut through the barriers created by sunk-cost effects and fallacies. It can give a voice to those who are typically excluded from decision-making, even if the decisions made directly affect them. Questions of authority, process and performance are put to one side, with these 'end-users' becoming welcomed and valued participants.

Co-creation also recognizes the role time plays within such settings: the solution is not imagined as a permanent one, but rather as the best available one within an evolving process, during which all participants, including the designer, can learn from each other. It is inherently experimental and iterative,

15   See Sanders, E.B.-N. & Stappers, P.J. (2008) 'Co-creation and the new land-scapes of design', *CoDesign*, 4.1: 5-18; and Voorberg, W.H., Bekkers, V.J.J.M. & Tummers, L.G. (2015) 'A systematic review of co-creation and co-production: Embarking on the social innovation journey', *Public Management Review*, 17.9: 1,333-1,357.

with each possible solution trialled and tested in place, and not imposed from without or above. This iterative process can, paradoxically, save time, since mistakes are not 'buried' by those in charge, but learned from, and built upon.

The main advantages of co-creation are its collaborative character and its emphasis on continuous improvement. There is no prescriptive model imposed, but usually a list of key questions that explore the problem; and these can change as the process develops. In fact, most co-creation workshops start by considering a simple list of goals. Information and communication technologies can be used to provide feedback in and after any meetings, and develop further tools for implementing solutions.[16]

Co-creation through Living Labs

Businesses and governments across the world are increasingly taking co-creation-led processes more seriously, since they can be harnessed to create user-supported outcomes in very different fields. They have the unique advantage of being able to position social and environmental needs at the centre of decision-making, and can be used iteratively to engage end-users throughout the design and development process.

The concept of the 'Living Laboratory' is tied to the use of co-creation and its iterative and pragmatic use of people, skills and technologies to solve what are often intractable problems. The idea of the 'living laboratory' was developed, in part, from the recognition of the value of linking new social media technologies with more open, collaborative decision-making processes.

Since the European Union first prioritized sustainable social goals, there has been an increasing interest in Living Labs within Europe. The European Network of Living Labs (ENOLL) now has about 350 affiliated members. It defines 'Living Labs' as

> ... user-centred, open innovation ecosystems based on a systematic user co-creation approach integrating research and innovation processes in real life communities and settings. In practice, Living Labs place the citizen at the centre of innovation, and have thus shown the ability to better mould the opportunities offered by new ICT concepts

16   Ballon, P. & Schurrman, D. (2015) 'Living Labs: Concepts, tools and cases', *Info*, 17.4: whole issue; and Franz, Y. (2015) 'Designing social living labs in urban research', *Info*, 17.4: 53-66.

and solutions to the specific needs and aspirations of local contexts, cultures, and creativity potentials.[17]

While in some ways Living Labs seem to represent a modern, more 'high tech' version of a cooperative – an organization that is collectively owned and works towards some shared purpose – Living Labs are inherently more flexible because the partnership is openly defined by the aim of the Lab itself. It is not necessary to limit the lab to a particular way of operating. The funding for the lab can also be very flexible, with the possible involvement of 'junior partners', something that is normally not possible with most cooperatives.

The Knowle West Media Centre, just outside Bristol, for example, is a successful Living Lab that attempts to address the now almost universal problem of post-industrial social disadvantage. The Media Centre manages to engage a large number of local people in a wide variety of projects – including a series of co-created design, photography, music and film projects – many of which are integrated with social and technological research projects. There have been significant educational and skill-development outcomes.

In one project, unwanted furniture from the local council was remanufactured into 500 pieces for a large client. The work was carried out in the Media Centre's 'Factory' – a computer-aided workshop – and was largely self-funded. As they might in a trial for an apprenticeship, a number of young people gained skills in helping an established designer make furniture, and went on from there to formal employment.[18]

Many of the Centre's projects actively make use of creative art, design and technology – teaching, for example, data visualization techniques, filmmaking and production, music studio production, and various other new media related skills. Each of these projects is co-created, maximizing end-user involvement, with the aim of developing the participants' skills, building a sense of community, and involving the participants in opportunities that would have otherwise been closed to them. All outcomes are also documented, with some projects becoming 'sites' for social and technological research for three participating universities.

17 See *European Network of Living Labs* (2016) 'About Us', http://www. openlivinglabs.eu/aboutus, accessed 10 January 2016; and see also http:// www.eggbrussels.eu
18 Knowle West (2015), Knowle West Media Centre, at http://kwmc.org.uk, accessed 1 November 2015. See also Hambleton, R. & Howard, J. (2013) 'Place-based leadership and public service innovation', *Local Government Studies*, 39.1: 47-70.

Whether such a site of cooperative innovation is called a 'Living Lab' or something else, three critical principles seem to be at work. Firstly, the participants are given clearly defined goals or aims, and they are committed to working towards them both collaboratively and iteratively. For example, in one large urban living lab in which I am involved, the aim is to reduce carbon emissions, through local design strategies, co-creation and technological innovations.

Secondly, they all make use of interactive 'social technologies', such as social media platforms and more specialized collaborative design tools, to share their work with others and to interact in the process of their collaborative work. They are more democratic in their organization than are most businesses, and committed to 'open' forms of collaborative work, where those who want to participate are welcome.

Thirdly, to work collaboratively and effectively with each other, they are all committed to some form of co-creation. This brings the first two principles together, and is usually structured as a series of open, strategic meetings where certain topics are worked through by all participants and end-users. It is the principle of democratic inclusion, especially of end-users, that distinguishes co-creation from other more limited and controlled forms of collaborative work.[19]

This 'democratic' thread that runs through all co-creative processes and therefore all living labs is about recognizing and utilizing the intrinsic value, experience and knowledge of the end-user, *whoever* this might be. This radical repositioning of the working social order, is the result of prioritizing knowledge and experience over authority for a particular end. As we saw in our little example from the children's hospital, it matters not if you are a senior doctor if what you are saying cannot be understood by your patients. Pretending that you are being understood will make little difference.

Co-creation in effect exploits the network, rather than the hierarchy's line of command. This is a critical point and explains why co-creation has become so important today, and also explains its close linkage to new communication technologies. By meeting (face-to-face or virtually) to solve a common set of problems collaboratively, and by interrogating the issues most relevant to these problems, all voices around the table can be heard,

19   See Franz, Y., Tausz, K. & Thiel, S.-K. (2015) 'Contextuality and co-creation matter: A qualitative case study comparison of Living Lab concepts in urban research', *Technology Innovation Management Review*, 5.12: 48-55, and Ind, N. & Coates, N. (2013) 'The meanings of co-creation', *European Business Review*, 25.1: 86-95

and knowledge that might otherwise seem marginal can be revealed. This seems particularly important where long established practices have side-lined the voices of end-users. Indeed, in social contexts where new technologies are being deployed, this involvement of end-users can be critical for their success.

Time and place play an important role here, for in co-creation it is assumed that the setting, such as in a Living Lab, will persist over time, and future participants or end-users should also play a role in informing its design and development. Whereas in many commercial settings the past and its memory can be erased as the old makes way for the new, in co-creation benefitting from the past is essential. This is because of its essentially collaborative and contextual basis: it matters where your end-users and stakeholders come from, and what their experience is. In fact, one important 'stakeholder' might be the environment itself, and this of course entails its history.

Co-creation assumes the central importance of the network over the hierarchy, and that each 'node' in this network has an important contribution to make, regardless of its social or technical status. This approach can create new, valuable knowledge, and recognizes that the lack of openness and transparency between 'top' and 'bottom' in most existing settings also undermines the capacity to collaborate across internal boundaries (such as between 'divisions' or 'departments').

As this suggests, co-creation in effect prioritizes the intrinsic values and goals of the participants referred to in the last chapter. By reducing the need to compete, or to position oneself within some hierarchy, it becomes possible to work more openly with others towards a shared goal. This makes co-creation most valuable from an environmental point of view, since it privileges deeper working relationships and an open sharing of knowledge. It favours understanding based on *influence* rather than on *cause and effect* alone. This makes it potentially useful in reconfiguring the linear processes responsible for many of our unsustainable post-cautionary problems.

Locating the precautionary

As we have seen, in the post-cautionary world of the linear economy an imagined future shapes the present: decisions are too often made based upon imagining future profits deriving from a particular product or service, and mentally clearing the path towards this goal. There is often little time spent on considering its 'sideways' social and environmental effects, or its broader material contexts.

In the fresh food section of most supermarkets, for example, the vision of perfection that is created to seduce the consumer results in a display of perfect rows of shining fruit and vegetables. This is the end result of a process that discards up to 40% of what is grown – the 'ugly fruit' that naturally occurs on most trees, plants and vines. Even more waste is generated along a lengthy supply chain created by a remorseless push to lower production costs for the retailer's benefit, and then more at the produce's end of life. Some estimates suggest half of all food is now wasted.

As many critics have noted, the supermarket's low prices come at a high environmental cost, and often also at punitive social costs for producers, truck drivers, and even shelf-stackers. The consumer too is reduced to passivity, just like the metaphorical pig in the pen of the pioneering supermarket chain, the 'Piggly Wiggly' stores of 1920s America.[20]

Even though they still dominate food provision, supermarkets now compete with a number of alternative, and often smaller scale retail outlets. Farmers' markets and organic stores are booming in many parts of the developed world, especially the USA, Canada, Europe and Australia. They can be more sustainable than supermarkets in some measurable ways, even if these are sometimes disputed.[21]

These more consciously ecological stores and markets generally work to reduce the waste created in the long supply chains of the supermarket system, prioritizing local, identifiable and seasonal produce. On one occasion I have come across a local store selling eight varieties of locally produced plums, something that most supermarkets would be unable, and unwilling, to do.

Secondly, these alternatives try to eliminate the deception and misinformation that dominate in supermarkets, in terms of produce origins, and the processes involved in the making or manufacturing of goods. They place a

---

20   Gille, Z. (2012) 'From risk to waste: Global food waste regimes', *Sociological Review*, 60: 27-46; and on the Piggly Wiggly stores' origins, see Freeman, M. (1992) 'Clarence Saunders: The Piggly Wiggly Man', *Tennessee Historical Quarterly*, 51.3: 161-9.

21   MacRae, R. *et al.* (2012) 'Empowering the citizen-consumer: Re-regulating consumer information to support the transition to sustainable and health promoting food systems in Canada', *Sustainability*, 4: 2,146-2,175; and see Carey, L. *et al.* (2011) 'Farmers' market consumers: a Scottish perspective', *International Journal of Consumer Studies*, 35.3: 300-306.

much greater emphasis on quality and freshness. Growers selling their produce at farmers' markets typically have no restrictive, time-based contracts
to fulfil, and do not have to cope with sudden and apparently inexplicable
drops in prices within such contracts.

Thirdly, in contrast to most supermarket shoppers, people buying in these
markets and stores are treated as 'members' of a community, each with their
own needs, and they are encouraged to talk to the producers or the store's
managers about what they are buying, perhaps trying or tasting individual
items, and choosing in the knowledge of where something comes from and
how it is made. They are not seen as passive, substitutable consumers, or as
merely so much measurable 'traffic'.

These markets and stores represent an attempt to reinvent a more sustainable style of provisioning. One model that seems particularly promising combines elements of the older cooperative store with elements of the
Farmers' Market, using online media systems to link the grower directly to
the store. I am presently involved in a small project investigating how such a
model might work, if it were to be applied in different locations.

In the Jetty Food Store, situated in the small picturesque tourist destination of Port Elliott, on South Australia's south coast, fresh food comes in
boxes with labels denoting their origins, such as 'Mixed heirloom tomatoes'
from 'Henry Smith, Mount Compass' (about half an hour's drive away). This
provides confirmation that one is buying local, seasonal fruit and vegetables.
There is a refrigerator with locally made cheeses, meats, milks and other fresh
foods nearby, a basket of breads sourced from a local bakery, and a selection
of local wines. Most goods in the store come from within 50 kilometres. Even
the dry groceries are sourced from local producers, where this is possible.[22]

Exploiting the flexibility of current technologies, the store is a hybrid of
old and new, of fast and slow, of global and local. As the co-owner, Stephen
Schmitz, says, his aim is to be able to sell 'the local, the seasonal, the small,
the unpackaged, and the imperfect.' Unlike in a supermarket, where a
grower must contractually promise a large volume of the same products, on
time, there are no such risks involved in supplying this store. In promotional
terms, there is also a better deal for the suppliers. Their names are clearly
marked on their products; they receive free publicity and a much higher
margin for their products. They can also sell things that they cannot sell
anywhere else – perhaps just one box of lemons.

22   I am very grateful to Stephen Schmitz for his willingness to talk about his store
     with me, and also to provide the photograph of its interior, here.

FIGURE 10.2: INTERIOR, JETTY FOOD STORE, PORT ELLIOTT, SOUTH AUSTRALIA

Photo: Stephen Schmitz (2015)

Stephen Schmitz and his partner, Peta Dougherty, are in constant contact with their growers and, at short notice, can pick up even small quantities in their van. Any waste from his store ends up as feed for their pigs, or as compost. While technically they might be driving more local miles per kilo of products than the supermarket, he employs up to 5 times as many local people per million dollars spent than a supermarket does, and this ensures that in social terms this model of local store is already more economically sustainable.[23]

23 Jetty Food Store (2015) https://www.facebook.com/jettyfoodstore, accessed 1 December 2015. Quotation from personal communication. On the problem of store wastes, see also Farrell, M. (2004) 'Composting at the world's largest natural foods supermarket chain', *Biocycle*, 45. 11: 27-30.

In contrast to large-scale monoculture-dependent provisioning systems like supermarkets that must rely on logistical efficiency, product substitutability and supply-chain compliance, the flexibility of small-scale, open systems like this store can provide a more varied, authentic, and experientially richer service – even if it may not be able to supply the same range of goods that supermarkets can offer.

This greater flexibility, local connectivity, more rapid response to seasonal changes, makes it more ecologically efficient. There is no systemic waste-making in this store, no elaborate system of supply chain enforcement and associated 'legal' manipulation of producers, nor any attempt to disguise or misrepresent goods that are for sale.

Towards sustainable consumption

This greater flexibility and resource efficiency is to some extent suggestive of the notion of a sustainable future in which elements of what is called the 'circular economy' can become more common. Gaining increasing recognition in Europe and China in recent years, the 'Circular Economy' has been defined as one that is

> restorative and regenerative by design, and which aims to keep products, components and materials at their highest utility and value at all times, distinguishing between technical and biological cycles.[24]

This is an attractive concept that has gained the attention of economists, policy experts and larger companies, concerned with the threat posed by resource scarcity. However, the social and behavioural aspects of this notion, as with most economistic constructs, remains obscure.

Taking the example of food provisioning, will we continue with supermarkets exploiting growers, truck drivers, packers and customers under this new economic model, simply because it suits its distant shareholders? Or will the circular economy really be able to tame the financialization, distancing and remorseless profit-taking, at all costs, that characterizes our new century's capitalism? Or will this remain, like so many other 'sustainable solutions' a matter of creating a few beautiful demonstration projects for their 'green' sympathizers to admire?

24   Ellen Macarthur Foundation (2016) 'Circular Economy', http://www. ellenmacarthurfoundation.org/circular-economy, accessed 1 January 2016.

The circular economy is an attractive idea because, with its emphasis on 'closing' the material and energy loop, it can result in a reversal of the conversion of labour into energy and materials that has marked our present 'linear economy' for so long. The Jetty Food Store, as I noted, employs about five times more local people, per dollar spent, than a supermarket does. Local soil companies I know here have similarly created employment and profit from 'organic waste'. Generating economic activity in this way gives value to the 'valueless' and generates employment where previously there was none. But this is happening at a local, more transparent scale. It is also happening in a regulated market, with good laws, governance, and a responsible judiciary.[25]

The size of the Jetty Food Store, its local setting, its connection to community and the evident pride the owners take in their environmental credentials, make it very different from a corporate business, run out of a boardroom in London or New York. The problem the Jetty Food Store addresses is not just one of calculable systems or measurable technological and economic relationships, but also more basic ethical and human ones, that few larger corporations seem to be much interested in, apart from the 'marketing edge' of producing 'green reports'.

This is the problem of the corporation itself, and the fact that it can operate within a far too loose ethical and environmental compass. Pretending to be a person, pretending to be obliged only to its board and shareholders, has enabled and thus encouraged many of the worst corporate environmental disasters of the late twentieth century, from Love Canal to Bhopal and more recently the oil spill in the Gulf of Mexico. A distant descendant of the infamous East India Company of seventeenth-century Britain, the modern corporation needs only to 'obey the law', which its concentrated monopoly power can often dilute to its needs. There is no obligation, under its present formulation, to follow the precautionary principle. This will remain the work of governments and much maligned intergovernmental organizations into the foreseeable future.

As this suggests, the potential strategies for change outlined here are necessarily a work in progress, and must involve all concerned, including many disciplines beyond design. What I have outlined here are some obvious principles to follow, not 'final' solutions in themselves. There is no starry-eyed

25 See Stahel, W. (2010) *The Performance Economy*. 2nd edn, London: Palgrave Macmillan; and the more recent discussion about potential influences in social practices, in Hobson, K. (2016) 'Closing the loop or squaring the circle? Locating generative spaces for the circular economy', *Progress in Human Geography*, 40.1: 88-104.

state of sustainability to attain, like light at the end of the tunnel, and no particular groups able to really control the direction of the world to their will, even if they might delude themselves that they can. We will, inevitably, reap what we sow, but at least we can work towards what is clearly, ethically and environmentally, better for all of us.

* * *

Shifting our attention away from the post-cautionary products and systems that dominate our lives, and from the sunk-cost effects their continuing production and consumption generate, is neither an easy nor straightforward task. This is why I have emphasized here the value of collaborative, incremental and localized change, using co-creation, with both experts and end-users, towards clearly defined goals. This involvement of voices that are usually silenced as 'unimportant' can help us develop more effective responses to our present crisis.

Emphasizing a return to understanding the services that products are supposed to deliver is an important first step in cutting through the power of the sunk-cost fallacy that established industries can generate. They will always answer our questions in one way – by justifying and 'explaining' their interests and present dominance. Returning to consider what each product or system 'is for' seems simplistic, but it is a means to unlock our collective, inventive creativity, and allow us to reconsider other ways of attaining the same goal in a less intensive, wasteful and damaging way.

While the precautionary principle is widely understood, its significance in the creation of value, and in the maintenance and development of communities and commercial relationships, is still neglected. Rather it has become the focus of lawyers and others interested in risk and uncertainty, one of several theories that might be usefully applied *after* the damage has been done. Precaution needs to be taken back into the design and development phase itself: we now have the 'big data' to make this possible. Why should we not use it?

Further reading

Ayres, R.U. & Ayres, L.W. (Eds.) (2002) *A Handbook of Industrial Ecology*. Cheltenham, UK: Edgar Elgar.

Cohen, M.J., Brown, H.S. & Vergragt, P.J. (Eds.) (2013) *Innovations in Sustainable Consumption: New Economics, Socio-technological Transitions and Social Practices*. Cheltenham, UK: Edgar Elgar.

Cooper, T. (Ed.) (2010) *Longer Lasting Products: Alternatives to the Throwaway Society*. London: Gower.

Ehrenfeld, J.H. (2008) *Sustainability by Design: A Subversive Strategy for Transforming Our Consumer Culture*. New Haven, CT: Yale University Press.

Ellen Macarthur Foundation (2016) http://www.ellenmacarthurfoundation.org, accessed 1 January 2016.

Fuad-Luke, A. (2009) *Design Activism: Beautiful Strangeness for a Sustainable World*. London: Earthscan.

Fry, T. (2009) *Design Futuring: Sustainability, Ethics and New Practice*. Oxford: Berg.

Manzini, E. (2015) *Design, When Everybody Designs: An Introduction to Design for Social Innovation*. Cambridge, MA: MIT Press.

MacBride, S. (2012) *Recycling Reconsidered: The Present Failure and Future Promise of Environmental Action in the United States*. Cambridge, MA: MIT Press.

McDonough, W. & Braungart, M. (2002) *Cradle to Cradle: Re-making the Way We Make Things*. New York: North Point Press.

McDonough, W. & Braungart, M. (2013) *The Up-Cycle: Beyond Sustainability – Designing for Abundance*. New York: North Point Press.

Papanek, V. (1995) *The Green Imperative: Natural Design for the Real World*. London: Thames & Hudson.

Sennett, R. (2012) *Together: The Rituals, Pleasures and Politics of Cooperation*. New Haven, CT: Yale University Press.

Seyfang, G. (2009), *The New Economics of Sustainable Consumption*. London: Palgrave Macmillan.

Stahel, W. (2010) *The Performance Economy*. 2nd edn, London: Palgrave Macmillan.

Thorpe, A. (2012) *Architecture and Design versus Consumerism: How Design Activism Confronts Growth*. London: Earthscan.

Vezzoli, C. & Manzini, E. (2009) *Design for Environmental Sustainability*. London: Springer.

Walker, S. (2011) *The Spirit of Design: Objects, Environment and Meaning*. London: Earthscan.

Walker, S. (2014) *Designing Sustainability: Making Radical Changes in a Material World*. London: Routledge.

Webster, K. (2015) *The Circular Economy: A Wealth of Flows* (online) at http://www.ellenmacarthurfoundation.org/publications/the-circular-economy-a-wealth-of-flows, accessed 1 July 2015.

Conclusion

Consumerism and its discontents

Consumerism today represents an unprecedented crisis of values, in ethical, social and material terms. Never before have so many resources and so much energy been used to produce so many goods for so many people. Never before have these hundreds of millions of people across the world been so ingeniously encouraged to buy, use and then throw away or upgrade – with increasing rapidity – what they have bought. This has resulted in a world of unsustainable material flows, and a world drowning in wastes, and the associated destruction of the larger environments on which we must depend.

The three-part structure of this book follows my attempt to answer three questions emerging from this unprecedented crisis: firstly, what are the psychological, social and material origins of contemporary consumerism from a historical perspective? Secondly, what are the dynamics that make today's consumerism so escalatory, expansive and increasingly destructive? And thirdly, what are the main principles and strategies that might slow this seemingly unstoppable trajectory and return us to more sustainable forms of consumption?

I began this book by emphasizing that over the last century or so we have had access to an historically unprecedented coincidence of abundant energy and resources and an increasing array of knowledge, skills and technologies able to exploit these. This has enabled a profligacy in consumption never witnessed before, at current scales, rates and environmental consequences.

Since the Second World War we have also been subject to a closely related ideology promising freedom from scarcity for all, through mass-consumption. In this fast consumerist 'linear economy', value is created by producing more goods for more people more rapidly, and substituting labour with energy and machines to increase productivity.

This 'growth economy' makes a continuous increase in the global mass-production of consumer goods seem essential, a recipe, as many have noted, for environmental collapse. Consumerism today is the 'state of mind and way of life' – an effective ideology – justifying and supporting this regime of ever-increasing productivity. It displays some unique and inherently destructive characteristics that I have tried to emphasize in this book:

1. Individualism and perfectionism

There is a deeply held emotive and moral dimension to consumerism, the aim of which is to 'improve' our lives in some way, even beyond fulfilling those needs required for achieving our capabilities within the bounds of a good life. It is a form of materialism and 'perfectionism', promising a 'better' life for everyone, at least in theory. This perfection has no stable, ultimate standard or reference point, but thrives on social comparison and competition, and thus is inherently escalatory and self-referential.

This notion of abundance for all first became the implicit promise of Western democracies, and was made explicit in popular culture, design and media, during the fifties and sixties. At this time, the newer, better, more luxurious or technologically advanced product promised to liberate the individual consumer from drudgery, improve her comfort, save her time, or provide her with some novel and exciting experience. Needless to say, this promise can only be fulfilled under certain optimal conditions, and with the income required to attain the promised improvement. This has resulted not only in an ongoing democratization of luxury but of aspiration, where rising standards create a continuous need to catch up to peers and social betters.

2. Comparison and social competition

By possessing the latest and 'best' product, the individual consumer can express her own identity and reveal her social position to others. In a society that seeks to privilege skills and qualifications over inherited status or wealth, comparison and emulation become important means to assert the individual's identity and social standing. In turn, this encourages and normalizes an extrinsic, competitive and comparative view of ourselves, as we must imagine and concern ourselves about how others might see us in an increasing range of contexts and scenarios.

This becomes an encouragement to engage in consumerism, and to try to raise our estimation in the eyes of others. However, since it is not always possible to achieve what we aspire to, consumerism is inherently disappointing for many, a cycle of small defeats in an ongoing struggle for higher standards, recognition and social parity, for respect and a place in the world. For those who seem to 'fail' or 'lose', this creates a culture of resentment, envy and frustration, which in some situations can descend into violence. For this intensification of social competition through 'invidious comparison' erodes the stable institutions and community relationships that have supported the more sustainable social and economic relationships of the past.

3. Deception

The commitments and obligations of contemporary consumerism typically involve deception. This deception encourages the consumer to believe in the transformative virtues of the promoted product, typically packaged in a story that relies upon an absence of transparency. This mutually beneficial ignorance encourages a separation of the staged representations of the ideal to be gained through a particular act of consumption and the often dirty and distanced domains of production and waste.

This plays a significant role in perpetuating our environmental crisis, for the consumer is never allowed to understand what she is holding in her hands, where it comes from, or even how it was made or by whom, and especially its distant environmental effects, even though such information could now easily be made available. Becoming a part of our ambient culture, this deception also habituates us to accepting an absence of truthfulness and transparency in public life, in governance and in the media.

4. Sunk-cost effects

Much of the deception described above derives from the massive sunk costs of our larger enabling systems, which have been built up over the last century or so. These generate sunk-cost effects and fallacies, which encourage a motivated reasoning justifying and explaining why these existing but unsustainable systems are so essential to the economy and should not be changed.

Blaming the individual for their presumed excesses in consumption, as I have tried to show, can divert our attention from the more substantial environmental impacts of these systems, and also the fact that most individual consumers are 'locked in' to them through many dependent relationships.

There is no doubt that the emissions generated by systems such as food provisioning, transportation, electricity generation and urban development and construction, contribute massively to climate change, but little progress has been made towards their 'de-carbonization'.

5. Waste making

To keep an increasing number of people buying more, more often, requires a rapid cycle of economic and material throughput; this involves encouraging consumers to devalue or 'discount' what they have with increasing rapidity and to more readily turn their products into waste. The problem is not just one of built-in obsolescence but a post-cautionary disregard of a whole-of-life perspective of the product and its impacts on the environment. Waste is what is deemed 'valueless'; so the 'old' must now be discarded to make way for the new, and more rapidly, supposedly for the sake of economic growth.

To generate this faster cycle of consumption and discard requires not only the deception noted above but a massive overproduction of goods, along with a matching overconsumption of resources and energy, to make, use and waste more rapidly. This can be seen in every domain, including fashion, cosmetics, hospitality, health, appliances, electronic products and building systems. This has immediate and long-lasting environmental consequences, contributing its own expanded footprint to climate change. None of this can be changed by improving product or process efficiency alone, as is too often assumed.

6. Post-cautionary production and design

Consumerism is increasingly dependent on what I have called here post-cautionary production and design, approaches to developing new products or systems that make few attempts to evaluate the environmental impacts of what is being produced. There are many examples of this, from the overproduction and dumping evident in fast high-street fashion, to the use of micro-plastics in cosmetics, and palm oil and trans-fats in food production.

Post-cautionary approaches in design and production are extremely costly to the environment and often to those they directly impact. They also waste time and money, typically taxpayer-funded efforts, undoing or mitigating the damage they wreak. As I have argued here, computerization gives us few excuses to continue with these commercially aggressive but high-risk strategies. These also contribute directly to the emissions responsible for climate change.

Principles to live and design by

From this brief summary of the main issues I have drawn attention to here, a number of important principles follow. These are primarily ethical principles that can help clarify what might be done to develop more sustainable forms of design and production for consumption, and the kinds of strategies these might involve. These may not provide practical solutions to our problems, but they do indicate where, and why, we should develop more substantial and better integrated strategies for change. They each relate back to the problems summarized above:

1. Truthfulness

Consumerism gains its power over us through deception and exploits the distancing of consumption from production enabled by globalization. So an important strategy to follow here should be a reduction in the distance, deception and misrepresentation it legitimizes. As consumers and citizens we deserve to know 'what's in the box'; we deserve to know that its makers are treated well, to a recognized international standard. We should not have to guess where our products come from, or how toxic their elements or parts might be.

There are a few good examples of how this might be approached, including that taken by the clothing company, Patagonia, which allows consumers to retrace the supply chains of the products they sell, and Fair-phone, a Dutch company that ensures the various components of their phones come from verifiable sources, and shares this knowledge with their consumers. Legislation demanding higher standards of product and service information could progressively nudge change in whole industries, following guidelines pioneered by companies like this. Technology can also be used more effectively to gain information about individual products and their components and origins. Honesty can be enforced through available legal instruments.

2. Transparency

A closely related principle to truthfulness is transparency, which is especially applicable in governance, supply chains and product and service management. A lack of transparency supports consumer deception, and can lead to the collapse of trust in a company as well as in the services offered by governments. This seems particularly important during a period of transition when governments as well as companies need to carry their audience with them, in a way that is free of factual deception, misinformation and manipulation.

The recent VW scandal is an excellent example of the damage wrought by a lack of transparency. To overcome more stringent US regulations an elaborate plan of deception was created in-house, misrepresenting emission levels of many diesel engines in use, a deception engineers must have well understood. The privileging of spin over transparency in this case has come, eventually, at a very high cost to the company, with legal proceedings now in their second year. This has also led to a collapse of public confidence in the brand, the company and its integrity, a hidden cost that might take many years to repair.

3. Respect

This principle is the social dimension of the first two principles, truthfulness and transparency. Too often advertising exploits social difference by implying a *discounting* of the consumer's intrinsic value, suggesting that we are not good enough *as we are* – for instance, girls are 'too fat', boys are 'not tough enough', etc. This can have long-term negative consequences on the well being of those subjected to it. This is one reason why France has recently banned ultra-thin models from fashion advertising. If we are all 'equal', then we are all deserving of respect *as we are*, not only as we might become if we bought the advertised product.

Despite the interest of marketers in this area, co-creation is still a neglected tool for achieving greater respect and equity in the field of production and consumption, in both commerce and government. Too many processes in corporate environments treat citizens and consumers with an assumed distrust, as mere 'consumers' or 'traffic' to be managed, superficially 'consulted' in often extremely rudimentary ways, and then locked out of decision-making, even where this directly affects them.

4. Non-substitutability

In recognizing the intrinsic value of human life, we also acknowledge that as people we are essentially non-substitutable, and like all parts of the natural world, unique in time and place. It is valuable for designers to recognize the dangers of applying the notion of substitutability uncritically from its industrial and economic origin to people, products or environments, as occurred in the example of 'consultation' above. No one wants to be just a number, but each of us wants to be treated with respect. Other creatures deserve this also.

As I have argued, there has to be a reduction in the presently rapid cycle of discounting or devaluation in objects and environments, and the wasting of resources and energy this requires. We might be able to rapidly substitute one product for another to extract value in the exchange, but the environmental tail of such exchanges is too long and costly, as most will now admit. Non-substitutability suggests the importance of preserving materials and energy wherever possible, and this leads to considering strategies in design like reuse, design for disassembly and durability, all approaches now generally used in design for sustainability.

5. Precaution

Consumerism is based in a post-cautionary economy that 'follows the money', even when there are likely to be heavy environmental and social costs involved. The many examples of post-cautionary products described above share a well-worn path that can be found in too many situations. This is characterized by a lack of transparency, intense competition, and a lack of concern with, or knowledge of, likely environmental or social consequences. Given the extraordinary advances in science and technology over the last 50 years, we no longer need to follow this approach. Instead, we can follow the ancient dictum of Hippocrates, 'first do no harm': given the vast resources of information at our finger tips, this is now much easier than it has ever been before.

Good design is necessarily intelligent precautionary design, mapping the relationships of an object in place and time, and exploiting the advantages of the past and building upon these. Lifecycle analysis, for example, has become increasingly sophisticated, and there are more and more examples of databases that share similar precautionary characteristics, from design databases on the impacts of material choice, to more sophisticated scientific ones, revealing the toxicity of similar chemicals. Greater knowledge and improved technologies have made these projects valuable. It should be possible now to 'design out' not only waste, but toxicity, and most unforeseen environmental consequences. This is one of the fundamental aims of the circular economy.[1]

***

It would require another, much longer book to apply these principles in depth. What is apparent from the various approaches currently being adopted to begin greening our industries, homes, cities, and way of life, is that the above principles are often understood but rarely implemented outside a few smaller demonstrator commercial or government settings. We need to shift from designing smaller projects that entertain visitors with the idea of some possible future sustainability, to normalizing sustainable consumption and production, scaling up through the kinds of strategies suggested here.

What often remains poorly understood is the role of consumerism itself and its enabling systems in contradicting, delaying or preventing the greening of our economic and social life. We need to actively steer consumption towards sustainable, circular forms of consumption. This will require, as I have suggested, a return to more carefully, slowly and enjoyably consuming as the 'custodians' of our possessions.

To achieve this, we need longer-life products, and more products that are leased through service-system agreements, and so can be cared for and remanufactured at the end of their lives. This will require legislation against many environmentally damaging throwaway products, and also against the advertisers, and the media's continuous encouragement to engage in damaging forms of 'fast' product-based consumption. Certainly, legislative change should include greater pressures on the post-cautionary misuse of design, marketing and advertising to increase sales, regardless of all consequences.

Addressing consumerism itself is critical in developing effective levers of change. There are two aspects to this. Firstly, in terms of material flows, we need both incentives and laws that make poorly designed, short-lived, unrecyclable goods unattractive, and not in the interests of the manufacturer. This is very much in line with the notion of a circular economy.

---

1   See for example 'Distributed Structure-Searchable Toxicity' Database (2016) at https://www.epa.gov/chemical-research/distributed-structure-searchable-toxicity-dsstox-database, accessed 1 July 2016.

However, we need to add to this approach one that confronts the continuing inner exploitation of the consumer; the deliberate creation through design and marketing of a sense of lack or inadequacy, and the exploitation of competitive, comparative values to achieve these commercial ends. This ideological dimension of consumerism might generate sales but it does so at a cost that is far too high in psychological, social and physical terms, and this is now well documented.

To achieve sustainability must include achieving sustainable consumption. This will require a radical reconsideration of material and social relationships involved in design, production and consumption, and a transformation of the governance of the market. We cannot afford to continue holding the individual solely accountable for the degradation of our environment, while allowing the producers behind this destruction to hide. Consumerism, certainly, is no longer 'somebody else's problem'.

About the author

Robert Crocker, D.Phil (oxon), teaches the history and theory of design and design for sustainability in the School of Art, Architecture and Design at the University of South Australia. Beginning his academic career as a historian of early modern science and philosophy, he became interested in social and environmental sustainability while working as a volunteer for a local pedestrian advocacy group. This led him to develop an interest in other aspects of social and environmental sustainability, and particularly the role of consumption and technology in generating our present environmental crisis. Recent publications include two edited volumes, *Motivating Change: Sustainable Design and Behaviour in the Built Environment* (Routledge, 2013) and *Designing for Zero Waste: Consumption and Technologies in the Built Environment* (Routledge 2012).